Buying Time
and
Getting By

Buying Time
and
Getting By

The Voluntary Simplicity Movement

MARY GRIGSBY

STATE UNIVERSITY OF NEW YORK PRESS

Cover photo by Gary Grigsby.

Published by
State University of New York Press, Albany

For information, address the State University of New York Press,
90 State Street, Suite 700, Albany, NY 12207

Production by Marilyn P. Semerad
Marketing by Anne M. Valentine

Library of Congress Cataloging-in-Publication Data

Grigsby, Mary, 1952–
    Buying time and getting by : the voluntary simplicity movement / Mary Grigsby.
        p. cm.
    Includes bibliographical references and index.
    ISBN 0-7914-5999-3 (alk. paper). — ISBN 0-7914-6000-2 (pbk. alk. paper)
        1. Voluntary simplicity movement.   I. Title.

BJ1496.G75 2004
179'.9—dc21
                                                                    2003050529

10 9 8 7 6 5 4 3 2 1

Contents

Acknowledgments

I am grateful to the people in the voluntary simplicity movement who shared their lives with me. Their generosity in giving their time and their candid discussions of the processes and struggles they experience in seeking to live simple lives made the research for this book possible. Other scholars, particularly standpoint and third-wave feminists, those engaged in cultural analysis, critical theorists, and sociologists of new social movements and cultural movements, must be acknowledged. Their work is the soil in which this analysis has its roots. Among these scholars are close colleagues and friends whose reading, comments for revision, and questions have been central in shaping this analysis. Thanks to Mary Jo Neitz, whose appreciation and understanding of the type of analysis I wanted to do, combined with her insightful questions and encouragement, were important in shaping my work. Thanks to Ellen Reese, whose detailed reading, suggestions for further reading, and careful suggestions for revisions helped me improve the depth and clarity of the analysis. Thanks to J. Kenneth Benson, whose critique and mentoring were helpful. Thanks to Anna Riley for her helpful comments, particularly her review of my analysis of race and ethnicity as constituting elements in the voluntary simplicity movement. Thanks to Jere Gilles for his comments and questions and for his enthusiasm for the topic. Thanks to Ted Vaughan, with whom I discussed this research at length early in its conception. Thanks to Barbara Barman-Julius for her excellent copyediting and proofing and to Nancy Ellegate and Marilyn Semerad of SUNY Press for their guidance throughout the publication process.

I also wish to acknowledge and thank the late C. David Anderson, Lottie Mae Mitchell, Fathy Soliman Elbana, and John Crighton, each of whom influenced my way of seeing the world and thus my work as a sociologist and this research. What I learned from each of them is with me in all I do.

To my mother and dear friend Mary Elizabeth Middlebrooks Anderson I am most grateful. Her encouragement and support throughout the time I have been working on the book have been important elements in making the work satisfying and in helping me to complete it.

Many thanks to Gary Scott Grigsby, my partner, who read and proofed early drafts of the book. During the time I was conducting research for the book Gary and I adopted various voluntary simplicity practices, in part because I wanted to understand the experience of practicing these techniques and in part because we both desire to align our personal practices with our environmental and social values. Gary's work as an environmental journalist and my research on voluntary simplicity came together and influenced our decision to change our own personal practices. In this way my research journey, which proved to be one of change and discovery, was accompanied by a separate but related partnership journey. Gary's support of the intellectual and personal journey this research represents for me, the parts of the journey we shared, and our love contributed greatly to making the process of doing the research a joyous one.

CHAPTER ONE

———•———

Voluntary Simplicity:
A Cultural Movement

People in the voluntary simplicity movement are concerned about environmental degradation, critical of conspicuous consumption and "careerism," and dissatisfied with the quality of life afforded by full participation in mass consumer society. Simple livers, as participants in voluntary simplicity are often called, maintain that a voluntary simplicity lifestyle is more fulfilling for the individual, creates a stronger community, and decreases environmental damage.

People in the movement believe that overconsumption is promoted by the dominant culture, which is materialistic, competitive, and destructive of the planet and human fulfillment (Elgin 1993a; Andrews 1997; Dominguez and Robin 1992). Simple livers say that there is no built-in or culturally established concept of "enough" in the dominant culture, which implicitly accepts a goal of working long hours for a wage under conditions that are often deadening and stressful. Dominguez and Robin and many in the movement maintain that work for pay for someone else is rarely fulfilling and undermines authenticity. They believe the economic drive for profit above all else promotes conspicuous consumption detached from any true measure of quality of life and long-term consequences. Participants in voluntary simplicity say they prefer to determine what is enough for themselves and earn only what they need to get by.

The voluntary simplicity movement offers ideology and techniques for arriving at a personal definition of what is enough and promises a more fulfilling life to those who consume in more sustainable ways, reduce clutter, and minimize activities they don't find meaningful. Simple livers try to get by on less conspicuous consumption and less income from waged work in order to buy time for the well-being of the global environment, and for themselves to pursue more fulfilling and pleasurable activities.

The alternative values and practices simple livers use to describe how they define voluntary simplicity provide insight into why these mostly educated, middle-class, white women and men ranging in age from their twenties to their eighties say they embrace voluntary simplicity, attend simplicity meetings, and seek to bring their use of money and time into alignment with their values.

What Is Voluntary Simplicity?

These are the accounts of some of the people in the movement about what voluntary simplicity is and why they practice it. Kevin, a rosy-complexioned, grey-bearded man in his seventies, who wears tan shorts and a T-shirt, fixes his intense blue-grey eyes full of a gentle kindness on mine and leans back against the wooden bench he and his wife Nita built into the compact basement apartment they share in the house Nita owns. He crosses his muscular arms across his chest and says,

> Well, the basic purpose [of voluntary simplicity] is to live more simply, live closer to the earth, and live simply enough so it takes very little to actually earn where you are so you can spend your time doing things you like to do rather than things that become the mandates that you do. I simplified my life, I stripped down, but I felt great, stripped down to my bike, had no money, but big deal. My security was not in my wallet, my security was in my head. And I found this was an easy way to live, the availability of just about everything was there no matter what you do. This is the way I've lived since 1970.

Nita, her reddish brown hair parted in the middle and pulled back neatly into a bun at the nape of her neck, is a youthful sixty-two. She wears a white blouse and one of her own creations, a full skirt with intricate embroidery around the bottom. As she leans forward over her knitting, eager to share why she practices voluntary simplicity, her dangling earrings sway gently. Her bright blue eyes and freckled face are as expressive of her strong feelings as are her words. She speaks rapidly and forcefully as she explains,

> One of the things I tell people [is], "I am founding mother of Over Extended Anonymous." And I say, "If I was just doing things I didn't want to do I would cut them out. But everything I'm doing is stuff I really want to do." For me I think it's being in a place that is not any bigger than you need physically or philosophically. I think some people need big space but I'm not one of them. Getting the stuff pared down so you have what's important to you. But it's not like you're taking care of and herding a bunch of stuff that does not matter. And using time in a way that seems really interesting and kind of fulfilling and appropriate. So you're not spending a lot of either time and money doing stuff you don't really want to do. I think it is a cumulative process. I can get up in the morning and there is a lot I want to do, and need to do, but there is not much that I have to do! So I think that's sort of nice!

Emily sits across the table from me in her sunny dining room in the three-bedroom home she owns in a working-class neighborhood. A bowl of fresh cherries picked from the cherry tree in her back yard graces the space between us on the table. The pink sweatshirt she has on emphasizes her white skin and rosy cheeks framed by short, smooth, dark brown hair. She cradles a cup of coffee in her hands, a quizzical look on her face as she mulls over how to explain why she opted out of corporate employment in her early fifties to adopt simple living. She speaks slowly and thoughtfully,

> I feel like what it is giving me now is ownership of my life and not just in a freedom-from-job aspect—that's sort of a minor, or maybe a medium part of it, but it is thinking about your life in new ways. And once you think about how to spend your money, I think then, for me, it opened up how I do a lot of other things, what possessions I have around, the people that I associate with, and it brought more of my other values to the fore.

Fred is clearly tired when we meet at seven o'clock in the evening. He says the work he does installing portable toilets is so physically taxing to him at forty-one, that he knows he can't keep doing it much longer. Fatigue lines his forehead and the creases around his soft brown eyes where they meet the sides of his brown beard. His shoulders slope over the table where he sits holding a glass between his hands on the table. We are in a restaurant where he wanted to meet for the interview. He felt the room he rents would be too cramped for comfort. As he warms to the topic some of the fatigue appears to drop away and he raises his shoulders and smiles a wry smile, sighs, tilts back his head, and tells me why he embraces voluntary simplicity:

> Well I guess being part of it for me is . . . it's become cliché: "Live simply so others may simply live." So it is that mix of environmentalism, but it is also corporate warfare [warfare against corporate interests promoting conspicuous consumption]. I'm very much inclined not to buy into "I'm a good person if I bought a brand new car, but if I didn't I'm not." More or less it is just a matter of self-respect. I don't know that I could live much differently and be at peace with myself. For me it's a place that I'm not a weirdo.

Barbara's dark brown eyes flash with the memory she is preparing to recount to me and as she swings her head quickly to glance at her husband Lewis, her long, straight, dark brown hair arcs out around her shoulders. Barbara and Lewis, who are both twenty-seven, often talk into each other's comments, one picking up where the other left off. At the time they decided to adopt voluntary simplicity Barbara was working on her Ph.D. in sociology and Lewis was completing his master's in environmental economics and debating whether to continue for a Ph.D. Barbara ended up deciding not to complete writing her dissertation and Lewis decided not to go on for a Ph.D. Instead, they decided to get jobs and invest in rental property. They aim to quit work in a few years and do volunteer work and other things they enjoy. Barbara's face is scrubbed clean and she has a peachy pink glow beneath her skin running from cheek to cheek across her nose. She is wearing a dark green, long-sleeved cotton top and jeans. She is barefoot and her long, slim legs are stretched out straight as she sits on the sofa in the living room of their home, a unit in the triplex they have bought. The door to the living room is open and a gentle breeze flows through the room as a neighborhood cat wanders in. Barbara says,

> We were both in [graduate programs preparing for teaching and research in academia] for lifestyle. [We thought] this would be

a nice way to work. We get all this time off in the summer and you don't have to be so stressed out in the day. But what we saw all around us was people who were stressed and did not have always fulfilling family lives. It took a long time before they got to the point where they could enjoy and relax. And we are not passionate enough about our subject. It wasn't enough.

Lewis, sitting in a chair opposite the coffee table from Barbara, nods his head as he intently follows what she is saying. His hair is dark brown, almost black, and closely cropped and he is clean shaven. He, like Barbara, is medium height and appears physically fit. He wears a navy blue cotton top and sweatpants without shoes. His legs are stretched out in front of him and crossed at the ankles. His expression is one of excitement, a smile on his face, his dark brown eyes alight with the memory of the moment as he shares the following account of what happened when he and Barbara read *Your Money or Your Life* (YMOL)[1] a popular simple living self-help book, together:

> We started to get really excited 'cause we started to think, well hey, we have choices, and we have options and you know maybe I don't need to finish this program that I am so miserable in. What I see as the goal, our version is not to live the simple life right now but to build the foundation for a simple life right now. And by reducing our need for material things through conscious decisions—that is what is going to help us do that. But in general I think it is about reducing personal resource requirements as far as material possessions so you have time for yourself and hopefully time for others. I see simplicity benefiting the individual and society itself. Right now most people in our lives are so wrapped up in being so busy without any end in sight. And I think a lot of people tell themselves they are going to get beyond this stage and they won't be so busy. But why is that true? It's not, unless you have a plan. And we have a plan!

Barbara picks up where Lewis left off and adds,

> For us it means, not that we are having a simple life right now, but that we have a goal. And we have just changed things around, yesterday. We think we're going to live in cohousing and we just bought a lot. But really all along the goal is to get through working so we can have time. For us the pivotal part

of YMOL is well, we don't have to work forever. We saw each other on and off all day in school and that is why we got married. We want to see each other. So for us it may be when we say "simplicity," we don't know exactly what the future will hold. It may evolve.

Wearing overalls, Brad sits with his arms outstretched on the table in front of him in the kitchen of the house he, his partner Jane, and friend Sandra rent near the campus where they are studying. He takes a deep breath as he prepares to outline why he chooses voluntary simplicity as a way of life. He has a direct gaze and a presence that makes me feel he is comfortable with himself and with me. At twenty-one he is nearing completion of his B.A. and planning to study sustainable agriculture in the future, aiming to have his own farm someday. He speaks looking directly at me, with no hesitation and with clear conviction and confidence in his voice:

> The basic idea is to practice what we preach, to find out what you think, and to make all of your decisions based on that. To take a job that you really believe is doing the right thing. To the best of your ability, to cut down on your driving and your consumption, if you don't fully believe in these things. And to remove all the clutter that we have in modern society from your life so you can become a better person or become closer to what you actually want to do, so you get control. Self realized. The ideal would be to do what you want to be doing all the time.

Most of the people quoted above have been inspired by books and workshops on voluntary simplicity and all have participated in study groups organized to support participants in striving for the simple life. The study groups are often referred to as "simplicity circles" (Andrews 1997) by participants.

Unlike some alternative movements which advocate withdrawing from or rejecting the mainstream, the voluntary simplicity movement advocates remaining in contact with the mainstream in some ways, such as through volunteer work, property ownership, investment, and buying goods and services from locally owned businesses. But other aspects of the mainstream, such as conspicuous consumption and seeking status and meaning through waged work, are rejected. Many in the movement advocate involvement at the grassroots level, where they believe community building can best be accomplished. The circles, workshops, literature, and networks—among those making meaning of their beliefs and practices through identifying themselves as practitioners of voluntary simplicity—support them in carrying the ideology and lived practices into the larger community.

The Voluntary Simplicity Cultural Movement

The ideas that are being worked on in the voluntary simplicity movement by people in circles and in books and the media draw on the dominant culture, earlier ideas, and cultures of resistance found in the environmental movement and to a lesser extent the feminist and civil rights movements, and diffuse through the culture. Voluntary simplicity encompasses a broad range of prescribed practices and is characterized by flexible and emergent ideology. Among participants, simple living is seen as a process, not something that one achieves as a stable state. This produces elasticity in terms of the range of practices present within the movement and gives insider status to those seeking to simplify as well as those who are closer to the ideals of simple living found in the how-to literature and described by simple livers.

Several of the core ideas of voluntary simplicity have currency with people outside of the movement. For instance, the belief that the planet's environment is endangered and that resources need to be conserved, the belief that work for a wage is not fulfilling and often requires people to do things they do not believe are right, the belief that society is unjust, and that social resources are not equitably distributed are all ideas found among people who are not part of the voluntary simplicity movement. Practices such as recycling, doing volunteer work, and buying locally grown food and goods extend well beyond those in voluntary simplicity as common practices.

Many of these ideas did not originate in the voluntary simplicity movement. Some voluntary simplicity ideas have origins that are quite old. Both Elgin (1993a) and Shi (1985, 1986) provide interpretations of the historical context of the voluntary simplicity movement. Shi traces the ideas of the movement back to the founding of the United States. Elgin emphasizes a coming together of a constellation of ideas that gained salience in the United States in the 1960s, including both Eastern and Western influences. Shi, an historian, emphasizes the importance of the experiences in the 1970s and 1980s in forming the movement. He discusses the work of Elgin (1993a) as linked with the "ecological simplicity movement" that emerged in those two decades.

The voluntary simplicity movement has brought ideas and practices together in a way that is distinctive and emergent. It is the power these ideas have in the cultural and economic context of contemporary Western society that indicates their sociological importance. Part of the power of the movement rests with the way it resonates with the thoughts and feelings of its participants and helps them to make meaning of the conditions of their lives as white women and men possessing cultural capital (Bourdieu 1984; Lamont 1992) that locate most of them in some significant ways as middle class in the late twentieth century in a patriarchal/capitalist United States of America.

This book provides insights into the ideas and experiences identified as significant by people trying to adopt or practicing voluntary simplicity today. It shifts the focus from a linear historical interpretation that centers on voluntary simplicity as primarily constituted of ideas, to the context of social change and the process of change that occurs in the lives of simple livers. Another reason this movement is sociologically important is because it raises issues more often implicitly than explicitly about how identities and groups (communities) are constructed and structured in relation to gender, race/ethnicity, and class hierarchies. Studying the voluntary simplicity movement offers a way of exploring these issues in the lives of the people involved in the movement.

The struggles of people in the movement to define themselves as worthwhile and good people and to establish practices that enable them to understand themselves to be living in keeping with their values result from social and cultural forces felt by others living under similar cultural and economic conditions. By asking how people's social identities (their biographies) are fashioned and altered over time (as they interact, put ideas into practice, and respond to the contexts in which they are located) and examining the role voluntary simplicity plays in the process, we can gain insight into the social nature of identity construction through an alternative lens. Studying simple livers allows us to understand one response to cultural and economic conditions and thereby to look at the cultural and economic conditions in a different way.

The voluntary simplicity movement does not formally recruit new members, imposes no strict guidelines or criteria for inclusion, has no officially sanctioned leaders, is not centralized or hierarchically organized, and is not aimed primarily at changing public policy. Schwalbe (1996) points to similar criteria, which characterize the mythopoetic men's cultural movement, as evidence that this movement is more cultural than social. Many participants are uncomfortable with the label "movement" applied to voluntary simplicity but end up accepting it for lack of a better way of talking about it. Most people practicing voluntary simplicity view it as the practice of bringing one's own personal values together with daily practice and maintain that it is through example that the movement will gain participants. Most disavow desire to indoctrinate others into thinking as they do relative to voluntary simplicity. For these reasons I choose not to refer to the voluntary simplicity movement as a social movement. It is a "loosely bounded" (Neitz 1994, 127) cultural movement that can best be understood through asking to what extent it is able to establish group boundaries and collective agents and whether people act as carriers of the values and practices of the movement.

The term "cultural movement" seems appropriate for the voluntary simplicity activities for several reasons. Those practicing voluntary simplicity view themselves as cultural change agents who will influence others to change by their example rather than through efforts to convert others. The alternative they say they represent is consistently defined against a construction of the dominant culture, particularly consumer culture. It is also responding to critiques of the dominant culture in less discursively direct ways. And perhaps most important the simple livers act as carriers of culture through circles and other networks in which they participate.

The more obvious sources for the development of a sense of group consciousness and for recruitment that supports the cultural movement are the simplicity workshops and support groups in which people in the movement often participate, and the movement literature that they read. In December 1997 there were 108 circles listed on the "Web of Simplicity" internet site, most in urban areas and most using either Andrews (1997) or Dominguez and Robin (1992) as guides for group meetings. In February of 1999, 218 study groups or circles were listed. In June of 2002, over 650 study groups were included in the database. The *Simple Living Journal* lists circles nationwide that have asked to be listed. The Seattle Phinney Neighborhood Association maintained records of known circles in the city until 1997. They discontinued updating the list because circles form and disband so frequently it was taking too much staff time to maintain the list. Any of these available records represent only a small percent of the total. The movement has resulted in circles forming in communities nationwide and in some other countries. Most circles use several specific readings that lead them to focus on a generally consistent constellation of concerns, at least initially.

Previous Research

Recently the movement has generated some interest among consumer economists and policy analysts who believe it offers useful prescriptions for reducing personal debt, combating environmental degradation, and influencing production practices that are more sensitive to long-term quality of life and sustainability (Goodwin, Ackerman and Kiron 1997; Schor 1998; Blanchard 1994). An excerpt of Duane Elgin's (1993a) quasi-scholarly work which describes the movement and advocates voluntary simplicity appears in *The Consumer Society*, a 1997 volume edited by Neva R. Goodwin, Frank Ackerman, and David Kiron. Elgin's chapter in this volume is titled "Living More Simply and Civilization Revitalization." It is drawn from a section of his book, *Voluntary Simplicity: Toward a Way of Life That Is Outwardly Simple, Inwardly Rich* (1993a). This appears to be the first published work to apply the name "voluntary simplicity" to this contemporary movement. Elgin adopted the term from Richard Gregg, a student of Ghandi's teaching who, in 1936, wrote a book titled *The Value of Voluntary Simplicity*. Responses to a survey questionnaire in *Co-Evolution Quarterly* in the summer 1977 issue provided data for Elgin's analysis of the movement. He argues that the data points toward a social trend that is gathering momentum and maintains that people practicing voluntary simplicity are "pioneers of an alternative way of living" (1993a: 109). His is an evolutionary theory of human life that incorporates the element of choice as central. His later work, *Awakening Earth* (1993b), is devoted to outlining the theory in more detail. In the late 1970s, when he gathered the data for *Voluntary Simplicity* and in 1981 when it was first published, he was employed as a social science researcher at Stanford Research Institute.

Elgin (1993a) found that most people involved in simplicity groups are white, middle class, and female. In a 1996 interview for the journal *Yes! A Journal of Positive Futures*, he indicated that women outnumber men in the movement two to one (van Gelder 1996). The survey data Elgin bases his findings on are limited to responses from subscribers to *Co-Evolution Quarterly*.

Etzioni (1998) draws from a range of secondary material about trends in contemporary society, including the works of Schor (1991), Elgin (1993a), and Ray (1997), among others, as well as media accounts of the voluntary simplicity movement, to support his assertion there is a broad social trend toward voluntary simplicity underway in affluent Western countries. He theorizes about the causes for the trend and what its impacts may be, arguing that the search for alternatives to consumerism as the goal of capitalism is the driving force of the trend.

Etzioni identifies three variations of this trend. First, "downshifters" represent a moderate form "in which people downshift their consumptive rich lifestyle, but not necessarily into a low gear" (621). For example, they dress down or drive beat-up cars, but might also own a boat (622). Another group are "strong simplifiers who have given up high-paying, high-stress jobs as lawyers, business people, investment bankers, and so on, to live on less, often much less, income. These people give up high levels of income and socioeconomic status; one former wall Street analyst restricts his spending to $6,000 a year" (624).² The third variation in the trend toward simplicity is the actual voluntary simplicity movement (625). Etzioni maintains that those in the simple living movement are the "most dedicated, holistic simplifiers" and "adjust their whole life patterns according to the ethos of voluntary simplicity" (625).

The focus of Etzioni's research is not on the voluntary simplicity movement itself, but on the broad trend he believes it is indicative of. For this reason he does not explore the movement in any detail beyond pointing out that it is "a small, loosely connected social movement, sometimes called the 'simple living' movement (that) has developed, complete with its own how-to books, nine-step programs, and newsletters . . ." (626). He maintains, "The rise of voluntary simplicity in advanced (or late) stages of capitalism, and for the privileged members of these societies, can be explained by a psychological theory of Maslow (1968), who suggests that human needs are organized in a hierarchy. At the base of the hierarchy are basic creature comforts, such as the need for food, shelter, and clothing. Higher up is the need for love and esteem. The hierarchy is crowned with self-expression" (632). It is the highest level needs that he believes voluntary simplicity can contribute to fulfilling.

Simple livers too believe that adopting voluntary simplicity requires having experienced having enough. They also point out it requires arriving at the understanding that fulfillment does not come from having more material things or from work aimed at making money or gaining status. They don't usually draw on Maslow's theory but they claim that having experienced affluence enabled them to recognize its limitations. Still, questions about how simple livers come to make the choice to adopt voluntary simplicity remain unanswered by Etzioni. After all, most people in affluent Western societies who have the option of maintaining a consumerist lifestyle and holding status occupations don't opt for voluntary simplicity.

Etzioni maintains that voluntary simplicity "if constituted on a large scale, would significantly enhance society's ability to protect the environment" because simplifiers use far fewer resources than conspicuous consumers (638). He also asserts that the more "voluntary simplicity is embraced as a lifestyle by a given population, the greater the potential for realization of a basic element of social justice, that of basic socio-economic equality" (639). He writes further,

> Voluntary simplicity, if more widely embraced, might well be the best new source to help create the societal conditions under which the limited reallocation of wealth, needed to ensure the basic needs of all, could become politically possible. The reason is as basic and simple as it is essential: to the extent that the privileged (those whose basic creature comforts are well sated and who are engaging in conspicuous consumption) will find value, meaning, and satisfaction in other pursuits, those that are not labor or capital intensive can be expected to be more willing to give up some consumer goods and some income. The "freed" resources, in turn, can be shifted to those whose basic needs have not been sated, without undue political resistance or backlash. (640)

Etzioni maintains that a combination of voluntary simplicity personal practice and policies that support basic needs for all can result in increased environmental sustainability and social justice. He does not look inside the movement critically or explore it from the participants' perspective as I do. Those in voluntary simplicity, including those whom I interviewed, don't generally talk about policy initiatives, instead focusing on the individual as the primary mechanism for change.

Etzioni's knowledge of the movement comes primarily from Elgin and media accounts rather than from empirical analysis of the movement based on close observation. His focus is on theorizing broad trends, not on the detailed understanding of the cultural and economic processes as they shape and are shaped by groups of people in their daily lives. I, too, am interested, at least in part, in understanding the social forces at work in the lives of simple livers but this research is centrally concerned with understanding derived from the particular and grounded experiences of people in the voluntary simplicity movement. This research draws on analysis derived from close observation and participation in simplicity circles and workshops. I turn to the accounts of simple livers about why they adopt voluntary simplicity, and what simple living practices are, as the starting point for understanding the significance of the movement.

Schor's recent work, *The Overspent American: Upscaling, Downshifting, and the New Consumer* (1998), includes a brief description of her interviews with a small but unspecified number of people in the voluntary simplicity movement in Seattle. She points to the movement as one that offers insights into how some middle-class people can resist overconsumption. Schor says she can't estimate the size or demographic composition of the movement with any accuracy but suggests that simple livers tend to be middle-class whites, have at least a college education, are more likely to be women, are unlikely to have young children living at home, and are more likely to be single, to have grown children, and to be "a little bit older."

Shor's primary concern is reducing debt and overconsumption among the middle class. She focuses on consumer culture and status consumption as pressures the middle class must resist and believes that if they can resist them, this will result in a slow change in corporate economic practices and divert cultural and social capital toward community service. Her assessment of the voluntary simplicity movement recognizes that it does not represent the society at large because, she says, simple livers have high levels of cultural and human capital which enable them to live on less. She also believes the absence of children from their lives is key to their ability to live as they do.

Schor's work came out not long after I began my research and confirmed the basic demographic features of the movement that my data suggests. But the usefulness of this data is limited for providing a sociological understanding of the movement or a sense of the reasons people come to participate in voluntary simplicity and the collective capacity of the movement.

Schor suggests that the voluntary simplicity movement may not last because simple livers may not be able to sustain their alternative lifestyles. She also believes they have the option of moving back into middle-class mainstream jobs whenever they want. But I find that the simple lifestyle is being sustained over time. I also suspect that most simple livers who have quit work probably could not move back into jobs that command salaries like they were making at the peak of their earning history after a few years out of the job market. None of the people I studied who had quit work had started working again in jobs similar to the ones they had previously held. One person who thought she might have to supplement her investment income at some point in the future made it clear she knew she could not get the kind of management position she had held and further that it would not be her choice of work at all. She had several hobbies that offered the possibility of making some income and she planned to pursue that angle if she needed money at some point. In any case, my data suggests that most people in the movement still work or are preparing to work. Most people I interviewed did reduce and change their consumption patterns, but there is a wide range of incomes and expenditure among simple livers.

To understand the transformative capacity and emergent culture of the movement, and how participants are socially located, requires consideration of a complex set of interrelationships of patterns that unfold over the lifetimes of people in the movement. These patterns emerge out of gendered, raced, and classed biographical histories and within the economic and cultural contexts in which simple livers are located. Most people in the movement who participate in simplicity circles don't have children, but some do. It may be more difficult to practice voluntary simplicity with children. But not having children is not a central reason for either practicing or not practicing voluntary simplicity. This research suggests that there is a constellation of orientations, circumstances, experiences, and practices and choices that unfold over time to orient people toward the practice of voluntary simplicity. These include the following: being well educated; experiencing dissatisfaction in waged work; being concerned about the environment; being uncomfortable with a consumerist lifestyle; being involved in social, environmental, or care-taking types of work; close exposure to how less fortunate people live; being single; not having children; being vegetarian; and using alternative medicine. This is not a linear progression, but is a process better understood through ethnographic analysis. It involves a coming together of individual biographies; relationships with other groups, individuals, and institutions; and geographical, cultural, and economic contexts to bring participants to assume the alternative worldview and adopt the practices of voluntary simplicity.

Though identifying the characteristics held commonly by people practicing simple living can help us understand them a little better, it is grasping the patterns that characterize their lives, how the circles work, and the networks they have that provides a fuller picture of the movement and what distinguishes simple livers from other groups. The key here is to understand how the ideas and practices of simple livers are drawn from, or are responses to, the surrounding cultural and economic environment. Further, it is important to consider how the social location, gender, ethnicity, and other characteristics of movement participants may lead them to respond to the world in certain ways that are consistent with the voluntary simplicity movement.

Much of what has been written about the movement has come from readings of selected books in the how-to literature and from reading Schor's work. In an article in *The Nation*, Vanderbilt (1996, 20) bemoans the fact that five books in this genre, including Dominguez and Robin (1992), landed on the best seller list because their prescriptions are trivial. He views voluntary simplicity as a luxury afforded the affluent. He suggests that the voluntary simplicity literature is a money-making activity for the publishing companies and authors and is well suited to preparing the middle class for their downward mobility brought on by "turbo-charged capitalism, that high-tech market without borders where the number of well-paying corporate jobs shrinks and that of the lower-paying service jobs blooms," leading to a scenario where "the hourly earnings of the bottom 70 percent of all Americans will decline, even as the total national income continues to increase" (20).

In an article in *Tikkun,* Segal (1996) maintains, "Advocates of simple living are expressing a value orientation that overlaps in important ways with that of the politics of meaning. They reject the idea that the good life is to be found in ever-higher levels of consumption. They argue strongly against rampant careerism and materialism. They opt for less money, less work, more time with friends and loved ones" but they "view the attainment of a simpler, more meaningful life as an individual project, not as a matter of collective politics" (20). Segal argues that a political agenda needs to be coupled with the voluntary simplicity movement and its central objective would be a society in which fundamental human needs can be met at modest levels of income.

Utne Reader devoted much of a 1998 issue to "stuff," or the clutter that results from over consumption and, in an article titled "Don't Buy These Myths," cites voluntary simplicity as a movement "[f]or those willing, as Schor puts it, to 'struggle against the dominant cultural assumptions about consumption' " (Madison 1998, 54), but that won't work for society at large. The analyses provided in these books and articles are arrived at without benefit of a close look at simple livers and their activities from the inside.

The Scope of the Book

Looking inside the movement is important not only because it offers the opportunity to understand the meaning making of simple livers about why they adopt voluntary simplicity but because it simultaneously offers access to their detailed accounts of these matters for analysis.

Through attending workshops, participating in a circle over time, visiting circles, and doing in-depth interviews with simple livers, I aimed to capture who these simple livers are, why they embrace voluntary simplicity, how they live, and what sorts of changes voluntary simplicity makes in their lives and potentially more broadly. How people become part of the voluntary simplicity cultural movement and how their commitment to simple living develops are central concerns of this book as are broader concerns about how the meanings of modern society are contested and negotiated by the symbolic expressions and values as well as practices of groups such as these (Neitz 1994).

The sketching of the relationships between women and men, of how status is established, how inequality is addressed, how and what kind of community is established, and how identity is constructed through the movement provides a lens through which to view the larger culture and how change is shaped. What broad cultural and economic forces are simple livers responding to as they seek to define what constitutes being a person of worth, what a good community consists of, what relationships between people should be like, and how inequality is to be addressed? How do their locations within the matrix of class, gender, racial, and ethnic categories that structure the relative power of groups in contemporary Western countries shape voluntary simplicity?

This book provides a sense of the cultural significance of the voluntary simplicity movement through offering an understanding of what the people in the movement are doing—how they are using the movement and what they are making with it. While access to the leaders of the movement was available and I did attend a workshop by one of these leaders, Cecile Andrews, my focus is on the everyday people who read the how-to books, attend workshops, participate in circle meetings, and struggle to live simply.

The "loosely bounded" (Neitz 1994, 127) nature of the movement makes it important to look closely at four levels: "First we need to study the individuals who are carriers of the culture; second, we need to study the ideas and practices that make up the culture" (Hall and Neitz 1993, 239). Third, the circles, workshops, and other networks people participate in need to be studied. And fourth, the broader cultural and economic forces that constrain, support, and shape the movement must be considered (Benson 1977; Collins 1990, 1993). This book looks at each of these levels to provide a sociological understanding of the voluntary simplicity movement.

Methods

I used qualitative research methods of participant observation at simplicity circle meetings and workshops, intensive interviews with simple livers, and textual analysis of the popular "how-to" and inspirational literature aimed at helping and encouraging people who want to practice voluntary simplicity.

I conducted participant observation in two simplicity circles, one in Columbia, Missouri, which I attended weekly for its duration of seven weeks during the fall of 1998 and the other in Seattle, which I attended once. I also gained detailed knowledge of a third circle because I interviewed four people who were in the same circle.

I was a participant observer at three workshops attended by a total of forty-four people. The first was taught by Cecile Andrews at North Seattle Community College in Seattle, Washington, on June 29, 1998. Twenty-five people attended the workshop. I was a participant observer at a workshop on voluntary simplicity offered by Peaceworks, an organization in Columbia, Missouri, devoted to promoting peace, environmental sustainability, and social justice, in the fall of 1998 at the local public library that fourteen people attended. In the winter of 1999, as a volunteer for Peaceworks, I organized a workshop for women on voluntary simplicity at Unity Center in Columbia, Missouri, that five women, in addition to myself, attended. A women's simplicity circle, of which I am a member, formed as a result of that workshop. I chose to be more a participant than an observer in this circle. But during the time I was writing this book I continued to think about the women's circle I was part of in comparison to the circles that are the focus of this analysis. The women's circle is not characteristic of simplicity circles, which are usually made up of both women and men and because all of the people in the circle, other than myself, have children. My experiences in this circle inform this analysis, especially in areas where there is a contrast with my experiences of the other circles I observed. Those contrasts are things I naturally have tried to understand.

In order to more fully understand the lives of group members, I conducted intensive interviews with fourteen people from three different circles, two in Seattle and one in Columbia, Missouri. I conducted interviews with ten people in Seattle and four people in Columbia. I designed sixty questions, many of them open ended, to guide the interview process. In most of the interviews I ended up not having to actually ask all of the questions because people discussed the areas I wanted to learn about without being prompted. Overall the people I interviewed were eager to talk about voluntary simplicity. In two cases I interviewed couples together and those interviews lasted the longest. I interviewed myself using the same guidelines used in interviews with other respondents. This self-interview and reflexive notes provide some of the data used in writing the reflexive portions of the book but are not included in the data used to characterize the voluntary simplicity movement in the analysis.

Textual analysis of twenty of the recommended voluntary simplicity books and many of the materials frequently referenced by those in voluntary simplicity also informs the analysis. Three texts emerged as central for the movement, and became the central focus of textual analysis appearing in chapter 2, because they are the ones most often discussed by informants. These three texts are Joe Dominquez and Vicki Robin's national best seller, *Your Money or Your Life: Transforming Your Relationship with Money and Achieving Financial Independence* (1992); Duane Elgin's *Voluntary Simplicity: Toward a Way of Life That Is Outwardly Simple, Inwardly Rich* (1993a); and Cecile Andrews's *The Circle of Simplicity: Return to the Good Life* (1997).

Theoretical Contribution

In this research I employ "grounded theory" (Glaser and Strauss 1967) that builds theoretical understandings inductively from the data gathered in combination with theory elaboration that involves making use of theories that "highlight some aspect of the situation under study" (Burawoy et al. 1991). Employing the process of theory elaboration I bring theories to bear on the data and synthesize, integrate, and sometimes refine existing theories in order to provide the fullest understanding of the data. Theoretically this book represents a serious attempt to bring together Collins's (1990, 1993) call for empirical analysis that explores the coconstruction of race, class, and gender and analysis of cultural movements that includes reflexivity.

Much of the literature on race, class, and gender focuses on the influence of the dominant culture and tends to overlook the dynamic identity work of transformative cultural movements. At the same time much of the literature on cultural and social movements tends to overlook how the cultural work of movements is shaped by race, class, and gender as coconstructing elements. The works that do consider them often give salience to one over others.

The theoretical approach taken draws on socialist feminist theoretical standpoint epistemology and empirical research aimed at teasing apart the intertwined and coconstructed categories of gender, race, and class inequalities (Collins 1990, 1993; Harding 1986, 1987; Smith 1987a, 1987b, 1990) and more recent studies that have often emphasized gender, race, or class inequality and are sensitive to the influence of culture in reproducing and transforming inequalities (Halle 1984; Fantasia 1988; Frankenberg 1993; Schwalbe 1996).

Feminist standpoint epistemology asserts that what we know depends on the historical location and position in social hierarchy of the knower. Women's knowledge of the world is different from men's. And knowledge among women varies based on their class, race, ethnicity, and other characteristics. This approach turns away from the "master theory" conception that one explanatory theory can reflect the knowledge of all people. This is a relationist perspective that requires knowledge that offers recognition of difference. The challenge is to understand, respect, and value diversity yet identify commonalities in the experience of different groups. This book is reflexive in two ways. It explores both the significance of the social locations of simple livers in shaping the voluntary simplicity movement and the significance of my social location in shaping the analysis of the movement in the book.

Another theoretical tradition this book links with is work that explores the role of social and cultural movements in social transformation. Here I draw generally on culture studies aimed at understanding the relationships of cultural movements (Neitz 1994, 1999, 2000, 2002) and social movements to social change and transformation (Johnston and Klandermans 1995; Laraña, Johnston, and Gusfield 1994; McAdam 1988). Of particular importance for this research is recent work that has incorporated gender analysis into the study of such movements (McAdam 1992; Mueller 1994; Neitz 1994, 1999, 2000; Schwalbe 1996; Seager 1993; Taylor 1996). This analysis is also linked to literature theorizing new ways of understanding class in the analysis of social and cultural movements (Halle 1984; Fantasia 1988). Most of these efforts have privileged gender, race, or class but have not addressed all three. This book extends this approach by including analysis of class, gender, and race in the study of the voluntary simplicity cultural movement.

Chapter Outline

Chapter 2 describes "The Ecological Ethic and the Spirit of Voluntary Simplicity," the dominant beliefs and ideal practices of voluntary simplicity prescribed in the literature of the movement that are used by movement participants in their efforts to live simply.

Chapter 3, "Getting a Life: Constructing a Moral Identity in the Voluntary Simplicity Movement," analyzes the struggles of people in the movement to define themselves as worthwhile and good people and the shared characteristics and experiences of people in the movement are discussed. In this chapter I explore efforts of participants to establish practices that enable them to feel they are living in keeping with their values, and to cope with the negative impacts they believe are caused by participation in conspicuous consumption and waged work by reducing their dependence on both in a process many in the movement refer to as "getting a life." I find that consumption is a key tool used in constructing a voluntary simplicity moral identity.

In chapter 4, "Gendered Visions of Process, Power, and Community in the Voluntary Simplicity Movement," I analyze what sort of community simplicity circles represent and what sort of community or collective capacity voluntary simplicity generates. Tensions in the movement are found primarily along gendered lines that stem from gendered conceptions of community, and the relationships that constitute community. These tensions are revealed to be linked to more complex tensions that involve gendered conceptions of what constitutes power and how to go about creating it, what a desirable community is, and how to build such community. Differences in the ideas of men and women in how the boundaries of the movement are defined, what a desirable community is, and how such communities can be built and the tensions that result are described. I argue that women's and men's contrasting understandings of autonomy and community and their differing relational styles and behaviors unfold out of the differing developmental experiences (Chodorow 1978) of white, middle-class women and men in the contemporary United States. I point to the possibilities and the limitations these tensions suggest for the collective capacities of the movement.

In chapter 5, "Looking into the Shadows: The Politics of Class, Gender, and Race/Ethnicity in the Voluntary Simplicity Movement," I argue that the relative positions of power of simple livers, based on how they are situated within the matrix of power relations defined by gender, class, race/ethnicity, and nation as categories through which power is structured, shape the voluntary simplicity movement in significant ways. I find that how simple livers are situated at the intersections of gender, race/ethnicity, and class privilege interlinks with the ideological work of voluntary simplicity to make them more likely to overlook the importance of public aspects of patriarchy and institutionalized power relations found in capitalism. I argue that even the changes they clearly advocate can't be fully realized unless they look deeper to issues of power, such as gender and racial/ethnic inequality, that they often claim are not issues of immediate concern to them. I will point to how their own accounts of their lives reveal that categories through which power moves and is structured, such as gender and race/ethnicity, are intertwined and coconstructed with occupational and consumer status hierarchies that they want to escape and see erased. I argue that these categories shape the identities and goals of individuals at the level of their biographies, in many ways forming the options they can envision and structuring the avenues available through which to achieve them.

But I also argue that the movement shifts dominant patterns of gender relations somewhat by resisting market intrusion into household production and rejecting traditional gendered patterns of household work and the male breadwinner role. I find that simple livers' rejection of the value of conspicuous consumption and status derived from waged work also signals their struggle to shift dominant cultural patterns associated with industrial capitalism in response to shifts in their experience of the labor market and their concern for the environment. But simple livers continue to value home ownership and owning rental property and other investments that provide them with income that frees them from the need to do waged work. They describe these practices in terms of supporting them in their efforts to be self-sufficient. They don't tend to deeply examine how their investment income depends on the labor and conspicuous consumption of others in the profit-driven growth economy with which they find fault.

Chapter 6, "New Tools and Old: Transformation and Reproduction in the Voluntary Simplicity Movement," examines the prospects for emancipatory social change through the movement. In this concluding chapter I summarize what the movement reproduces and transforms. I also identify the "highest meanings" (Touraine 1995) of the movement, the possibilities it opens up for consideration. In this chapter I suggest ways movement participants may extend the emancipatory capacity of the movement and document recent efforts by some of the prominent advocates of voluntary simplicity to establish networks with business funding sources and higher education research expertise to establish a policy research agenda for the simplicity movement.

This chapter concludes that the voluntary simplicity movement, though small and imperfect, is part of a broader cultural shift that some argue is well under way. It offers a model for generating alternative practices that work locally to reduce the level of need for money, work, and consumption while increasing involvement in the community and leisure time activities. But individual decisions about work and lowered consumption that characterize the focus of the everyday people in the movement are not enough; policies that support these choices and enable less privileged people to adopt them more readily are also needed. Linked to a political agenda the goals of the movement point to shifting over time to a no-growth economy, a shrinking work week, health care reform, limits to urban sprawl, ending discrimination against part-time workers, wage equity globally, lower levels of consumption, product development linked to long-term environmental sustainability, and a vital local economy and neighborhoods and communities that are organized based on sustainability.

Conclusion

I am sympathetic with the desire of people in the movement to achieve self change and cultural change. I am committed to helping piece together understandings that provide common ground for action on the part of differently situated groups who share the desire to alter the "relations of ruling" (Smith 1987a, 1987b, 1990). I want my research to promote the full participation of women and marginalized groups in the organizing of social relations and to support their ability to practice self-definition (Combahee River Collective 1982; Collins 1990). I don't view this as something I want to achieve just for others but for myself with others.

The similarities between my own location within dominant social hierarchies (as a middle-class, white, Western, educated woman) and those that characterize many in voluntary simplicity, plus my basic agreement with the values the movement seeks to support, made my own reflexive work and arriving at the critique within this analysis challenging. I chose to do research on the voluntary simplicity movement because the ideas associated with the movement resonated with me as hopeful. They still do. I hope that those within the movement may benefit from having a sociological analysis offer them a new perspective on their activities. And those who are critical of voluntary simplicity may also benefit from reflecting on how they respond to social and cultural forces in comparison to simple livers.

The greatest pleasure in writing this book was spending time with simple livers and learning about their lives. Most of the people I encountered eagerly shared accounts of their struggles to live good lives based on voluntary simplicity values. Their stories continue to inspire me to try do the same thing. Their struggle, even with its limitations, is a significant example of resistance in the face of deeply embedded and powerful social and cultural forces that encourage mass consumerism, result in unsustainable use of natural resources, and foster social inequality.

The next chapter, chapter 2 "The Ecological Ethic and the Spirit of Voluntary Simplicity," describes the ideology and practices advocated by the popular literature of the voluntary simplicity movement. Many people in the movement say these ideas and suggested practices are important in their choice to adopt a voluntary simplicity lifestyle.

CHAPTER TWO

———•◦•———

The Ecological Ethic and the Spirit
of Voluntary Simplicity

This chapter describes the patterned themes in the voluntary simplicity movement literature in order to identify the distinctive and essential elements of the movement ideology that informs the practices of many of its participants and attracts them to the movement. Of course, not all proponents of voluntary simplicity concur on the details of ideology and practice—not at all. The ideology and practices are constantly being reworked and elaborated. New information is brought into the movement and ideas that are diffused and reworked, external to the movement, cycle back into the movement. Plus the terrain within the movement is contested and the culture emerging in circles and among simple livers is fluid and open to alterations.

The voluntary simplicity movement is so "loosely bounded" (Neitz 1994) and changing so quickly that to claim to capture essential elements of its ideology and practices means doing so for only a moment or two in time. And yet, the movement does have distinctive contours that have continuity. There are several consistent patterns in what voluntary simplicity writers make salient, downplay, or leave out of their accounts. They focus on a loss of sense of meaning and fulfillment in life on the part of individuals, environmental degradation and impending environmental crisis, and the demise of strong communities as interrelated problems. They maintain that these problems are caused in

25

large part by a consumerist lifestyle among affluent Westerners who are caught up in fast-lane careers and a cycle of work and spend.

The solution is to reduce careerism and consumerism through voluntary choice on the part of affluent individuals. At the heart of voluntary simplicity ideology is an ecological ethic that asserts that all things in the universe exist in interdependent relationship and that human beings have the responsibility and power to shape future evolution of the world in positive or negative ways. Simple livers believe that adopting a voluntary simplicity lifestyle will shape a positive future, while maintaining a consumerist lifestyle will shape a negative future.

The authors of the literature do not focus on altering differential power between groups through policies aimed at structural change or the idea that powerful groups are invested in maintaining control over resources, and are therefore interested in denying such power to other groups. Instead they tend to use evolutionary analogies to explain the present situation. The ideas and practices being worked on in the voluntary simplicity movement literature, by groups of people in circles, and by individuals creating lives they define as simple, draw on the dominant culture, earlier ideas such as the Puritan value for frugality and simplicity, and the environmental, feminist, and to a lesser extent the civil rights movements selectively.

Voluntary simplicity authors draw from a repertoire or "tool kit" of available ideas and practices to construct "strategies of action" (Swidler 1986, 273). They rework the ideas and weave together selected elements in a unique way. The strategies of action are not built from scratch as means-ends activities but are chains of actions that depend upon available cultural and structural materials. This way of conceiving of the significance of culture shifts our thinking away from focusing on culture as the source of "ultimate ends or values toward which action is consistently directed" (Swidler 1986, 273) to a view of culture as a set of available tools that may be used in a variety of ways by participants in voluntary simplicity.

This analysis views culture as beliefs, rituals, symbols, customs, and artifacts which are not just ideas but which are found in emotions, practices, and the physical aspects of life. Rather than viewing culture as ideology and practice as material, this perspective recognizes the two as mutually constituted and entwined, as coconstructed. This extends the concept of a dialectically related production of culture and material relations of production to an interembedded form of relationship (Hays 1994). The model of culture I work from assumes that culture's influences on action and the ways groups use culture is multifaceted and varies depending upon contextual circumstances.

The ideology found in the movement literature and used by movement participants in their efforts to live simply offers an emergent model of new ways to organize action and to structure human communities that engage participants in active competition with the dominant culture and other cultural models as well.

Overview of the Voluntary Simplicity Movement Literature

The theoretical ideas and ideal practices of the voluntary simplicity movement are best exemplified in a handful of books recommended at workshops by workshop leaders, mentioned in the *Simple Living Journal*, included on simplicity-oriented web sites such as the simple living network (http://www.slnet.com/), and that informants say are good.

The first text of the movement that I encountered was an audio tape of Cecile Andrews's book *The Circle of Simplicity: Return to the Good Life* (1997) that I checked out of the public library in the midwestern college town where I live, because they didn't have the book in print in the collection. I was curious about the movement because the ideas described resonated with me as hopeful.[1]

Even now, when I think about the book it draws up the image of the walk I took as I listened to the tape. I walked along a nature trail that winds through the old established neighborhood where I live close to campus, in a duplex nestled among houses inhabited by a high percentage of faculty and other university employees, mostly middle-income families. It was the late summer of 1997 and the trees that arched over the trail offered welcome shade from the summer sun. The crinkled cotton skirt I wore swished with each step I took and created a gentle breeze that felt good against my legs. A light, seemingly luminescent layer of dust rose from the trail and swirled around me.

As I listened I felt like I knew Cecile Andrews, that we had something in common. I suspected that not only was she a person of substance and, as was later confirmed, that if I met her I'd like her. But I also felt uneasy with the framing of problems and the comfortable orderly connections to solutions offered. She was constructing a path to salvation, identifying and describing the problems faced and the solutions to them. The integrated set of beliefs and practices were flexible enough for people to find comfort within them and the solutions to problems were couched so that the necessary changes in personal practices called for would be possible. A tension developed from the start between my desire to live in such a manageable world, as constructed in her book, and my inability to fully accept the worldview offered, with neatly defined problems and solutions, as complete and fully workable.

Mine is a less certain path, full of questions about a world that I often experience as fragmented, full of conflict, a path strewn with the brambles of past seasons and new growth, and the voices of other people, many of whom don't necessarily experience the world as I do, identify the same things as problems, or envision the same solutions. I inhabit a world that I can hope to understand only partially. I like to think my education has widened the view from my window but I know I still occupy a geography that limits the contours of my capacity to envision alternatives and that I need always to be mindful of this. I have glimpsed too many contradictory constructions of reality to accept one in which the variables are so tidily correlated. The tension between totalizing and fragmented accounts is one I feel keenly in describing the voluntary simplicity movement.

Among simple livers the three most frequently discussed texts of the movement are Duane Elgin's foundational work, *Voluntary Simplicity: Toward a Way of Life That Is Outwardly Simple, Inwardly Rich* (1993a); Joe Dominguez and Vicki Robin's *Your Money or Your Life: Transforming Your Relationship with Money and Achieving Financial Independence* (1992); and Cecile Andrews's book, *The Circle of Simplicity: Return to the Good Life* (1997).[2] The latter two are often the books used to start off simplicity circles. In the circles I studied, participants tended to be familiar with both books and one, or both, were read and discussed as part of the circle activity.

The other "how-to" and inspirational books of the contemporary voluntary simplicity movement generally also follow in the traditions established by works written by Elgin, Dominguez and Robin, and Andrews. *Getting a Life: Strategies for Simple Living, Based on the Revolutionary Program for Financial Freedom, Your Money or Your Life* by Jacqueline Blix and David Heitmiller (1997), Wanda Urbanska and Frank Levering's *Simple Living: One Couple's Search for a Better Life* (1993), and Linda Breen Pierce's *Choosing Simplicity: Real People Finding Peace and Fulfillment in a Complex World* (2000) describe people's efforts to simplify. Blix and Heitmiller go into great detail about following the "Your Money or Your Life" (YMOL) program advocated by Dominguez and Robin (1992). The forward to Breen's book is written by Vicki Robin. Breen, who advocates adopting the simple life, describes the experiences of over two hundred people who have simplified their lives. Two widely circulated videotapes aired on PBS stations across the nation,[3] *Affluenza* and *Escape from Affluenza*, provide a good overview and synthesis of the ideas and practices of the movement presented with an eye toward diffusion to the broader culture. There are also several books and a couple of journals devoted to how to live cheaply. Some of the most often cited are Ernest Callenbach's *Living Cheaply with Style* (1993), and Amy Dacyczyn's *Tightwad Gazette*, a newsletter that has been compiled into three collections. Dacyczyn also wrote *The Complete Tightwad Gazette: Promoting Thrift as a Viable Alternative Lifestyle* (1999) that brings together tips on saving money drawn from issues published over a six-year period.

Some books focus on one or another of the themes that are drawn together by the major works in the movement. Several works devoted to reducing clutter, eating a sustainable diet, and saving time and money on cooking and household chores are used by simple livers as guides for achieving some of their goals. Michael Fogler's *Un-Jobbing: The Adult Liberation Handbook* (1997) is a good example of a book in the genre that deals with work from a voluntary simplicity perspective. Rich Heffern's *Adventures in Simple Living: A Creation-Centered Spirituality* (1994) focuses on living a spiritual life through voluntary simplicity. Janet Luhrs, the editor of the *Simple Living Journal,* has compiled a topically organized collection of strategies for living simply and stories about successful simple livers titled *The Simple Living Guide: A Sourcebook for Less Stressful, More Joyful Living* (1997). The simplicity circle I visited in Seattle was reading and discussing sections of Luhrs's book.

There are also some works that have been categorized by the publishing industry as simplicity books because they have "simple" or "simplicity" in the title but which don't always sit well with people in the movement. Two people mentioned they were not comfortable with Elaine St. James's works. St. James, a former real estate investor turned simplicity author, has done several books that deal with managing time, clutter, and money. Among the best known of her works are *Simplify Your Life: 100 Ways to Slow Down and Enjoy the Things That Really Matter* (1994) and *Living the Simple Life* (1996). She had been included in a voluntary simplicity program at the Phinney Community Center in Seattle as a guest speaker but was not among speakers at the Seeds of Simplicity Conference in Los Angeles in 1998 where the key leaders of the movement were represented (1998).

The Problems and Solutions Focused on in Core Texts

The literature of voluntary simplicity maintains that environmental and social problems come from an economy and culture that produce greed, stressful and unfulfilling work conditions, and overconsumption.

These conditions derive from an economy that is run purely for profit and growth and that fosters mass consumer culture rather than the true well-being of the earth and its populations. Other problems, such as a "sleeping sickness of the soul" (Andrews 1997), financial insecurity, and a lack of control over time and money are described in terms of being derivatives of overconsumption and stressful and unfulfilling work.

The solutions these authors prescribe are, first, to realize that everything exists in relation and that humans have a place in the cosmos with all other creatures, and second, that people must acknowledge it is their choice and responsibility to bring themselves back into alignment with nature by reducing consumption and gaining control over their time so they can become mindful. Doing this will also result in a more pleasurable and fulfilling lifestyle. This will be achieved through the individual actions of simple livers who will simultaneously wrest control over their own personal destinies and act as cultural change agents in creating a sustainable ecological culture.

The Ecological Ethic of Voluntary Simplicity

The core ideology and practices advocated by those in the voluntary simplicity movement are imbued with an ecological ethic that maintains that all things in the universe exist in interdependent relationship to one another and that human beings are damaging the sustainability of a continued harmonious cycle of these interdependent relationships through relentless consumption of the earth's resources. They believe the push for economic growth and social and cultural patterns of work and overconsumption that support it are at the root of the problem.

Dominguez and Robin's account of the relationality of all things is an example of the perspective found in the core texts of the movement. They write, "The fact that we are literally made of the body of the earth means that all of life is one creation, unfolding everywhere all at once. We belong. We are one human family, part of the family of life. What binds us together is stronger and more fundamental than what keeps us apart. In some strange way, life is living us as surely as we are living life. . . . The dream of 'everyone having enough' has been with us as a species for thousands of years, yet has never been fulfilled" (1992, 139–144).

An overarching theme running through the movement literature is a belief that global environmental deterioration threatens life on earth. In *Voluntary Simplicity*, Elgin outlines an evolutionary picture of the development of civilizations and cautions:

> Unless creative actions are taken soon to move beyond the industrial era, we will move deep into a harsh winter of civilizational breakdown.
>
> The signs that mark our entry into a stage of civilizational crisis are many; for example, debt-burdened and stagnating economies, the loss of a compelling sense of social purpose, special-interest groups that override the public interest and create political gridlock, overwhelming bureaucratic complexity, and inability to respond to critical problems in the local to global ecology. These challenges are so severe that industrial-era civilizations must make fundamental changes if they are to survive. . . . It is no accident that experiments in simpler living are blossoming at the very time that industrial-era ways of living have entered a time of crisis. Ecological ways of living will provide an essential foundation for building postindustrial civilizations. (1993a, 163–164)

For Elgin the understandings of the problems to be solved by voluntary simplicity are found in a grand evolutionary perspective that requires humans to participate in shaping the future evolution of the world. In this view human beings are now faced with the choice of living sustainably to foster the survival of human civilization or assuming responsibility for its demise if they continue to overconsume. To avoid environmental apocalypse an ecologically sustainable culture must develop. Elgin argues that voluntary simplicity represents a shift toward an "ecological era" and away from the "industrial era."

Andrews connects widespread indications of personal anomie to ecological degradation in the following way: "As the outer world sickens, so does our inner world. Everything around us is dying. Global warming, the hole in the ozone layer, polluted air and water, depleted topsoil, deforestation: With the earth dying how could we feel alive? The sicknesses of people and the planet are linked" (1997, 9). The ideology of voluntary simplicity presents a potentially apocalyptic vision of the future, one that is actually widely circulated in the society, but voluntary simplicity authors maintain that humans choosing to simplify can prevent it. Voluntary simplicity ideology emphasizes human responsibility and ability to control the environ-mental future of the world through making choices in keeping with an ecological ethic.

Most simple livers I interviewed have a vision of the future that includes the very real possibility of environmental collapse and feel it is their responsibility to use daily practices that reduce their contribution to the processes that will cause such an outcome. One source indicated a person involved in the movement in Seattle suffered a mental breakdown in connection to stress about Y2K and environmental collapse in 1998. Though none of my respondents has suffered a breakdown linked to these concerns, several did express strong concerns about environmental degradation and what the future might be like if voluntary simplicity is not widely adopted. Informants were also often conflicted over whether environmental collapse can, or will, be prevented.

Elgin is sensitive to the psychological discomfort that the prospect of civilizational collapse presents for simple livers but makes clear that there is hope for a positive future. He writes:

> It is psychologically demanding to consider the breakdown and transformation of civilizations. This is not an abstract process, as we are the persons who must live through it. A venture into this realm of inquiry may bring—as it has for me—considerable psychological discomfort. All of the hopes and fears that lie in uneasy though quiet repose in our everyday lives become starkly visible as we consider the depth and scope of change that lies ahead. Our anxiety about transformative civilizational change is lessened when we realize that it is part of a natural and purposeful process. To see the organic nature of social evolution, we need to separate the deeper currents of change from the surface turbulence that occupies so much of our public attention. (1993a, 164–165)

Elgin's more recent work (1997) drives this home and extends his early theory drawing on the concept of the collective consciousness of Carl Jung. The huge web of creation is described by Elgin as both a mystical web of constant creation and a realistic, often scientifically argued, set of ideas blending mysticism, puritanism, and positivism to propose that the conscious evolution of humanity has become possible. According to Elgin one of the key enablers of this is communication media, and the lifestyle of voluntary simplicity is both a response to this new consciousness and a catalyst for it. Elgin also draws on the ideas of Abraham Maslow (1968) to argue that despite the rise and fall of many civilizations there is an overall process of evolution toward a self-reflective and self-organizing global civilization that suggests higher levels of human development. He claims Western psychology, Eastern philosophical traditions, and major religious traditions support this view (1997).[4]

Elgin provides a particularly clearly outlined set of ideas that lead to the conclusion that voluntary simplicity promises a shared vision of the future of the planet as one in which conflict is not necessary and an ecological ethic prevails. Competition is not useful. Cooperation is the way to relate to others (1993a, 1993b). The ecological ethic provides the framework for integrating the "strategies of action" for the alternative culture of voluntary simplicity.

Global Inequality: How Much Is Enough?

The group that is singled out as the primary contributor to environmental degradation is the middle-class consumer in Western countries, especially in the United States. The middle class is caught on the treadmill of overconsumption and overwork created by a culture driven by profit at all costs.

Dominguez and Robin and Andrews draw on Alan Durning's book *How Much Is Enough? The Consumer Society and the Future of the Earth* (1992). Durning maintains there are three global classes; the consumer class, the middle-income class, and the poor. The consumer class includes all households whose income per family member, per year, is above $7,500. The middle-income class includes those who earn between $700 and $7,500 per family member. The poor are those who earn less than $700 per family member per year. Durning asserts that the global middle-income group that consumes at significantly lower levels than the global affluent is the group that people should aspire to emulate because it represents a better model for those who truly care about environmental sustainability.

Each of the authors argues that the Western middle class or consumer class must accept responsibility for depleting the earth's resources and make a commitment to reducing its overconsumption to facilitate everyone in the world having enough. Dominguez and Robin express this idea in the following way: "Initially, responsibility is about identifying when you have enough and stopping there—for your own well-being. Ultimately responsibility is about everyone in the world having enough, and finding ways for all of us to get there—for the well-being of the earth. We become response-able to life itself" (1992, 137–138).

Elgin, Dominguez and Robin, and Andrews each maintain that individuals must determine what is enough for themselves. There is no externally defined measure of enough imposed on the individual; instead, individuals are in control of judging how much is enough for them. Elgin writes: "Balance occurs when there is sufficiency—when there is neither material excess nor deficit. To find this balance in our everyday lives requires that we understand the difference between our personal "needs" and our "wants." Needs are those things that are essential to survival and our growth. Wants are those things that are extra—that gratify our psychological desires. . . . Only when we are clear about what we need and what we want can we begin to pare away the excess and find a middle path between extremes. No one else can find this balance for us. This is a task that we each must do for ourselves" (1993a, 147–148). Dominguez and Robin introduce a "fulfillment curve" that shows the relationship between the experience of fulfillment and the amount of money we spend:

> Part of the secret to life, it would seem, comes from identifying for yourself that point of maximum fulfillment. There is a name for this peak of the Fulfillment Curve, and it provides the basis for transforming your relationship with money. It's a word we use every day, yet we are practically incapable of recognizing it when it's staring us in the face. The word is 'enough.' . . . Enough for our survival. Enough comforts. And even enough little 'luxuries.' We have everything we need; there's nothing extra to weigh us down, distract or distress us, nothing we've bought on time, have never used and are slaving to pay off. Enough is a fearless place. A trusting place. An honest and self-observant place. It's appreciating and fully enjoying what money brings into your life and yet never purchasing anything that isn't needed and wanted. (1992, 25)

Simple livers are empowered to determine for themselves what is enough without being judged by either those who have less and might accuse them of greed or those who value status consumption and prestige occupations and might judge them as less worthy. They can have the sense of being in control of choices they make to simplify and are supported in saving and investing not as a greedy activity but as an activity that fosters reduced environmental damage.

Consumption as a Cultural Tool

The problem that receives the most attention in the literature in terms of solutions and prescribed practices is consumption. Problems associated with work-related stress and long hours run a close second. Voluntary simplicity authors maintain that human fulfillment and physical health are threatened by the dominant consumer lifestyle and values associated with Western consumer society. They blame advertising and other media for pressuring people to consume things that are damaging to the environment.

The practices advocated combine personal frugality with environmentally conscious purchasing and lifestyle choices that seek fulfillment from doing volunteer work, creative activities, and spending time in nature rather than buying "stuff." Elgin advocates rejecting "identity consumption" to find "authentic" identity. He writes:

> Four consumption criteria, developed by a group in San Francisco while exploring a life of conscious simplicity, go to the heart of the issue of balanced consumption:
>
> Does what I own or buy promote activity, self-reliance, and involvement, or does it induce passivity and dependence?
>
> Are my consumption patterns basically satisfying, or do I buy much that serves no real need?
>
> How tied are my present job and lifestyle to installment payments, maintenance and repair costs, and the expectations of others?
>
> Do I consider the impact of my consumption patterns on other people and on the earth?

> This compassionate approach to consumption stands in stark contrast to the industrial-era view, which assumes that if we increase our consumption, we will increase our happiness. However, when we equate our identity with that which we consume—when we engage in "identity consumption"—we become possessed by our possessions. . . . Our identity becomes not a free-standing, authentic expression in the moment, but a material mask that we have constructed so as to present a more appealing image for others to see. (1993a, 148–149)

Elgin focuses on the connections between altruism and the expression of authentic self that can be achieved through rejecting mass consumer values.

Cecile Andrews advocates resisting mass consumption and media pressure to consume, reevaluating the dominant culture's standards for housework, self-presentation, and home decor, and links changes in these practices to gaining self-actualization. Building relationships with other people and working to promote vital local communities are also central for her. Andrews devotes the whole of a chapter to consumption. She writes:

> Many experts give us only thirty to forty years before we reach the point at which our damage to the environment becomes irreparable. Much of the damage is the result of things we buy. The production of every single product means we have used up some of the earth.
>
> How can we save the earth? . . . [I]t is just as important to reduce the rate of consumption by major industrial countries. For instance, we have more cars, we drive more, we have bigger houses, we have more air conditioning, we fly more, we eat higher off the food chain. American houses are twice as big as they were forty-five years ago; we have more shopping centers than high schools; we drink more soft drinks than tap water. In our time-starved lives we turn to environmentally expensive conveniences: prepared foods, disposables, clothes dryers and kitchen appliances. We're using up nature. (1997, 49–50)

Andrews suggests that mass consumers have sold their souls for convenience and status. The consumer lifestyle, according to Andrews, results in spiritual emptiness which characterizes modern American life. She writes, "People feel an emptiness, a sense that life isn't all it could be. Albert Schweitzer called it our "sleeping sickness of the soul." Why a sleeping sickness of the soul? Is it because we have sold our soul for comforts and conveniences, for status and success?" (1997, 2). Andrews blames shopping and television for many social problems, including the loss of community life. She maintains, "The underlying idea of consumerism is the idea that more is always better. If more is always better, that means you will never have enough, so you will never by satisfied. You'll never really enjoy what you have. You will be bored and cynical. You will always be yearning for something you don't have. . . . The reason we consume is because we are empty and trying to fill up that emptiness. . . . Much of our emptiness comes from not meeting our real needs for self-esteem and community. We all must have a sense of our own worth, a sense of being valued. But our uncaring society has undermined it" (1997, 58). Andrews provides a long list of suggestions for reducing consumerism: avoid advertising, don't shop as entertainment, research every purchase, and develop your own personal slow-down mechanisms, like delaying a purchase to make sure you really want to make it. Andrews explains that reducing consumption does not mean people are not being loyal Americans, pointing out that consumption serves corporations, not the majority of people in the United States. She cautions her readers not to confuse national loyalty with corporate interests. She writes, "We are forsaking our values of life, liberty, and justice for all by consuming, not by reducing our consuming" (1997, 64).

Dominguez and Robin draw on Paul Wachtel's book *The Poverty of Affluence* (1989) to support their position that more material possessions do not necessarily produce greater happiness. They, like other voluntary simplicity writers, question the belief that more is better and link it to the evils of the rat race and environmental degradation. They write:

> Paul Wachtel, author of *The Poverty of Affluence*, calls into question our reliance on "more is better" as the solution to all our yearnings. He shows how our frantic pursuit of more ends up working against the very ends it's designed to serve, security and fulfillment: . . .
>
> You lose the ability to identify that point of sufficiency at which you can choose to stop. . . .
>
> Modern economics worships growth. Growth will solve poverty, the theory goes. Growth will increase our standard of living. Growth will reduce unemployment.
>
> What we overlook is that the fuel of economic growth comes from nature, and even under the best of circumstances, nature is not infinitely abundant. Resources can and do run out.
>
> We have come to believe, deeply, that it is our right to consume. If we have the money, we can buy whatever we want, whether or not we need it, use it or even enjoy it.
>
> Beyond the constitutional rights of free speech, assembly, due process, and so on, there is the right to have anything you want, as long as you are willing to pay for it (or at least promise to pay for it . . . on time). Environmentalists who question the right to buy a new gas guzzler or social activists who

question the cost to society of one person's owning a forty-five room house while others sleep on the street are maligned as interfering with the rights of free individuals. Now we aren't questioning the right to own private property. We are simply highlighting how profoundly we have taken our right to consume to heart, and perhaps placed it above other rights, privileges and duties of a free society. (1992, 12–13, 17)

Dominguez and Robin believe that what is required is a shift from an ethic of growth to an ethic of sustainability which requires us to transform our relationship with money and the material world: "Transforming our relationship with money and re-evaluating our earning and spending activity could put us and the planet back on track" (1992, 21). They emphasize the power of money, both in terms of its ability to command the earth's resources and its symbolic significance.

Each of the central texts of the movement gives serious consideration to mass consumption as a major cause of environmental and human problems. And the general prescriptions in each are quite similar.

The Oppression of Waged Work

The theme of disappointment and dissatisfaction with waged work runs through the voluntary simplicity literature. Dominguez and Robin attack what they call "jobism." They write, "Along with racism and sexism, our society has a form of caste system based on what you do for money. We call that jobism, and it pervades our interactions with one another on the job, in social settings and even at home. Why else would we consider housewives second-class citizens?" (1992, 5). These authors view jobism as an important social issue and place it as a form of caste system just like racism and sexism. Along with many who adopt voluntary simplicity, they view work as a major source of disappointment and dissatisfaction in their lives. They experience their need to earn money to survive along with cultural pressures to practice status consumption in keeping with the dictates of the dominant culture as the greatest oppressions they are conscious of suffering under.

In each of the voluntary simplicity texts there is a sense of economic insecurity being an issue. The texts mention concerns with job insecurity and scarcity, and instability of career trajectories among reasons to adopt voluntary simplicity (Andrews 1997; Dominquez and Robin 1992; Fogler 1997). Dominguez and Robin make these claims:

For many people, material possessions went from fulfilling needs to enhancing comfort to facilitating luxury—and even beyond to excess. We went from individual national economies to an increasingly global economy.

Over time our relationship with money—earning it, spending it, investing it, owing it, protecting it, worrying about it—has taken over the major part of our lives.

Most of us spend much more than 40 hours out of the week's total of 168 hours earning money. We must take time to dress for our jobs, commute to our jobs, think about our jobs at work and at home, "decompress" from our jobs. We must spend our evenings and weekends in mindless "escape entertainment" in order to "recreate" from our jobs. We must occasionally "vacate" our jobs, or spend time in the doctor's office to repair our job-stressed health. We need to plan our "careers," attend job seminars or union meetings, lobby or picket for our jobs.

With all that time and money spent on and around our jobs, is it any wonder that we have come to take our identities from them?

When we are not taking our identity from our jobs, we are identified as "consumers."

The material progress that was supposed to free us has left us more enslaved. (1992, xix–xxi)

Dominguez and Robin are questioning several key cultural and economic structures generally taken for granted in the dominant culture and embedded in the institutional structures of contemporary Western societies. They are questioning the notion that it is natural or desirable for a profit-and-growth-driven economy to be taken as given. They are questioning the instrumental rationality that characterizes economic relations in capitalism. However, they don't identify capitalism itself as a central contributor to the relations they seek to change. They are questioning the idea that more material wealth is better. They believe that, beyond a certain level that provides for essential needs and a little more, material wealth is not beneficial. They are questioning the necessity for people to have to do work that is alienating. As the preceding quote demonstrates, voluntary simplicity offers people neatly linked and simple ideology and practices that make meaning of history and the present in ways that support rejecting waged work. It empowers individuals and small groups to take charge of changing their own participation in social relations that take alienated and rationalized waged work as given.

Dominguez and Robin believe people should do only enough waged work to save and invest capital that generates income adequate to support them at a level they individually arrive at as enough for them to live comfortably. They should then quit working for a wage. What does this accomplish? Dominguez and Robin and many of their readers say it reduces environmental damage, frees up jobs for other people in a tight job market, gives simple livers financial security and freedom from worry about money, and allows them to have time to do more meaningful things and to carry the spirit of voluntary simplicity into the world by example.

More meaningful activities may include any number of things, but a high priority for Dominguez and Robin is promoting community service through volunteer work. It is assumed that doing volunteer work will meet social needs better than waged work. Dominguez grew up poor in New York City and struggled to get a job on Wall Street. He lost his first job because the firm collapsed. When he got another job, he decided to save every penny he could and invest it so he could quit work and live off of interest income. His aim was to feel financially secure and to have a sense of self-sufficiency. He found he could live on $7,000 a year. He invested in treasury bills. Of course, the reality that goes unrecognized by Dominguez and Robin is that he, and all of the other people following the plan in *Your Money or Your Life,* may feel self-sufficient once their investment income is adequate to meet their living expenses but they are still dependent on the economy aimed at profit and growth for their investment income.

Bringing this set of ideas together in this way creates a unique attitude toward waged work, consumerism, and the accumulation of wealth. Accumulate enough to maintain a frugal lifestyle, that is comfortable for you as an individual, and then quit so you can be free of the pressures of rationalized work for a wage which almost always dampens your authenticity and is not fulfilling.[5] You accumulate wealth to allow you to escape from an occupation that is rarely a calling so you can use your time to pursue what is a calling. In this way voluntary simplicity offers the promise of financial security, freedom from working for a wage, greater choice and control over time to become self-actualized, and feelings of being a good person by "leaving as light an environmental footprint as possible," as one simple liver expressed to me.

Andrews and Elgin do not come down as hard on work for pay as do Dominguez and Robin. They both criticize contemporary working conditions that deaden rather than enhance life, but they continue to hold out hope that some work for pay can be fulfilling. Andrews presents the idea that what is important is to pursue your passion, be it for pay or not. Elgin describes worthwhile work as a "calling."

The ideology links the desire to save the environment and humanity from the chaos of global environmental collapse and the desire to save themselves from the immediate discomfort of having to work long hours at deadening jobs or practice status consumerism. The literature identifies both dominant cultural consumerist practices associated with postmodern social control and rationalized waged work associated with modernity as forms of domination and suggests alternative consumption practices and ways of surviving that are doable in contemporary society.[6]

The Green Triangle

Dominguez and Robin and Andrews use the "green triangle," a conceptual tool, in explaining how voluntary simplicity works to solve these problems of overwork, overconsumption, and environmental damage. The green triangle is credited to Earnest Callenbach (1975, 1993), who first described it in his futuristic utopian novel, *Ecotopia* (1975). Though Elgin does not mention it explicitly, his reasoning is quite similar and he cites the works of authors who do mention it. In his 1993 book *Living Cheaply With Style: Live Better and Spend Less*, also popular among simple livers, Callenbach draws on the concept of the green triangle to promote frugal spending habits. Callenbach describes the green triangle as follows:

> The three points of the triangle are environment, health, and money. The principle that relates these three points is: *Anytime you do something beneficial for one of them, you will almost inevitably also do something beneficial for the other two*—whether you're aiming to or not.
>
> [Y]ou can start at any point of the Green Triangle. Let's assume you do something beneficial for the environment, like walking or bicycling instead of driving your car. You cut down pollution emissions, you reduce smog and lung damage, you decrease acid rain, and you may help postpone the greenhouse effect. But you'll also help your health, because you get more regular exercise and you'll save money on gas, oil and car depreciation. (1993, xiii)

Dominguez and Robin draw on Callenbach's concept of the green triangle. They assert that time is money and if you save money you are not just saving your "life energy," you are also saving the planet. Here's how it works:

> Earnest Callenbach, author of *Ecotopia* (a future fantasy in which Northern California, Oregon and Washington secede from the union to form an ecologically sound society), observes that your health, your pocketbook and the environment have a mutually enhancing relationship. If you do something good for one, it's almost always good for the other two. If you walk or bicycle to work to reduce your contribution to green house gases you are also saving money and getting great exercise at the same time.
>
> It isn't just an odd coincidence that saving money and saving the planet are connected. In fact, in some sense your money is the planet. Here's how.
>
> Money is a lien on earth's resources. Every time we spend money on anything, we are consuming not only the metal, plastic, wood or other material in the item itself, but also all the resources it took to extract these from the earth, transport them to the manufacturer, process them, assemble the product, ship it to the retailer and bring it from the store to your home. . . . [T]here are some environmental costs that aren't included in the price, what economists call externalities: the pollution and waste we pay for in other ways—lung disease, cancer, respiratory problems, desertification, flooding, etc. (1992, 213)

These voluntary simplicity authors use the green triangle concept to bring what is best for the individual together with what is best for the planet in a neatly worked out set of interrelationships.

The solution to the problems identified can be addressed through the individual actions of simple livers. Voluntary simplicity gives practitioners a sense of control over their destinies and the ability to act as cultural change agents rather than feeling helpless or alone.

Elgin writes:

> As individuals we are not powerless in the face of this monumental change. Opportunities for meaningful and important action are everywhere: the food we eat, the work we do, the transportation we use, the manner in which we relate to others, the clothing we wear, the learning we acquire, the compassion-

ate causes we support, the level of attention we invest in our moment-to-moment passage through life, and so on. The list is endless, since the stuff of social transformation is identical with the stuff from which our daily lives are constructed.

[W]e are each uniquely responsible for our actions and choices in this pivotal time in human evolution. There is no one who can take our place. We each weave a singular strand in the web of life. No one else can weave that strand for us. (1993a, 192–193)

Elgin maintains there are three possible paths ahead of humanity. Humanity may face collapse caused by "perpetuating the status quo and running the biosphere into ruin" (189). Stagnation can result if "citizens are passive and rely upon remote bureaucracies and technological solutions to handle a deteriorating local-to-global situation" (189–190). Or revitalization can occur if people will "directly engage our predicament as individuals, families, communities, and nations" (190) through grassroots involvement.

The world that is often experienced as out of control and fragmented is viewed by simple livers as actually well ordered and intricately interconnected, and everyone and everything is part of it. For those in voluntary simplicity each individual originates from the whole and must be honored as a unique part of the whole of nature. People in voluntary simplicity believe contemporary patterns of waged work and consumption play key roles in obstructing a harmonious relationship with nature based on an ecological ethic. The green triangle is an example of a conceptual tool that simple livers use to affirm, at a very concrete level, the positive impacts of their lifestyle.

No Personal Blame

According to the voluntary simplicity literature, individuals should not be blamed personally for the ecological crisis; instead the problem is viewed as culturally and economically produced. People are greedy and seek status through consumption and occupation because media, their reference groups, and the way society is structured promote this attitude. Blaming or negative judgments of others are discouraged as unproductive in solving the problems. Elgin expresses the idea this way: "There is no one to blame for our movement into a stage of civilizational transition. Who can be blamed when the problems we face are intrinsic to the intertwined structure of life in which we all participate? The views and values that arose in realizing the potential of the industrial era were fitting for that time. Now these same views and values are becoming increasingly ill suited for carrying us into the future. Although no one is to blame, we are all responsible for where we go from here" (1993a, 173).

Dominguez and Robin caution against negative judgements of oneself as well as others: "Judgment (blaming ourselves and others) is labeling things in terms of good and bad. . . . On the road to transforming your relationship with money and achieving Financial Independence, you will find that judgment and blame do not serve. *Discernment*, on the other hand, is an essential skill. Discernment is sorting out the true from the false, separating the wheat from the chaff. . . . Aligning your spending with this faculty is the key to Financial Integrity" (1992, 74).

Andrews gives particular emphasis to the cultural forces contributing to over consumption. She writes, "If we are looking at the forces in our society that make us greedy, the ease of consumption is one. But maybe you think that consumption is an individual decision, that no one is forcing us to buy. Theoretically that's true. But, when you analyze the forces driving us to consume, you realize it is a systemic problem, not just an individual failing. . . . [W]e are victims of propaganda that we are almost powerless to resist. Our materialistic way of life is shoved down our throats every minute of the day, and because we are so cut off from meeting our real needs, we are even more vulnerable to marketing's message" (1997, 16–17). Andrews holds that our culture virtually forces us to consume too much. According to her, the mass of unthinking consumers as well as those who have come to voluntary simplicity from affluent lifestyles are not to blame, but voluntary simplicity adopters have separated themselves from the unthinking masses by becoming simple livers and have assumed responsibility for change that will help to prevent an apocalyptic breakdown of the environment.

The authors say they don't believe that conflict results in positive change. Andrews devotes a small section of her book to explaining that people think more clearly when not under attack. The people in the movement don't want to be attacked or to attack other people. Perhaps the political climate of the late 1980s and early 1990s, which was not very receptive to the activist pressures for change they had at least in part identified with, may have contributed to making this approach attractive.

In theory, anyone who is seeking to simplify can be included in the movement no matter how wealthy or what lifestyle they are leading so long as they are trying to move to a simpler life. There is tension within the movement regarding being nonjudgmental, but in the literature the idea is that all should be welcome and not be judged or blamed.

The Influence of Other Movements

Environmentalism, feminism, and to a lesser extent the civil rights and gay and lesbian liberation movements are mentioned in the movement literature. Voluntary simplicity authors draw some ideas from these movements and at times claim similarities with them. As was discussed earlier in this chapter, Callenbach's (1975, 1993) concept of the green triangle is employed and elaborated by each of the authors to link human health, wealth, and the well-being of the environment into a neatly interconnected and mutually harmonious relationship if people adopt voluntary simplicity. Alan Durning's (1992) *How Much Is Enough? The Consumer Society and the Future of the Earth*, done under the auspices of the Worldwatch Institute's Environmental Alert Series, is also cited by Dominguez and Robin, Elgin, and Andrews. Andrews cites Carolyn Merchant's *Radical Ecology* (1992) but she makes use of Merchant in a very general way to point to the need for a relational rather than dominating stance toward nature. Prescriptions for sustainable living are drawn from a wide range of sources and aim at being things people can do without withdrawing from the mainstream and that are possible in urban as well as rural communities. Overall the ecological ethic expressed in the voluntary simplicity literature seems to echo ideas held by deep ecologists such as Devall and Sessions (1985), but the authors do not cite works by deep ecologists or refer to them, so it is difficult to know if there are any direct links.

The big problems according to the texts of voluntary simplicity are overconsumption, the pressures of working in a rationalized society, and being cut off from our authentic self by a culture that is driven by profit and is destroying nature as an object.

The Puritan Heritage and the Spirit of Voluntary Simplicity

The key authors discussed make a connection between voluntary simplicity and the Puritans. Elgin says voluntary simplicity is influenced by Christian,

Eastern, Early Greek, Puritan, Quaker, and Transcendentalist views. He says the following about Puritan views:

> Paradoxically, although the United States is the world's most blatantly consumerist nation, the simple life has strong roots in American history. The early Puritan settlers brought to America their "puritan ethic," which stressed hard work, temperate living, participation in the life of the community, and a steadfast devotion to things spiritual. Puritans also stressed the golden mean by saying we should not desire more material things than we can use effectively. It is from the New England Puritans that we get the adage, Use it up, wear it out, make do, or do without. Although the Puritan tradition tended to be hierarchical, elitist, and authoritarian, it also had a compassionate side that encouraged people to use their excess wealth to help the deserving poor. Puritans were not opposed to prosperity itself, but to the greed and selfishness that seemed to accompany excessive abundance. (1993a, 50–51)

The television program *Escape From Affluenza*, which is available on videotape, also includes a discussion of the continuity between contemporary voluntary simplicity values and the values of the Puritan pilgrims and Andrews writes, "When we create a new vision of life, we need to build on what we cherish in our past. To feel a sense of dignity, a nation needs to have a sense of pride in its heritage—we have seen it as African Americans recapture their roots, as women reclaim their history. Our founding fathers and mothers advocated the simple life, warned against excess and shallow materialism, exhorted us to develop the inner life. Along the way, we've forgotten this, but now people are remembering. Recapturing the simple life is a return to the good life" (1997, xxi).

Dominguez and Robin critique the linkage the Protestant ethic makes between waged work and a calling but value the frugality exemplified by Benjamin Franklin. They write:

> The final piece of the puzzle (why work has lost it's vitality) snaps into place when we look at the shift in the religious attitude toward work that came with the rise of the Protestant ethic. Before that time work was profane and religion was sacred. Afterward work was seen as the arena where you worked for your salvation—and the evidence of a successful religious life was success in the world of business.

So here we are at the end of the twentieth century. . . . Our jobs now serve the function that traditionally belonged to religion: they are the place where we seek answers to the perennial questions 'Who am I?' and 'Why am I here?' and 'What's it all for?' (1992, 224–225)

Dominguez and Robin advocate separating our idea of work as a calling from work for a wage. This means redefining work and realizing that finding "right livelihood" through waged work is not likely. So what they recommend is: "When at your paid job you can value your life energy by working efficiently, diligently, intelligently and for the highest remuneration possible. When doing the rest of your work, you can value your life energy by working efficiently, diligently, intelligently and with the greatest degree of enthusiasm and love you have in you" (1992, 231). They believe that being fulfilled in a calling is rarely possible through waged work. They advocate doing things we enjoy, but in particular doing volunteer work as a calling. They say, "Volunteering is the epitome of self-expression— choosing what you do based on an inner prompting."

They maintain, "You can continue to work for your own needs and desires, to buy more possessions or experiences, or you can work for something larger than yourself that gives to others and the world. You can consume or you can create" (1992, 281–282). The people in the contemporary voluntary simplicity movement say they are influenced by the Puritans but are also quick to note they are not into self-denial.

The ascetic lifestyle the Puritans advocated has been and continues to be an influence in modern culture and economy. And, not surprisingly, ideas regarding frugality and simplicity in the voluntary simplicity movement have been traced by some back to the ideas held by the Puritan founding fathers of America (Shi 1985, 1986; *Affluenza* 1997, *Escape from Affluenza* 1998). But the differences between the daily life circumstances and desires of simple livers that support the rise of the spirit of voluntary simplicity and those that supported the rise of the spirit of capitalism are profound. To understand why the people in the contemporary voluntary simplicity movement draw on some of the ideas of the Puritans and not upon others in creating their unique voluntary simplicity ideology we have to look at the context of their lives in contemporary America. The ideas themselves are given meaning through the ways they are used by people in the movement today. The Puritans looked to God and sought salvation in the afterlife. Simple livers look to the choice human beings make to live in keeping with the ecological ethic and seek fulfillment in this life through living simply.

People in voluntary simplicity, confronted with evolutionary science that points to the demise of human life, have done "ideological work" (Berger 1981, 1995)[7] that enables them to believe in a modified form of evolution, one in which humans can intervene to change the process (Elgin 1997).

The contemporary voluntary simplicity movement is dedicated to resisting the impacts of bureaucratic rationalization that Weber ([1904] 1958) associated with the "iron cage." Voluntary simplicity authors are most specifically resisting pressures from the rationalization process at work in the market and work for pay as a necessity of life. They advocate pulling production and reproductive work back into the private sphere of the household and extended private sphere of the local community. They often apply a similar methodical and calculated approach to reducing consumption and waged work and to pursuit of meaningful activities as that described by Weber of the Puritans seeking salvation. Yet simple livers seek connection with the enchanted world outside of the iron cage of rationalized work and consumerism as a way to achieve whole selves and as a way to save the planet. The ecological ethic enables simple livers to feel connection with the enchanted world of all creation through adopting the beliefs and practices that are the spirit of voluntary simplicity.

Other sociologists have noted similar reactions in other contemporary groups. Michael Schwalbe (1996) saw enchantment as a driving force in the mythopoetic men's movement. Mary Jo Neitz (1999) has found the same to be true of contemporary Wicca. These groups offer participants a place to connect with others who have similar experiences and to explore alternative ways of being.

In the social sciences generally we are seeing a critique of the rationality and the Enlightenment assumptions about the nature of reality and the basis of knowledge. Is the voluntary simplicity movement a popular culture movement that is also breaking with the Enlightenment project? I don't think so. There is a paradox in the movement regarding this issue. Its adherents question the knowledge of experts as the basis of knowing but turn to data derived by means of the scientific method consistently in their arguments. They accept an evolutionary understanding of history, but elaborate it to include human choice as the key influence in the process. These tensions within the movement about what constitutes knowledge and how best to construct it are of vital importance to the direction the movement may take and what sort of transformative potential it has. These tensions are not explicitly discussed but are undercurrents present almost all of the time in circle meetings.

Followers of the movement seek reunion with nature, and yet they continue to highly value efficiency and using time well. What they want to escape is the confines of a niche in the cogs of bureaucracy, not the tools provided by the Enlightenment for managing in the world. Simple livers believe life energy spent earning money to survive is not what gives life meaning. For them a penny saved is still a penny earned but earned to enable them to buy time away from rationalized waged work. Theirs is very much a real world to be understood through experience. What they do reject is the validity of expert knowledge over their own lived experience if the two conflict.

Weber believed interests are the driving force behind action, but that historically unfolding ideas determine the substance of interests. Yet if ideas such as the ones discussed in this chapter shape ethos, then "[W]hy did the ethos of ascetic Protestantism outlast its ideas" (Swidler 1986, 276)? Swidler suggests that "what endures is *the way action is organized*, not its ends" (276). She maintains that reliance on "moral work on the self to organize action" is an enduring feature, not the particular end toward which such work is directed. With this in mind, those engaged in voluntary simplicity can be understood, at least in part, to be carrying forward the moral work on the self and way of action that Weber identified as central in shaping modernity and at the same time to be resisting rationalized work, consumerism, and the McDonaldization process (Ritzer 2000) which have been shaped by this mode of action historically.

Conclusion

The core texts present the dominant culture's pressures to consume and work to get money to survive, establish social status, and construct identity as the most salient forms of oppression. Simple livers are resisting aspects of the rationalization process (Weber [1904] 1958) as it manifests in the market economy and bureaucratically organized workplaces. They often describe these effects in terms of their personal experiences in waged work.[8]

The two books widely used in circles, Andrews's (1997) book, which offers a seven-step program toward voluntary simplicity, and Dominguez and Robin's (1992) book, which offers a nine-step program toward financial independence, both take self-help approaches that are then connected to fulfilling hopes of broader social change. There are elements of consciousness raising, self-help, and concerns with broader cultural and economic change in these works. No cohesive set of political goals or activist practices is included, but the sense of individual change leading cumlatively to broader cultural and economic change is found in all of the three core texts.

Voluntary simplicity ideology offers middle-class, white hetero-sexuals a perspective that allows them to discuss their suffering, to try to understand the sources of their oppression, and to figure out what they can do to cope or change the circumstances that cause their discomfort. The most powerful form of oppression felt by this group tends to be the increasingly rationalized waged-labor market and cultural pressures to engage in status consumption often accompanied by varying degrees of concern about the environment and social problems. The voluntary simplicity literature and the group support model that some of the literature recommends allows them to connect with other people who have the same experience and arrive at ways to lessen or eliminate the pressures they feel are most uncomfortable in their lives, the pressures of downsizing, increasingly limited autonomy in decision making, job insecurity, and pressures to work long hours and consume status goods. It also relieves them of the need to fight directly with powerful, privileged people in the society, as some of them have experienced doing earlier in their lives. It empowers them to reject being blamed or judged by people in the mainstream or marginalized groups who might criticize white middle-class people. And it gives them a place where their condition, their social location, is the acknowledged norm.

In *Escape from Affluenza,* a television program about simple living, the impression that the movement represents a diverse group that includes racial and ethnic minorities and people in different socio-economic groups is constructed. Despite the fact that all of the people in the movement who I interviewed acknowledge that it is a largely white, middle-class movement, people in the movement want to be inclusive and want the movement to reach beyond its present confines.

The alternative of voluntary simplicity is constructed in contrast to certain aspects of mainstream culture which include consumer culture, working in the "rat race," and the demise of grassroots community self-sufficiency in the dominant culture. Status consumption and human worth judged by occupational status derived from the values of the dominant culture are rejected and an alternative way of establishing human worth that values living an integrated life devoted to self-fulfillment and service is constructed.

The solution for the problems identified, according to voluntary simplicity, rests primarily with the global middle-income group with whom most of them identify. It is this group that has the primary responsibility for being cultural change agents who reshape their own identities and lifestyles, and through doing so generate the start-up energy needed to propel the cultural shift required to move into the "ecological era" (Elgin 1993a, 1993b) and prevent environmental disaster. If you practice voluntary simplicity you are different from the greedy mass consumers who mindlessly follow harmful cultural patterns. You are a member of a unique and special group of people who are different, in a good way; you are on the cutting edge of what is the spirit of the future, the spirit of voluntary simplicity. According to the voluntary simplicity literature, living in keeping with the ecological ethic will enable humans to have enough and more and to live fulfilled and pleasurable lives in harmony with nature and each other.

The voluntary simplicity movement ideology, as it is reflected in the movement literature, is an emergent and fluid set of "strategies of action" (Swidler 1986, 273) that both struggles with and draws from the dominant culture. The ideology of the movement is also a product of power relations that reflect an effort to influence the use of resources toward the preferred interests of simple livers. Interests are thus important in shaping ideas, and ideology can serve interests through its potential to construct and regulate action (Swidler 1986, 280). This points to the need to shift analytical attention beyond concern with doctrine to the processes of adjustment, interaction, and change in the daily lives of movement participants. To fully understand the significance of the ideology found in the texts described in this chapter and embraced by people in the voluntary simplicity movement entails exploring why the movement gives prominence to this set of ideas at this time. Such understanding requires analyzing the material interests that influence these processes of selection and construction (Marx 1978) and the situations of relative power (Collins 1990) held by this group as well as the structural constraints and historical circumstances within which participants in the contemporary voluntary simplicity movement struggle for dominance.

To understand why these ideas are chosen and combined with other ideas in a particular way, chapter 3 looks more closely at the people who are simple livers and the cultural and economic circumstances that surround and bear on them in twentieth-century America and asks what kind of "identity work" is taking place. Chapter 3 describes patterns in the biographies of simple livers that help explain why some of these ideas are so appealing to them. It considers what role voluntary simplicity plays in how people's identities are fashioned and altered over time and the structural locations of simple livers and their material interests. Bringing these ideas together in the way the movement does gives them a way to construct moral identities as good people, to find self-acceptance and inner resources that allow them to exert their independence from the mass of consumers and workers in the "rat race," and to redefine themselves as simple livers instead of greedy, soulless "consumer zombies." It allows them to see themselves as fulfilled in a calling instead of being, as one informant said, "wage labor slaves" while at the same time supporting their interests in maintaining adequate access to resources and gaining more control over how they spend their time.

CHAPTER THREE

Getting a Life:
Constructing a Moral Identity in the Voluntary Simplicity Movement

People in the voluntary simplicity movement are engaged in a struggle to define themselves as worthwhile and good people. Resisting participation in conspicuous consumption enables them to feel they are living in keeping with their ecological and social values. Some also reduce their participation in waged work so they will have more time to pursue community and creative activities they consider worthwhile, and have a more fulfilling and pleasurable lifestyle. Simple livers frequently refer to this process as "getting a life" (Blix and Heitmiller 1997).

Shifts in consumption practices aimed at reducing environmental deterioration serve as a key tool used to give tangible evidence that simple livers are no longer like other middle-class, Western "consumer zombies" or status-seeking careerists whose lifestyles are judged by those in voluntary simplicity to be responsible for the current environmental crisis and at the root of many social problems. In one way the process of "getting a life" in the voluntary simplicity movement can be understood as identity work aimed at remaking the self as a moral identity while simultaneously resisting the rationalization process (Weber [1904] 1958) and the forces of McDonaldization that increasingly characterize contemporary society globally (Ritzer 2000).

Voluntary Simplicity Moral Identities

The voluntary simplicity moral identity involves both caring about the environment and others and caring for oneself. Simple livers are quick to say it is not about self-denial but about self-fulfillment. They reshape meanings based on their identities as middle-class, white, Westerners from their relative positions of power at the intersections of the categories of class, gender, and race/ethnicity in such a way that they clarify the qualities and practices of a good person who looks like them and construct those qualities and practices so they are achievable for themselves.

I use Schwalbe's definition of "identity work": "By identity work I mean anything we do, alone or with others, to establish, change, or lay claim to meanings as particular kinds of persons. As individuals, we must do some kind of identity work in every encounter. We do this when we give signs through dress, speech, demeanor, posture—that tell others who and what we are, how we are likely to behave, and how we expect to be treated. We do it also when we reflect on the meanings of our identities and try to reshape those meanings. This can be done alone, in thought or writing. Most identity work is interactive, however, since it is by engaging with others that we create and affirm the meanings that matter" (1996, 105).

How people in voluntary simplicity are biographically located within the matrix of existing social hierarchies is important because their relative power and the sense of oppression they experience as a result of their location shape what they are struggling for and against, the ideology they develop, the practices they advocate, and the type of moral identity they construct.

The type of identity work done by women and men to achieve a voluntary simplicity moral identity varies because of their differing locations of relative power and the aspects of contemporary culture that they reject with the support of voluntary simplicity ideology. Their material interests also influence the voluntary simplicity ideas they generate. Voluntary simplicity moral identity construction is in part shaped by shifts in cultural, social, and economic relations in the global economy that produce discomfort and insecurity for some simple livers but which also give them relative advantages in terms of access to resources. As the economy becomes increasingly competitive and streamlined, downsizing and efficiency measures become the norm. Many workers experience disillusionment and a sense of insecurity relative to waged work. This came up in many of the interviews I conducted with simple livers. Even those who had not lost jobs voiced similar ideas about the job market in general. So in one way voluntary simplicity can be understood as a response to shifts in the economy and job market that make middle-class simple livers less secure economically and increase work-related demands upon them.

Simple livers consider themselves middle class because of relatively high educational levels and their sense of personal agency. Most had not always been middle class in terms of family of origin. Most had achieved middle-class income or had moved into middle-class occupations at some point in their lives, but had not tended to stay there for a variety of reasons. Most had changed jobs over time and done quite different kinds of work throughout the history of their employment. Often they said they had chosen to make changes. But other reasons included losing their jobs, having accidents, and having health problems. Two of the people I interviewed had experienced painful downward mobility and were using the movement, at least in part, to hold onto middle-class identity. Respondents also tended to have had work experiences that brought them into contact with less advantaged people. These experiences tend to play a role in making them sensitive to the critiques of the dominant group they look like. Most view home ownership and investments positively as ways of achieving self-sufficiency that enables people to be economically secure and to spend their time on more meaningful activities than paid work.

The identity work of simple livers engages in altering two dichotomous sets of definitions (Collins 1990) and the practices they believe are involved in constituting them. They take issue with the high relative value the dominant culture assigns to affluence, which they contrast with frugality and simplicity. And they question the elevation of masculine characteristics of domination and competition over feminine characteristics of cooperation and relationality found in the dominant culture. They associate the high value for masculine characteristics with the domination of nature and the rise of competitive rather than cooperative relations with nature and others. They construct a new set of meanings in which affluence in the form of overconsuming is defined as unfulfilling, destructive of the environment, and a reflection and cause of social disintegration. Simplicity, which offers enough and a little extra, is defined as helping to sustain the environment and balance human relations and communities.

By targeting affluence associated with being white, Western, middle-class, overconsumers and focusing on changing consumption practices, simple livers claim a voluntary simplicity moral identity and claim a shift of the meaning of white, Western, and middle class from greedy overconsumer to simple liver.

Voluntary simplicity moral identity preserves connection to a mainstream identity in some ways. This serves the interests of simple livers in maintaining economic and cultural capital recognized and negotiable in the dominant culture, but elaborates it to accommodate a lifestyle and values that reject work for a wage or occupation and typical middle-class status goods consumption as worthy. It embraces ecological and social right livelihood as the path to becoming an authentic, fulfilled self who builds sustainable communities and saves the planet from environmental disaster. Identity work is necessary when people discover that old meanings don't suit their new circumstances (Schwalbe 1996, 107). And for simple livers the new circumstances include their discomfort with the "rat race" of waged work and consumerism and concern for the environment. Moral identities as simple livers emerge out of a process in which ideology and prescribed practices are coconstructed with others through ideological work (Berger 1981, 1995). Simple livers share practical knowledge of how to get by and act based on voluntary simplicity values in a given setting.

The moral identities simple livers construct are responses to and draw from the dominant Western culture. They are also influenced by cultures of resistance to the dominant culture (Fantasia 1988) found in the environmental movement, and to a lesser extent the feminist, civil rights, and gay and lesbian liberation movements which have critiqued the dominant culture. And they are also responding to critiques of the hegemony of the dominant culture by providing a voluntary simplicity alternative.[1]

Gender, racial, and class identities, according to Schwalbe (1996), can become problematic when groups compete to define identities in ways that better serve their own interests. Problems over matters of meaning, clarity, and worth of identities may arise. Simple livers are dealing with just this sort of problem. It arises from the competing definitions of moral identities they are responding to as they are at the same time struggling with hegemonic culture for the power to redefine what the lifestyle of a worthwhile white, affluent, Westerner is.

Simple livers resist the dominant culture on some points. In other respects they continue to draw on it (Swidler 1986; Hays 1994; Neitz 1999) and claim to be the carriers of its best features. People in simplicity circles identify themselves with the given categories of middle class, white, and heterosexual and also say they are well educated. They see themselves as rich in social resources, what Bourdieu (1984) calls "cultural capital." But they say even though they look like the mainstream, they are different.

Simple livers don't reject the categories of Western, white, heterosexual, and middle class that they occupy but they seek to remake them as good by rejecting the affluence (in the form of overconsumption) that being in these categories often provides. They also reject some aspects of masculinity they associate with the dominant culture such as competitiveness, violence, and domination and claim for all feminine traits of cooperation and relational interdependence they value.

Simple livers don't take on redefining the meanings of being white and Western directly in the ideology of the movement, as they do affluence and masculinity. But they use Western (white) traditions such as the Puritan value for frugality and simplicity and liberal democratic ideas of self-sufficiency, civic responsibility, and human self-actualization to reclaim the good parts of a Western (white) heritage and reclaim it as a potentially culturally rich category. This is not done discursively in overt opposition to people of color who have criticized whites, but in a form that deflects the critique from simple livers and assumes, rather than asserts, that color is irrelevant as a category that signifies a voluntary simplicity moral identity.

Simple livers believe they are better situated than the poor to understand that affluence does not produce happiness and fulfillment because they have experienced having more than enough. Informants in every age cohort, ranging from twenty to eighty years of age, consistently indicated to me that they were able to embrace voluntary simplicity not only because they had experienced enough, even luxury at some point in their lives, but because they also had experience living simply or being different in some way when they were young and therefore knew it was not something to fear.

Each has experience in early development of being distanced from the mainstream middle-class consumer culture, and each made meaning of this distance as positive in some way. Eight of the fourteen respondents grew up in working-class families. Six of the respondents indicated they grew up in middle- or upper middle-class families. All of these had something in their experience that had marginalized them relative to the mainstream, such as moving many times, going to a Quaker school, or being the child of immigrant parents.

Many had very good memories of lean times when they were young. In those times, they felt close to family and part of a community that they enjoyed. Both of the respondents over seventy and one who was sixty-two brought up the Great Depression as a time of close community and solidarity under hardship and all three surprised me by saying they believed another depression would be good for Americans. These are descriptions from four informants about growing up simply.

Nita (62 years old): Well when we were growing up, I think we actually were poor but I didn't know it, you know. We had a great time. We didn't have a car until I was in high school. My dad never made more than 5000 bucks a year. There were six of us all together.

Brad (21 years old): [I] grew up on a farm and my parents were really poor. My dad is a butcher and my mom raised us until I was seven and then she went to work at a convenience store three days a week. It was during the farm crisis and we were paying for a farm. And my Dad is making about $15,000, he's working for his parents and she was working part time so we did not have much money at all. There were three of us (kids). We were all close, too. And so we always just made it work somehow. We always had everything we wanted. I thought it was a good thing we were in the food business I guess. [He laughs]

Peter (49 years old): There was a scarcity of resources when we grew up and so we got nourished in different ways. Mutual contact with kids and working together on our paper route. Our big thing was a drive in the country.

Emily (52 years old): I was going through my photo album. It kind of takes you back through your whole life. I was noticing how much entertaining I did when I lived in very small places when you have no money. I think there is a way of supporting each other, and you are more—you need the family more. I see this in my neighbors. One set are welfare people, but the family [is] always together helping each other. Now in my family, we have all been blessed financially. We are all OK financially. We are all doing pretty well and so there has been this norm of independence. So we don't help each other out. So in going back to the photos, I thought, gosh, I entertained when I lived in a place beneath the freeway where there was heck of a lot of noise. And I see a picture of my brother and my nephew laying on my bed watching TV. Part of it is either relying on people or relying on money. And when you have the money to always buy you'll buy the service.

Closer relationships with family and community are associated with their younger days, when many recall having less money but closer relationships with others. But most agreed that having enough was crucial to choosing voluntary simplicity and feeling in control of the process of simplifying was essential. While informants rarely spoke of this in terms of class privilege, their achieved class status clearly was an important part of their accounts. Emily explains it this way: "You have to have a certain level of affluence to decide to adopt voluntary simplicity. [I read] a great article about women going into convents after being CEOs but you don't see secretaries out of college doing that." Most felt that having enough or being affluent for a time enabled them to realize that money and material wealth did not provide the fulfillment they wanted. All distanced themselves from being poor because of having social and cultural capital that the poor lack. They maintain the poor will tend to believe that if they can attain affluence they will be happy. They also believe that they have superior knowledge than those who are still caught up in consumerism and jobism. They tend to view this group as a herd of mindless sheep who can't be blamed because they are entrapped in the dominant culture's values. It is the simple livers, therefore, who are the central catalysts for change.

Gendered Voluntary Simplicity Identity Work

Through collective identity work simple livers collaborate to preserve parts of their identities and to change the meanings associated with them. And they collaborate to change other aspects of their shared identity: "In this way it redounds to the benefit of the identity holders who collaborate to help each other define what they are as a kind of people" (Schwalbe 1996, 105). In the case of simple livers the collective identity work they undertake involves glossing over some differences among themselves, most significantly differences between the experiences of women and men and the impacts of the differences in their experiences on the identity work they need to do to achieve a collective voluntary simplicity identity. This collective identity work is different than work done to signify who and what they are as individuals (Schwalbe 1996, 105). Taylor and Whittier define collective identity as "the shared definition of a group that derives from members' common interests, experiences, and solidarity" (1992, 105). For these authors, "collective identity is seen as constructed, activated, and sustained only through interaction in social movement communities (or submerged networks, in Melucci's [1989] terms) and as shaped by factors such as political opportunity structures, the availability of resources, and organizational strength—in other words, matters of resources and power" (1995, 172). It is just this sort of identity work that participants active in simplicity circles are engaged in.

Rejecting careerism and mass consumer values of the dominant culture and adopting voluntary simplicity moral identities has different implications and requires different types of identity work for men than it does for women because men and women have different developmental experiences as middle-class whites who have grown up in the twentieth-century United States (Chodorow 1978). These men and women as groups also experience different expectations and pressures from the dominant culture. And they occupy differing relative positions of power to dominant institutions. Men and women in voluntary simplicity are in one way involved in trying to remake those aspects of masculine and feminine gender identity that they experience as negative. How they use voluntary simplicity reflects different unmet identity needs in men and women.

Because the movement ideology is more critical of hegemonic masculinity[2] than traditional femininity,[3] people in the movement tend to be more conscious of its efforts to redefine masculinity. But the movement also advocates women freeing themselves from the dominant cultural standards of housekeeping, grooming, and dress.

The Use of Consumption in Voluntary Simplicity Moral Identity Work

"Getting a life" involves the process of rejecting both jobism and conspicuous consumption. But it is consumption that is the key tool used by most simple livers in the work they do to attain a simple living moral identity.

For the purposes of this analysis, I define "consumption" broadly to refer to the selection, purchase, use, maintenance, repair, and disposal of any product or service. Typical market distinctions between production and consumption tend to blur when examining the lives of simple livers because they often shift some production into the home and make goods, or at least parts of goods, themselves. While consumer goods often have important uses in terms of supporting human survival, food to eat, shelter from the elements, and so forth, much of the literature on consumption recognizes that consumer goods and services are also important in terms of their symbolic functions or meanings.

Consumption is a social process that is a source for the construction of identity and social relations (Appadurai 1986; McCracken 1988; Mukerji 1983; Seager 1993). Consumption has both the self-expressive use in which people symbolize unique aspects, personal qualities, values, and attributes, reflect personal history, and signify relationships and "categorical" uses in which group membership, social position, and status (Bourdieu 1984; Schor 1997, 1998; Veblen [1899] 1965) are established by people in social-material terms (Appadurai 1986; Campbell 1995; Lury 1996; McCracken 1988; Miller 1995; Mukerji 1983; Seager 1993).

Altering consumption was the topic of rich discussion and clearly important for everyone I interviewed. Many in the movement aspire to save enough money that they can quit or reduce work. But changing work often takes time and getting to the point where they no longer need to work is not always achievable, so consumption tends to offer more immediate evidence of change. Overconsuming is judged to be a greedy and destructive practice that must be replaced with frugal, green, and grassroots community-building consuming practices. Simple livers emphasize consuming primarily items with use value that support basic needs for food, shelter, and clothing and goods or experiences that are deeply fulfilling to them such as time spent in nature and materials needed to do creative work. For many it also implies developing mindfulness or a better capacity to experience and enjoy the present fully. Food is usually the most important area of consumption for simple livers, but any type of consumption reflects similar identity work being done.

Daniel works only intermittently, as he needs cash, and rents out rooms in the house he owns for his regular income. This gives him the time to pursue his passion of rock climbing. He, like many simple livers, tries to eat low on the food chain, a mostly vegetarian diet because it is viewed as environmentally more sustainable. He describes his grocery shopping this way:

> Groceries end up being a *very* significant part of my disposable income, my budget. I eat a lot of food and I like to buy gourmet foods. I don't eat out often, though, and I don't buy packaged or processed things. Most of what I buy is raw, whole natural food but because I keep an eye towards cost I decide to go to different venues to get different products. So for example I know that I really enjoy Nancy's nonfat yogurt and I get that by far cheapest at a PCC which is the cooperative organic foods chain. But there are many things like dried bread,

toast crackers, canned sardines, and many prepared foods that I get very cheaply at a small Chinese grocery in northeast Seattle. And then there are the items that I can buy in bulk at Costco and I generally don't like to support a huge—I see it as a heartless, spiritless, communityless operation like Costco, but some things are about half-price there. So I end up going about five places to get my groceries and it is not as complicated as it might seem to a lot of people 'cause I don't do a single trip for a single purpose. If I go out of my house I combine a lot of other errands with it and fortunately a lot of times when I am going to a far-off place for groceries I can also stop in on a friend. And so it is not a forty-five-minute commute by bicycle just to get cheap cantaloupe and cheap beets. I am sure it is a lot nicer, I mean I have some close friends who just go to one supermarket and they have incredible allegiance to that one supermarket, and if they can't get it, they ask the manager to bring it in. And usually they will. So they get all that they want at that one place and it is pretty speedy compared to all the time I spend gathering up my groceries.

Daniel lets me know that in keeping with voluntary simplicity values he uses much of his disposable income on the essential of food, not on conspicuous consumption. Usually simple livers say that most of our spending should be for food and shelter. Daniel lets me know that he is not denying himself pleasure but enjoys food, one of the simple pleasures people in voluntary simplicity sanction. The next statement confirms that he is frugal; he does not eat out often and waste money on higher-costing meals, a practice that may also encourage wasted energy and food in the restaurant kitchen. This locates him in terms of one of the many points of debate being worked on in the contested terrain of the movement. Some people advocate eating at locally owned restaurants to support the local economy while others maintain eating at restaurants is undesirable. Daniel neatly links his position on restaurants with his environmentally sustainable practices of not buying prepackaged or processed foods, which restaurants may do. His frugality is demonstrated by traveling to five stores by bicycle to obtain the cheapest, least prepackaged, and most environmentally sensitive products he can afford. Like most other simple livers Daniel experiences tension between buying green and buying cheap. He weaves in his participation in a community in Seattle by mentioning that he usually stops off to visit friends on the way. He also lets me know he uses an environmentally sound means of transportation, a bicycle, rather than a car. And in conclusion he separates himself from those who take an easier route by going to only one grocery store, a chain store, rather than the simple living one. He says it is not as complex for him as people think but it is easier for those who don't do what he does and shop at one chain store. In this way he hints at his superiority, his simple living moral identity, without criticizing others. After all, he claims they are his friends. This is a typical motif in the accounts of simple livers who claim they don't want to be blamed for the world's problems and they don't blame others. Everyone is in the same circumstance on the planet earth and we all have to work together to prevent ecological collapse. But simple livers show that they do more than those who don't practice voluntary simplicity.

The way consumption is structured affords the sense of a high level of control over choice and its complexity offers ripe ground for developing ideology and practices that prescribe necessary analysis and research regarding consumption. Daily practices such as resisting advertising by not watching television, buying at thrift stores and from local co-op grocery stores, sharing tools, and growing fruits and vegetables instead of buying them give evidence of simple livers' difference from the mainstream of consumers and affirm to themselves that they are strong independent thinkers who do not give in to social pressures to conform.

The process of bringing more production into the household, which some simple livers are doing, involves a profound alteration of the relationship of production and consumption that characterizes modernity and a blurring of the lines between them, but also is central in the identity construction process of simple livers.

In order to achieve the goal of having choices about how they spend their time and control over it, all of the people interviewed believed that they had to carefully manage, monitor, and decrease consumption. In order to be able to buy time they had to make other buying decisions selectively, carefully, and frugally. Simple livers invest time in consumption to cut costs in monetary terms, but they also maintain it increases the quality of consumption (the pleasure of consumption in terms of needs or uses, physiological sensation, imagined pleasure, and signification). They shop for and buy sustainable products. But they also consume through repairing, maintaining, sharing, trading, making, growing, using, and experiencing.

Consumption practices of simple livers are culturally purposeful activity. But unlike the findings of Veblen ([1899] 1965) and Simmel

(1950) regarding consumption, their consumption is not aimed at achieving higher social status within the dominant culture or of imitating a group considered superior because of material wealth. They are trying to remake the symbolic meanings that construct class/status in such a way that modernist conceptions of desired levels and modes of consumption, wealth, and personal control over the earth's material resources are reevaluated and do not carry the same positive symbolic meanings.

As discussed in detail in chapter 1, Etzioni (1998) argues that those in the voluntary simplicity movement—along with less intense simplifiers he identifies as downshifters who give up some consumer luxuries and strong simplifiers who give up high-paying, high-stress jobs—represent a shift to postmaterialist values which can be understood, at least in part, by drawing on Maslow's theory of the hierarchy of human needs. Etzioni maintains that these groups of people rejecting luxury consumption have satisfied their needs for creature comforts and are turning to their higher needs. Indeed his description supports my finding that they are privileged by class advantage. He writes, "[V]oluntary simplicity is thus a choice a successful corporate lawyer, not a homeless person, faces; Singapore, not Rwanda" (632).

Etzioni suggests that the three types of voluntary simplicity point to a shift toward the consumption of knowledge objects rather than consumer objects, which he maintains are less environmentally damaging forms of consumption. But a more reflexive approach reveals a danger in adopting this logic because it sets up an assumed experiential superiority for the affluent and attributes to them a higher level of needs and understanding of what is best for human well-being, which also happens to be better for the environment, thus establishing once again the superiority of the relatively privileged. And we are still left with the question of why all affluent people are not making a shift away from modern consumerism.

People adopting voluntary simplicity are not simply responding to fulfilling the sort of natural progression theorized by Maslow from one level of need fulfillment to the next. How needs are fulfilled, and what human needs are defined to be beyond the most basic requirements of food, clothing, and shelter are socially and culturally constructed. People adopting voluntary simplicity are engaged in a cultural struggle to redefine what the values of society should be, and these values and the practices they advocate clearly serve their identity needs and material interests.

The activity of simple livers is aimed at gaining cultural and symbolic advantage over the dominant system of signification (Donald and Hall 1986) by establishing a system that marks social status through simple living instead of through status occupations that pay well and high levels of consumption. But their activity also attempts to respond to and deflect critiques of those viewed as primary carriers of the dominant culture of Western whites (with whom simple livers might be grouped by cultural critics). The ideology responds to specific aspects of the critiques to empty out the content that is criticized and to fill the category of Western white with an alternative definition that allows people located in the ascribed categories to claim a different set of characteristics. Instead of being greedy and wasteful "consumer zombies" who are responsible for the destruction of the environment, they are ecologically sensitive, self-sufficient, self-actualized, caring, simple livers.

Simple livers engage in imitation of groups defined as lower status by the dominant culture, those Durning (1992) defines as the global middle-income group who live on between $700 and $7,500 a year. This is the group that they are more interested in looking like and they use consumption as the key signifier through which to accomplish this goal. Most simple livers don't actually live on under $7,500 a year but most do focus on reducing their spending on consumer goods.

They do not aspire to working the same kinds of jobs the global middle-income group does, or the same kinds of hours they work. Nor do they propose a major shift in resource distribution through voluntary simplicity. The immediate change they advocate is a voluntary change in resource consumption by the affluent. They aspire to looking like the global middle-income group only and most significantly in terms of consumption. Even here they are selective in how they pattern their consumption based on their comparison group. McCracken points to this same dynamic in his analysis of consumption claiming that "imitation that occurs may be expected to be not the wholesale appropriation of a symbol or a style, but a selective borrowing that works to preserve some of the qualities of the subordinate group even as it allows them to claim the status of the superordinate group from whom the borrowing occurs" (1988, 98). McCracken assumes that the imitation will be of a higher status group but simple livers are imitating a group defined as subordinate by the dominant group and trying to redefine their own group as superior through identification with the subordinate group whose consumption practices they believe are better for the environment and human communities.

Most of the people I interviewed try to evaluate purchases carefully based on the information they have regarding ecological, community-building, and human rights concerns and balance their buying decisions between buying environmentally friendly products and supporting local producers and buying cheap goods or bargains that are often available through chain stores. Consulting friends and other circle members, picking up information from organizations, and reading magazines and books are all common ways of getting information that helps in consumer choice decisions. Because most of the people I interviewed live on limited incomes, price matters greatly to them. Often simple livers will weigh issues of cost against other concerns in making a buying choice. For instance, several people indicated they could not afford to buy all of their food at a local co-op and had to buy some food from regular grocery stores despite the fact they would like to do all their food buying at the co-op.

Meanings reside in goods (Appadurai 1986; McCracken 1988; Mukerji 1983). These meanings derive from the culturally constituted world. Since simple livers are attempting to shift meanings it is no surprise that they make use of goods which are tangible objects that can serve to give substance to new meanings for the collective of simple livers and to other groups they are in discourse with. The internal consistency in the range of consumer goods they buy is collectively arrived at and constrained by the contexts in which they live, the capitalist economy, and the welfare state. And it is also enabled by the contexts in which simple livers live. In Seattle, for instance, with its extensive public transportation system and cooperative food stores, simple livers are supported in not using personal cars as much and being able to buy locally grown organic foods.

The constellation of consumption practices that signify a voluntary simplicity moral identity is the result of the interplay of product availability, available institutional features of the context, geographic location, collective meaning making, and biographical histories of participants in the movement. One important factor that shapes the biographical histories of participants in the movement is their gender.

The Gendered Use of Consumption in Voluntary Simplicity Moral Identity Work: Autonomy and Self-Restraint

The two types of core identity stories told about becoming involved in voluntary simplicity are gendered. Men say they have always been simple livers and that the movement has caught up with them. Women say they have not always been simple livers but have always been uncomfortable living within the constraints of the dominant culture and that voluntary simplicity has freed them to fulfill their authentic selves.

Men in the voluntary simplicity movement are challenged with reconstructing the category of masculinity as good rather than bad. They do this by drawing selectively on existing cultural scripts and by claiming things as masculine that have been defined as feminine in the dominant culture, as did the men in Schwalbe's (1996) study of the mythopoetic men's movement. The men in voluntary simplicity find traditional masculinity problematic and are trying to reject it because "the logical outcomes of . . . society's socialization process that teaches males to become men by engaging in and supporting behaviors which, if internalized fully, logically lead them to interact destructively with others" (Franklin 1988, 2–3) is uncomfortable and painful for them. They say they don't want to be competitive and to try to dominate others and that they value cooperation and caring.

The different ways that women and men attain the freedom they associate with voluntary simplicity moral identity become clear through analysis of the stories they tell about why they adopted voluntary simplicity or what it means to them. Emily's account is typical of women:

> I feel like it is giving me new ownership of my life and not just in freedom from job aspect. That's sort of a minor or maybe a medium part of it but it is thinking about your life in new ways, and once you think about how you spend your money, I think then for me it opened up how I do a lot of other things. It opens up consideration of other things—what possessions I have around, the people that I associate with—and it brought more of my other values to the fore. You know, being a vegetarian I've been ridiculed. I don't watch TV, that is another. And I've chosen to be childless and living singly. There's a lot of aspects where you just start kind of becoming weirder and weirder. And I guess Nita [she laughs] is kind of out there on the weird range. . . . She has been a good role model in that aspect.

Emily, like most simple living women, describes voluntary simplicity as supporting her autonomy from demands of the dominant culture that she work for a wage, practice gendered and status consumption, and marry and have children, among other things.

Roger's account of his interest in voluntary simplicity is typical of men I interviewed: "I found that I was already leading that kind of life. And when I heard of voluntary simplicity I was like, 'Oh wow, that is interesting! There are a bunch of people out there who have the same ideas that I do.' So one reason I feel I really like the idea of voluntary simplicity is it was my idea first!" Roger, like most men in voluntary simplicity, sees his own adoption of voluntary simplicity as something he did on his own. He does not focus on support from others in achieving autonomy to do as he wishes. Most men say they never cared about conspicuous consumption. They claim to have always exerted self-restraint rather than the dominance they could command. Interestingly, this story rarely includes not having ever cared about occupation or work. In fact, former occupational status is described in rich detail and at length by many of the men. It was often returned to by the respondent several times and in some cases respondents resisted moving on in the interview.

For the men, status continues to be linked to occupation outside of the movement despite their ideological position that worth is not derived from occupational status or money. Letting go of the breadwinner role, which is central for masculine gender identity construction in the dominant culture, requires different identity work of the mostly heterosexual men adopting voluntary simplicity moral identities than it does for women. What they are willing to give up financially and in terms of status occupations in order to become simple livers along with how well they are able to get by comfortably are central in this aspect of their identity construction. Handling finances well, being frugal, and most importantly knowing how to save money by shopping wisely are all part of getting by well. Plus men build positive masculine identity through demonstrating they are knowledgeable about how to get things cheaply, repair, maintain, and make things and through sharing skills and equipment with others. Shopping for groceries and household goods, largely defined as a female role in modern consumer society, are redefined by simple living men as masculine through stressing frugality, using self-restraint, and in some cases producing things on their own.

Men generally reject conspicuous consumption (often claiming that they were never materialistic) and rather than drawing on discourse about past conspicuous consumption and how they gave it up, to construct identity or status, they talk about how they have always been frugal. And, in some cases people see themselves as always having been frugal but also describe earlier lifestyles that were not frugal.

Women in voluntary simplicity say they were never comfortable with the lifestyle they had. They say they always had a sense of not being able to be their true selves. For them voluntary simplicity provides support and a way to assert their autonomy in the face of pressures from the dominant culture and others to conform in terms of gendered consumption and traditional gender roles. They describe this in terms of finding their authentic selves and for a number of the women this also involves connecting with other women. Emily expresses her experience of voluntary simplicity this way:

> Voluntary simplicity has opened up this broad spectrum of how I could lead my life. Once you let go of the work thread as the primary thing it is like an adventure. The job was never a good fit for me personally because I'm an introvert and being in sales is more of an extrovert thing and I found as I aged it got more energy draining. I am at this stage in my life I prefer reading books by women authors. I feel like their voices are the voices I want to listen to now. Maybe I got off on the male spectrum too much in my job, the money earning thing. The competition was more the male thing and so now it is just a different focus. I think women have allowed their lives to be more multidimensional so there are greater points of contact when in conversations.

Women don't construct identity by making heavy use of their past or present occupations, though they will describe this as a phase in their development and as ultimately not fulfilling. They tend not to talk for very long about it or to care as much about rich detail of their many accomplishments in their careers.

They also tend to claim that they were overconsumers or collectors. One woman collected beanie babies and teddy bears and said her three-bedroom house where she lived alone had been so full of collectibles she was pressed to find space to accommodate new acquisitions. At the time I visited her home there were no teddy bears or beanie babies in sight in her living room, dining room, kitchen, or bathroom, the rooms I saw while there conducting the interview. She said she had sold or donated the bulk of her collections and was in the process of disposing of the last ones she had. Household goods (often found as bargains), clothing, shoes, fabric and sewing materials, knitting materials, things purchased while traveling, magazines, and books are some of the things people I interviewed discussed as the things they had overconsumed or collected. One woman said she had filled her house with pieces of broken furniture that she bought inexpensively with plans to repair. Then she never got around to repairing it. It cluttered the house, but much of it was virtually unusable. As part of her voluntary simplicity work she had stopped buying broken furniture and gotten rid of the pieces she had acquired. One woman described how voluntary simplicity supported her desire to stop buying and wearing makeup and reducing the quantity of clothing she bought. Most informants maintain that they did not find typical consumption activity fulfilling. They never liked certain aspects of it, for instance, the atmosphere of shopping at malls, feeling pressured to buy by the expectations of others, and costs of products in certain contexts.

Regarding attitudes toward shopping, women describe the unpleasant feelings they have in certain contexts and also are concerned with resisting external pressures to practice consumption, while men tend to focus on frugality and self-control as the sources for avoiding spending money and as the reason they avoid malls. Here again the pattern of concern with autonomy in women and self-restraint in men emerge.

Robert Prus and Loren Dawson's (1991) study, "Shop 'til You Drop: Shopping as Recreational and Laborious Activity," found that shopping tends to be viewed as a more laborious activity when one experiences a confused, constrained, and irrelevant sense of self in shopping situations. Simple livers, like those in Prus and Dawson's study who viewed shopping as labor rather than recreation, cited time, pressures from others to consume, monetary restraints, and dislike of certain kinds of purchases and shopping contexts as reasons for their dislike of shopping. Shopping emerges as an activity through which the self finds expression in, and becomes subjected to, the situations at hand (Prus and Dawson 1991, 160). But unlike the respondents in Prus and Dawson's study, simple livers also cite their values and critique of conspicuous consumption as grounds for their dislike of shopping in certain venues and they link this to their physiological and emotional discomfort in such settings and with shopping. Prus and Dawson do not consider gender as a variable in their analysis. Interestingly there is variation along gender lines among simple livers. Women mention certain contexts and types of products as the source of their discomfort in shopping more often than they mention cost, while men mention cost as the source of their discomfort and a preference not to buy at all more often. Women, for instance, describe not liking the feelings they have when faced with the artificial environment and product diversity in malls and find they have difficulty concentrating.

Nita and Kevin's discussion of their grocery shopping and food production reflects themes similar to those in Daniel's account, and highlights the gendered moral identity work being done by men and women in which men are distancing themselves from identities as dominant, controlling users of the earth's resources and establishing themselves as cooperative and self-constrained frugal people who, though they could be competitive successful businessmen, are leading the way to voluntary simplicity. And the women are establishing themselves as self-actualized autonomous people who make their own choices about what is desirable for them rather than being influenced by cultural dictates and the opinions of others:

Nita: We have a big vegetable garden and we shop at a co-op and QFC (a chain store).

Kevin: We don't shop there all the time because it is not that close. QFC is two blocks away.

Nita: We probably have some differences about spending too. We had a little argument about toothpaste a while back because Kevin got this toothpaste . . . I did not like. He said it was a lot cheaper. I said, I get expensive shampoo—well hell it lasts months—$8 instead of $1.50 over three months. He had to finish the toothpaste! Kevin does grocery shopping, cooking, dishes. I do vacuuming and wash, mending and stuff.

Kevin: I hate doing wash.

Nita: I think getting things locally is very important. I have never been in the big mall in Auburn and I will never go there because I think malls are destructive to neighborhoods. I often don't get the cheapest thing, I consider quality, I don't buy stuff made in China. I get things locally [even] if they cost more than going to Northgate and I get stuff I like and to me that is an advantage of not having much money: you can choose what you spend on carefully.

Kevin: I do the grocery shopping and I do it a different way than most people. I go with a list. And if it is not on the list, unless it is something I can really use, or really need, that is in the produce department—that's where my shopping really starts. I don't like processed foods or packaged foods because of the waste. And the trim [from produce] goes into the compost for my garden.

In this discussion we have a rich example of gender identity work being done to establish voluntary simplicity moral identities. Kevin does the grocery shopping, a task often assigned to women in the middle-class dominant culture. But he emphasizes that he does it with an eye to frugality and very methodically, exerting self-control and restraint. Kevin explains he goes with a list. He only buys items he really needs or can use. He, like Daniel, avoids processed and packaged foods. Nita points out they shop at the co-op and a chain store. Kevin explains they opt for the chain store at times because it is closer. In this way he is responding to our shared knowledge that voluntary simplicity ideology generally views co-op shopping as preferable. Nita brings up the theme of shopping locally even if you have to pay more and of avoiding malls and asserts the power of voluntary simplicity to enhance choice. Kevin explains his methodical shopping practices. He outlines what he does and does not do. The focus for him is not on choice, but on restraint, the restraint necessary for an identity associated with hegemonic masculinity to be shifted to a masculine voluntary simplicity moral identity.

Nita and Kevin establish that they share the reproductive work equally and in ways that please them both. They are balanced, in harmony. Nita points to her autonomy in consumer choice as a voluntary simplicity practice. She also points to the equal division of labor based on preferences and skills, not stereotypical cultural dictates. Kevin participates in elaborating this by saying he hates doing laundry, thus affirming they share work to suit them both.

They continue talking about their food production:

Kevin: Of course I can pears. We have the trees. I dry them and I make wine out of it.

Nita: See that big thing over there? [she points] That's called a dryer. And it has six shelves in it. We can dry fruit in it. And another thing we have is called a soft cooker. You can just throw batches of fruit in there and you just steam it and the steam gets the juice out and when you are through steaming it for several hours the pulp that's left is totally tasteless and the juice has all the flavor.

Kevin: You can make juice concentrate.

Nita: Yeah and some becomes juice and some of it we make into wine but it's a good way, you know, and when the fruit comes in you just have tons of it. You got apples till you just can't stand it; you got pears! We got a couple of apple trees, we got pears, we got lots of berries.

Kevin: Normally we end up with a surplus, maybe four gallons of raspberries at the end of the season. Normally we put it in the freezer and we still have stuff in the freezer.

Nita: And sometimes you are just trying to get rid of stuff any way you can—just overwhelming.

Kevin: Yeah, so at present we have stuff left over from last year even this year in the freezer. We have frozen strawberries, we have frozen rhubarb, we have frozen raspberries, we have frozen blueberries.

Nita: But we have to make jam pretty soon.

Kevin: Yeah, cause we have too much stuff.

Nita: When we make jam we do it all day. Just kinda empty the freezer out and start over. We make one batch because making jam dirties the whole kitchen whether you are doing one or twenty so you might just as well do it all at once and then you only have to clean up one time.

Kevin: Uh-huh. [We grow] just about anything that grows in this part of the world.

Nita: We have kale, lettuce, brussel sprouts.

Kevin: Got broccoli out there too. Tomatoes and peas, snow peas.

Nita: Snow peas, beans.

Kevin: We always grow snow peas because they are four dollars a pound in the market.

Nita: I love growing snow peas and they grow like weeds.

Kevin: They are a good crop around here . . .

Nita: If you don't buy much, that helps. And if you buy from thrift stores that helps.

Kevin: And if you stay away from packaged foods.

Nita: And if you have a good trading network. Now we have a "free" sign and when there is something we don't want, raspberry bushes we have too many of or something, or other three-dimensional things, we put them out front with a "free" sign on them. You can just get rid of enormous quantities of stuff. And, you know, we call our friends and say, "Do you need any of this? Don't buy them 'cause we have tons."

Kevin: But you also need cooperative neighbors. That is the big thing you gain—cooperative neighbors who throw their grass into your compost piles as a good example because we don't have any grass.

Nita: Yeah, the reason Kevin has not starting making beer yet is we loaned our beer-making stuff to a kid who is making it and when we get it back we'll make it and then let him have it again.

Kevin: The reason I make beer is that it tastes just like what I get at the store and it costs a fraction of what I'd pay at the store. I can make fifty bottles of beer for less than ten bucks.

Nita and Kevin have brought much of their food production back into their home, growing and processing fruits and vegetables in abundance. The dominant culture's model of the gendered division of labor is replaced by one that supports Kevin in establishing a heterosexual, masculine voluntary simplicity moral identity through being a master gardener, good cook, carpenter, and frugal shopper rather than a breadwinner. They describe the abundance of food they grow. Nita animatedly talks about the surplus they have and how they preserve it and share it. But Kevin brings up saving money as the reason for growing snow peas when he says, "We always grow snow peas because they are four dollars a pound in the market." Kevin is putting the emphasis back on frugality, not abundance. Nita focuses on the joy of growing the peas in response to this and says, "I love to grow snow peas and they grow like weeds." She is asserting her pleasure in the choice to grow peas while Kevin is asserting his restraint in the form of frugality as the basis for growing snow peas. They establish simple living moral identity through the consumption practices they describe, which demonstrate the combination of frugality that lowers ecological damage, self-sufficiency, abundance, and choice that support self-fulfillment and pleasure, and cooperative relations in their community which voluntary simplicity promises. Nita expresses her autonomy, even willfulness, through her consumption practices while Kevin expresses his self-restraint through his frugality.

These findings point to patterns similar to those identified by Neitz (1999) and are consistent with Chodorow's (1978) analysis of the different developmental patterns of girls and boys in modern Western nuclear families in which male children raised largely by women must break with their mothers in order to individuate as masculine. They thus develop distancing and autonomous relational patterns while girls who do not experience the need to break with their mothers to identify as feminine tend to be highly relational and not to develop autonomy. Chodorow's model has been criticized for taking as given the white, middle-class, twentieth-century Western nuclear family. This is true but, in the case of simple livers, most actually grew up in such families. Chodorow's analysis also focuses too exclusively on the psychological development of children in relation to the family without an adequate grasp of the institutional framework and material advantages males gain from adopting the dominant masculine modes of relating. We must examine both material interests and developmental patterns to understand the way simple livers construct their moral identities.

Neitz (1999) outlines how women in contemporary Western society enter into religious experience having experienced more constraint than their male counterparts and having had less experience of willfulness and autonomy. She theorizes that women require a different spiritual path to develop "whole selves" than the "paths which men have traditionally walked" because of the different experiences of men and women (1999, 11). For Neitz, whose definition of autonomy I employ in this analysis, autonomy is composed of two aspects:

> First there are the social structural constraints that have limited women's autonomy in terms of what women could do in public spheres and defined her responsibilities in the private spheres (e.g., Walby). While only a part of women's experience, these constraints—and the degrees to which religion has been instrumental in defining and enforcing them—have been extensively documented across many societies. In addition some feminist theorists have also suggested that the role of women

as mothers in the nuclear family facilitates the development of autonomy as the central characteristics of adult males and relationality as the central characteristic of adult females in the twentieth-century Western society. Autonomy here is contrasted with the quality of relatedness, rather than constraint that is imposed from outside. (1999, 11–12)

While "fasting, abstaining, covering the body, and celibacy" (Neitz 1999, 13) might be the appropriate prescribed spiritual practice for men because it serves to balance men's experiences of power and autonomy with constraint and self-denial that is characteristically prescribed in religious traditions that emerge from male dominated cultures, Neitz maintains, such practice is not likely to make women more whole. So it is not surprising that women simple livers use voluntary simplicity to support them in identity work aimed at gaining higher levels of autonomy while men use it in identity work aimed at self-restraint that supports them in rejecting aspects of masculine identity they view as negative such as being competitive and seeking to dominate others. The men are engaged in identity work that rejects embracing power over others, which is the common practice of dominant men. (For men to have power is to dominate: power over. For women to have power is to have autonomy.) So for men to consciously try to stop at autonomy is to display a nondominant form of power.

Among simple livers men give salience to discussion of frugal self-restraint while women tend to discuss the autonomy and pleasure it helps them achieve. In this way men and women are doing identity work through voluntary simplicity that meets unmet identity needs derived from the differing developmental experiences and structural constraints faced by many women and men in contemporary Western society in order to arrive at a voluntary simplicity moral identity.

Fulfillment through Voluntary Simplicity: Pleasure and Satisfaction

Being fulfilled through adopting a simple lifestyle is a sign of voluntary simplicity moral identity. Simple livers point out that voluntary simplicity is not about self-denial but about true self-fulfillment. Women simple livers' accounts of their fulfillment often include descriptions of the body's sensations coming together with the meanings they attribute to their actions. Men more often describe feelings of satisfaction with the frugal lifestyle.

Attaining skills of gardening, canning and preserving food, cooking, sewing, knitting, and carpentry is valued highly among simple livers. The materiality of production and consumption as one process and the grounding of the process in the material, the stuff of which the earth is made, affirms their connection to the web of life. For instance Kevin made his own beer and said he liked doing it because it saved so much money. Several people grew vegetables and fruit and canned, froze, preserved, and dried foods. And frequently the way they talk about these processes is as though the process of making things is a form of consumption because it gives them an experience that is pleasurable or satisfying. For instance when Nita sews clothes she consumes the pleasure of the sewing, the touch of the fabric, the experience of being in the flow of creating something. She also describes being close to other women as she sews as part of the pleasure of the activity. She loves the visual stimulation by the object she is making for use as clothing or chair seat covers or drapes. Plus Nita views her sewing as creative work that builds community. Here she describes how sewing her own clothes builds community and does a neat bit of moral identity work to redefine the meaning of having many clothes, which she likes:

I sometimes feel guilty because I have hoards of clothes and I'm always making more and redoing the ones I've got. But a friend of mine said, "You know, you shouldn't look at it that way. Those aren't really clothes—those are your artistic expression." . . . So I felt better because it is a little ridiculous. But I really like doing things with fabric and fibers. . . . I can wear them, and the other thing about clothes that you make yourself is [that they] are like an invitation to conversation. People come up to talk to me who don't even know me. The way I dress [is] a "hello" in a way. It tells a lot about who I am without having said anything even. I really think if more people made clothes, found different ways to dress—it is a really community building thing because you know more about people. [I] was at a meeting of the open space committee and I was working away on a hem and this woman who I've known for years came up and she says, "You mean you make all those clothes you wear? I thought you had found a neat shop somewhere!" But people really do come up! And, see what I mean, if everyone is dressing the same you don't really know anything about someone when you meet them.

Nita infuses her sewing with meaning beyond simple use value. She says she enjoys the physical act of the work. She views the clothes she sews as artistic creations that help build community as well as save resources since she often makes her clothes from used clothing. She smiles with delight when she glances at the ordered stacks of fabric displayed on an oak shelf in her living room.

According to several of the women, what you choose to acquire has to be selective and is therefore more pleasurable; that is, pleasure is said to come from making choices carefully, having fewer things, and having mastery over the things in your environment and yourself in making proper choices for yourself as a unique individual. Plus life becomes simpler in some ways because there are fewer acceptable ways and venues through which to acquire things and fewer things that are acceptable to acquire. This sense of pleasure and heightened importance of choice in the process of consumption, along with the use of goods, help to make the moral identity of simple livers tangible to themselves in ideas and bodily sensations and to others.

Neitz too finds that for the women in Wicca she studies, the body becomes a tool for a positive expression of the will (1999, 13;16–23). Neitz concludes if women were to seek wholeness then "woman's spiritual discipline would encourage expression of the will and a movement toward autonomy" (1999, 23) rather than denial of the self. Neitz finds men are drawn to neopagan religion in part because they may experience less autonomy in their daily lives than they might have at a previous era and "at the same time, they experience less cultural reenforcement for the traditional disciplinary practices of bodily renunciation" (1999, 24). She also finds that other men are drawn to Wicca because it offers them pleasure in indulgence in bodily desires that leads to ecstasy rather than wholeness/holiness (1999, 25).

Among simple livers many of the women are clearly using voluntary simplicity to support them in gaining autonomy, just as women Wicca are using their practices to experience a sense of autonomy, and bodily sensations play a role in this experience. But most of the simple living men I interviewed make use of voluntary simplicity to practice discipline through frugality that is akin to the ascetic traditions of self-denial associated with male-dominated religious traditions described by Neitz (1999, 9–10). Even though some male simple livers have experienced reduced autonomy in comparison to men in earlier eras, as had the men Neitz studied, the men in voluntary simplicity did not describe seeking pleasure for themselves through voluntary simplicity in the same way the women did. The men say they find satisfaction in the voluntary simplicity lifestyle but they more often describe it in terms of self-restraint and right livelihood.

Gender Roles

Male simple livers reject aggression, competition, and emotional detachment, claiming they are pacifists, don't want to compete and make lots of money, and don't want to dominate others. They say they want to be part of a meaningful and fulfilling community. They don't want waged work or the male breadwinner role to define them. Kevin expresses his desire for a partnership that is not based on his fulfilling the breadwinner role in this way:

> And another thing too is personally, as far as looking for a wife was concerned, I was looking for someone who was independent. I was just sick to death of dragging some woman behind me. And that is something Nita is notorious for being. And I think it's great! I think it's great. And simplicity is part of that. You see, one of the problems is that too many people equate security with dollars. And it does not have a God damn thing to do with it!

Kevin asserts his ability to feel secure without necessarily assuming the breadwinner role or focusing on making money. Rejecting the breadwinner role and the desire to compete with and dominate others leaves the mostly heterosexual men with the need to do identity work that constructs an alternative masculine identity for them as relational and caring without giving up being masculine.

The movement ideology rejects the male breadwinner role and status occupations and prescribes practices that don't rely on gendered work. The men turn to cultural scripts they have access to such as individualism, past occupational status, being financially independent, being a shrewd buyer, and being good at making, repairing, and maintaining things and at sharing skills, all of which are dominant expressions of masculinity.

The women reject feminine gender roles as defined by the dominant culture. They reject dominant cultural patterns of gendered consumption (Weinbaum and Bridges 1978). Most mentioned advertising and popular culture depictions of the *Good Housekeeping* standard of household work as things they reject. One woman proudly asserted she does no ironing. Another said that she quit wearing makeup and plans never to wear a skirt or hose again in her life. And several also made it clear they are resisting the traditional caretaker role. This is what Pam says about being a caretaker: "I tired of doing the caretaker all my life and I'm kind of getting to the point where I think I'm enough. If somebody else wants to take care of me that's fine, but I just can't take care of anybody else anymore." Voluntary simplicity also supports women in asserting autonomy in close relationships. Nita expresses her independence as a simple liver by describing the equality in her relationship with her husband.

> One of the things you should know is we don't pool our money. We have been together nineteen years now but we got married about three months after we met. Because it was too much hassle to figure out how to make things even. I own this house. While he was working he paid $100 a month rent but now he just gets some of the grottier jobs. Kevin pays more into the food fund than me because he eats more. We halve expenses on the car but other than that we do our own expenses so if I want to buy a $60 needlework book I just find the money for it. So we feel it is a much simpler way of doing things because you are not limited to doing what you can talk the other person into thinking is okay. So it works really well.

Access to money, how housework is distributed, and autonomy in making consumption choices are explicitly interconnected in Nita's account. The idea that money represents life energy found in the voluntary simplicity ideology supports the approach she describes.

Women in the movement engage in identity work aimed at establishing more autonomy for themselves relative to the dominant culture and society and in relationship to men but they do not face pressure from the movement ideology to change their ways of relating.

Resisting the influence of media and the dominant consumer culture and resisting pressures to consume and work from family, coworkers, and friends are part of identity construction for many simple livers. Women tend to discuss these pressures as significant more than men do. Both men and women see themselves as strong, independent individuals who make their own decisions and choices and don't allow others to pressure them to participate in status seeking or self-fulfillment through occupation or overconsumption.

A distinctive aspect of the ideology of voluntary simplicity is that it stipulates that self-aware human beings recognize their connection to everything in the universe and especially to the earth, with which they are directly and most importantly connected. At the same time, autonomy relative to other people and groups is supported and this validates men whose capacities for relating have been shaped by the dominant family structure in the twentieth-century Western societies which encourage them to display autonomy rather than an orientation toward intimacy and relationality (Chodorow 1976, 1978; Johnson 1988; Rubin 1983).

But at the same time, the value that voluntary simplicity places on relationality to all things enables a sense of deep connection and relationality to other people and to all other things in the universe without necessarily requiring major shifts in gendered relational behavior on a day-to-day basis. For this reason men can make a shift in identity without necessarily reflecting on how much of a shift in relational behavior they actually demonstrate on a daily basis. This offers the possibility for them to see themselves differently.

The material and emotional interests of men in this group, most of whom want partnerships with women, are actually likely to be served by developing relational skills. There is evidence these men may sense they are increasingly disadvantaged by a lack of well-developed communicative and relational skills and have come to recognize they will be better able to find partners if they develop them. Some expressed a desire to develop the ability to talk about emotions and develop intimacy with women and other men. Most single male simple livers express a desire for partnerships or marriage.

Feminist literature (Blumstein and Schwartz 1983; Hochschild 1989; Walby 1990) suggests men continue to be advantaged over women in heterosexual partnerships because women continue to assume higher levels of responsibility for reproductive work even as they are increasingly continuously engaged in paid work. Women also tend to do more of the caring work of the family and more "emotional labor" (Hochschild 1983) both in the workplace and at home. And men tend to continue to dominate decision making about how resources of the household will be used and to use an unequal share of them (Walby 1990; Hochschild 1989).

This being the case, the cultivation of relational skills by these men and their assertion that they are not insensitive or incapable of expressing emotions and that they don't want to dominate nature or other people can in part be understood to be a shift in behavior shaped by their self-interested desire to succeed in the partnership market. That is, the men describe a worldview in which partnership holds potential material and emotional advantages for them. And at least some of the single men are also experiencing difficulty getting partners. They sometimes express very directly their desire for a partner who can earn money. They don't tend to express the desire to command reproductive labor of partners to reduce their own, but often they speak in terms of mutual emotional support. The fact that the single men believe having a partner earning money will improve their own financial and emotional situation suggests they assume they will gain some leverage over how the resources of their partner are allocated.

Most single women express ambivalence regarding partnerships and marriage. Emily, a fifty-two-year-old divorced heterosexual with a bachelor's degree in journalism who achieved "FI" and left her job as an HMO executive, expresses her attitude toward partnership in this way: "I'm not interested [in partnership] and I feel like I never wanted to be married when I was married. So I feel pretty comfortable with this lifestyle." Carol, a divorced heterosexual in her late forties with a master's degree in social work who is employed as a social worker, sums up her experience this way: "I've had relationships. That is not something I do well. I stay away from it because I don't do it well. . . . The man thing does not work for me. Isn't that amazing? Twenty years! People can't imagine an interesting life without."

Peter, a divorced forty-nine-year-old heterosexual with a master's degree in whole system design employed as a highway construction surveyor, describes the following as part of his ideal for living simply: "I'd be in a love relationship and I'd be living with someone. I'd be exchanging . . . spiritual, mental, social, emotional, physical connection and be getting nourished through and with her and that would automatically change things much more than I am doing one step at a time with doing my spread sheet on my finances and all that stuff. . . . Relationships, yeah, yeah. I'd say I'm in a shitty place in terms of relationships with women. But it's getting better. . . . I was married when I was a senior in college and I have *always* wanted to be married.

The women tend to be financially able to support themselves and to value autonomy. Their high educational levels and ability to earn good incomes without depending on the income of a man reduces the advantage men have had in dominating women in partnerships. Single simple living men may be responding to their lessening advantage in the partnership market by adopting a more relational style. This is not to suggest that they are not sincere in the changes they are trying to make in themselves, but that it is a complex sort of change that involves both material and emotional interests as well as the values they assert.

Single women doubt that men will support them emotionally or give them autonomy in relationships and they often describe past relationships where their financial and emotional resources were drained by men.

Voluntary simplicity ideology views the world as one powerful energy flow with no real separation between the natural and cultural worlds. Simple livers empower themselves by taking responsibility for healing the earth because they see the power of the cosmos to nurture as endangered in the face of ecological disaster. For men, voluntary simplicity offers the chance to experience oneself as a nurturer and the psychic reunion with the mother (earth) without necessarily having intimate relationships (Miller 1983), being in a partnership, or becoming a father (Ehrenreich 1983). But it also offers the sense and in some cases even the experience of relating to others in a new way that is more cooperative, gentle, and caring (Nardi 1992). It supports women in rejecting the devaluation of the female. It also offers women the opportunity to experience themselves as nurturers without actually being caretakers, having partners, or being mothers because it gives high value to contributions to community made through creative work, volunteering, and living sustainably—all things women can do without devoting themselves to caring for a family, being in partnerships, or having children.

Overall women simple livers tend to be single and childless. Most are ambivalent about partnerships with men, and those who do partner tend to establish partnerships in which they negotiate a relatively high degree of autonomy. Identities of simple livers are constituted in relation to being in nature, not in terms of dominating it. And there is a recognition that female ways of relating are of value (Bernard 1981; DeVault 1991; Feguson 1984; Gilligan 1977; Raymond 1986; Ruddick 1989). What is missing is a full consideration of the extent to which female and male relational qualities are culturally and economically constituted.

Ours is a society critiqued for abandoning male children to be raised by mothers alone and thus producing men who become detached from their own emotions and needs, and who are shaped into power hungry misogynists acting in an effort to avoid the grief and pain of their attempts to separate from their mothers, in order to become men (Chodorow 1978), with little support or contact from their fathers who are absent, at work, moved on to other families, or emotionally unavailable (Chodorow 1976, 1978; Dinnerstein 1976; Johnson 1988; Rubin 1983). This is the product of a particular form of nuclear family and relationships within the family, culture, and economy of contemporary society in which most of the men in voluntary simplicity grew up.

Men simple livers are attempting to reject the pain inflicted upon them by the dominant culture and the features of the dominant culture that reward the painful break with the mother/others in the form of occupational status and power over women. This also implies rejection of misogyny and competition that have, in large part, provided the basis for masculine identity and relationships with other men in the dominant culture. While some have characterized men's desire to avoid competition and the breadwinner role as a sign of self-indulgence, socially condoned irresponsibility, and detachment from others (Lasch 1978), in the case of simple livers, Ehrenreich's discussion of her "ambivalently" contingent "more optimistic reading" seems a better fit. Ehrenreich writes:

> If the male revolt has roots in a narcissistic consumer culture, it is equally rooted in the tradition of liberal humanism that inspires feminism. "Roles," after all, are not fit aspirations for adults, but the repetitive performances of people who have forgotten that it is only other people who write the scripts. Traditional masculinity, as the men's liberationists argue, is a particularly strenuous act and, as feminists have concluded, it is an act which is potentially hazardous even to bystanders. As the male revolt moved past paternalism (represented by the "good" husband and provider), and then past a kind of macho defiance (represented by *Playboy* and the Beats), it moved toward an androgynous goal that most feminists—or humanists—could only applaud. The possibility of honest communications between the sexes has been increased, so has the possibility that men may be willing to take on more of what have been women's traditional tasks . . . or so we may hope.
>
> Finally, the male revolt can be seen as a blow against a system of social control that operates to make men un-questioning and obedient employees. If men are not strapped into the role of breadwinners, perhaps they will be less compli-ant . . . as white-collar operatives of the remote and unac-countable corporations that are, increasingly, our substitute for elected government. Thus, on the optimistic side, a case could be made for putting the male revolt in the long tradition of human efforts toward personal and collective liberation—in step with feminism and with some broad populist impulse toward democracy. (1983, 170)

These men want close relationships with women in partnerships and with men in friendship. They do not want to objectify the earth or other people. They are rejecting the breadwinner role that requires men to bear the responsibility of economically supporting women, assigns women to the domestic sphere, and also encourages men to repress, deny, and project their emotional needs.

For women, voluntary simplicity reasserts the value of qualities assigned to them by the dominant culture such as nurturing and cooperation and maintains that it is those qualities that need to be adopted by all people, men and women, if the planet is to survive. Voluntary simplicity shifts the meanings of masculine and feminine identity of the dominant culture away from strict gender roles and gendered household work but it does not deconstruct the sex/gender system that shapes the context within which they do their voluntary simplicity identity work. And they don't specifically problematize and then question the idea that men and women are essentially different in relational and behavioral ways based on sex.

Conclusion

The process of remaking the self as a moral identity through the voluntary simplicity movement involves rejecting significant aspects of hegemonic culture. Participants disavow the value of work for a wage or occupational status seeking and reject typical middle-class status goods consumption. Simple livers are uncomfortable with their privilege, which they say derives from being affluent Western consumers. They are responding to the critiques of environmentalists most directly but are also responding to the critiques of the civil rights movement, feminists, the gay and lesbian liberation movement, and postcolonial critiques of the values and practices of the dominant but no longer hegemonic, presently contested, culture associated with the global economic system and Western power.

On the one hand they are directly responding to, and aiming at, resisting a worldview that adheres to the values they associate with the industrial era in which being affluent through dominating and exploiting nature and other people, and being white, male, and Western was constructed as the highest moral identity. The critiques of the dominant culture have impacted upon them powerfully enough that they are compelled to remake themselves, at least in part, in response to them. The critique of the dominant categories exposes the groups who fill them as exploitive, oppressive, and destructive. Simple livers tend to agree that the industrial era, propelled, in their view, by a male-dominated, nature-dominating, competitive Western culture, has been destructive of the environment and human well-being. But they are also engaged in a less obvious struggle with these critical cultural discourses for defining power.

Simple livers adopt voluntary simplicity because they want to reduce their own negative impact on the environment and to feel they are good people. They also want to reduce the discomfort they feel from waged work and mainstream pressures to obtain status.

Voluntary simplicity is different from Protestant asceticism or hedonistic sensuality. Simple livers seek a pleasurable and fulfilling lifestyle that is compatible with being a good person. But they also adopt voluntary simplicity because they don't want others blaming them for environmental degradation or telling them what they need to do differently to be good people. They want more clarity and certainty about what the qualities of a good person like themselves who is affluent, Western, and white are. They don't want others defining this for them. They want to be in charge of defining what a moral identity for themselves and their group is. The idea that there should be no blaming of others and that individuals must decide for themselves what is enough supports them in this aspect of their identity work.

People who adopt voluntary simplicity construct a moral identity that distances them from some aspects of being mainstream that make them uncomfortable by framing problems of environmental destruction and social injustice and the solutions for solving these problems in ways that mesh with the personal discomforts simple livers experience in rationalized work and cultural pressures to conform to consumerist values. Voluntary simplicity allows them to adopt changes that are possible for them to make and to feel that by doing this they are acting as cultural change agents and good and moral people. At the same time it supports them in continued connection to some parts of their identities that are more mainstream, such as being heterosexual and well educated, which help them in getting by.

The criteria for establishing a voluntary simplicity moral identity invite people to reject conspicuous consumption and some values of upper-middle-class status on the one hand, but enables well-educated, middle-class people to remain, in some significant ways, connected to their social and cultural capital and class privilege on the other. For instance, their ability to own homes, invest so they can earn interest income and choose to reduce consumption rather than being forced by lack of resources to do so is based in having economic, social, and cultural resources. Simple livers reclaim the simple living values of self-sufficiency and frugality and associate them with the Puritans, among other groups, thus maintaining a symbolic connection to the early colonizers of the United States, the dominant group in the modern era (Elgin 1993a; Dominguez and Robin 1992; Andrews 1997).

The movement offers the promise of broader cultural change derived from the cumulative change that will result as more individuals choose voluntary simplicity, thereby leaving in place a liberal democratic conception of the relationship of the individual to the collective. Participants believe that by living simply they set an example that will be noted and then followed by others and maintain that the whole of society can be changed in this way. Simple living moral identity involves supplanting the high value for affluence with a high value for voluntary simplicity and frugality. It also involves establishing an identity in which the simple livers experience themselves as balanced in terms of masculine and feminine characteristics.

Voluntary simplicity offers a convenient and compelling solution for them because it focuses on their chosen reduction of consumption and time working as a solution to reducing their relative affluence and achieving a moral identity, rather than targeting changes in the structural distribution of resources primarily, which would be much more difficult to achieve and potentially threaten the relative advantage they have in terms of access to resources.

The movement glosses over conflict through "ideological work" (Berger 1981, 1995), but the ideology is "contested terrain" (Berger 1981). The choices about which tools from the tool kit to use and how they will work are emergent (Swidler 1986; Hall and Neitz 1993). People are developing their own interpretations and approaches and sharing them, not following a set pattern despite the prescriptions offered in books, journals, and workshops. Structural constraints, and historically derived circumstances, influence possible choices (Hall and Neitz 1993; Swidler 1986). But within these limits there is flexibility, and those in the voluntary simplicity movement live in contested terrain where the possibilities for the introduction of new questions, ideas, and practices can and do emerge.

Simple living moral identity constructed through the movement does shift dominant patterns of cultural meanings assigned to affluence and poverty, stereotypical masculine ways of relating, and femininity in significant ways by questioning the value of the dominant culture's definitions of affluence and masculinity and offering a voluntary simplicity alternative. Gendered patterns of moral identity construction supported by the movement allow men to distance themselves from characteristics of masculinity they view as negative and to embrace cooperation and emotional connection. Women are supported in their orientation toward cooperative network building and at the same time tend to use part of the movement ideology that emphasizes self-defined values and goals to assert autonomy.

But simple livers tend to assume that differential gendered power within voluntary simplicity is eliminated by embracing the values of cooperation and relationality. They don't problematize issues of power within circles, their own relationships, or even within the movement more broadly. But not acknowledging power does not mean it is not present. Tensions along gender lines appear in circles and impact on the ways boundaries are set and status is established, and on the collective capacity of the voluntary simplicity movement. Chapter 4 analyzes these features of the voluntary simplicity movement.

CHAPTER FOUR

Gendered Visions of Process, Power, and Community in the Voluntary Simplicity Movement

The primary sites of collective identity building and boundary setting for the voluntary simplicity movement are support groups, which are often called simplicity circles by people in the movement. Simplicity circles offer rich data about the interactions in the everyday lives of simple livers through which the collective capacities of the movement are constructed and negotiated over time. People ranging in age from the early twenties into their eighties, mostly white and with incomes that vary substantially, often participate in the same circle. Most circles are made up of men and women. Circle participants join in a limited collective identity based on several very basic common ideas and practices and the broadly defined goal of linking personal practice to values. The areas that respondents consistently interpret in similar ways are few. But they generally agree that overconsumption is a serious issue and voice concerns about the environment. Most also believe waged work is not organized to serve human needs of workers and is problematic.

The sort of community that voluntary simplicity circles represent and the type of collective capacity that voluntary simplicity generates are shaped by tensions along gendered lines that exist in the circles. These tensions stem, in large part, from gendered conceptions of what constitutes power and how to go about creating it, what a desirable community is, and how to build such community.

For the most part, neither the women nor the men perceive tensions in the groups to be gender based. Instead they connect them to individual differences and interests. Participants in voluntary simplicity make meaning of the contested terrain within the movement largely through frames of understanding that don't help them to transcend the differences that exist along gender lines or to grasp and grapple with the contradictions these differences represent for the movement.

Circles initially tend to have more women members, but become male dominated over time. The two circles I studied in Seattle, which had been meeting for six years and two years respectively, had both become male dominated. One of the circles I participated in in Columbia, Missouri, also became male dominated.

In ideal typical terms women emphasize community building from the private sphere, collectivism, caring (Gilligan 1977), mutual respect, and self-transformation (Barnett 1993; 1995; Stall and Stoecker 1998) that reduce the separation between private and public spheres.

Men emphasize opposition to the dominant culture, confrontation in the public sphere, individualism, tolerance, and the desire to transform others. It is important to note that these orientations are ideal types and that men and women do not always fall neatly into these categories in all contexts or absolutely consistently over time, but that overall in discourse and practice women and men do clearly follow these patterns. There were no clear and consistent exceptions to this pattern among my informants though there are variations in the strength of these orientations among both men and women.

These findings are generally in keeping with the recent work by Stall and Stoecker (1998), in which they outline the existence of two types of gendered urban community organizing: the Alinsky model, "which focuses on communities organizing for power," (729) and what they call the "women-centered model," (729) which focuses on organizing relationships to build community. They find that, in practice, men tend to favor the Alinsky model and women tend to favor a women-centered model of organizing which is associated with women's community organizing efforts (Barnett 1993; Bookman and Morgen 1988; Naples 1991, 1998; Payne 1989; Robnett 1997; Stall and Stoecker 1998; Taylor 1996, 1999; Weiss 1993, 1998; Weiss and Friedman 1995; West and Blumberg 1990). As Stall and Stoecker explain, "Building a mobilizable community is called community organizing" and it can "refer to the entire process of organizing relationships, identifying issues, mobilizing around those issues, and building an enduring organization. Community organizing is localized, often prepolitical action that provides the foundation for multilocal and explicitly political social movements" (730). These authors point out that these models are rooted in distinct traditions and vary along several dimensions, including "conceptions of human nature and conflict, power and politics, leadership, and the organizing process" (729).

The similarities between organizing efforts using the women-centered model and those advocated by the ideology of voluntary simplicity are striking. Both include problematizing at least some aspects of the split between public and private spheres; both tend to draw in activities which do not fall smoothly into either category. For instance, the women-centered model and voluntary simplicity ideas both extend the boundaries of the private sphere to include the neighborhood and imply an extended private sphere that links private life, close community, and civil society rather than accepting them as separate spheres (Bernard 1981; DeVault 1991; Kaplan 1982). For example, a couple who encountered a woman living on the street in their neighborhood invited her to live with them until she could get back on her feet and find a job. They arranged for her to share in their household work and assisted her in seeking work. After four months of living with them she had gotten a job and was able to get a place of her own. A group of women organized a weekly sewing group and tea at the housing project in their neighborhood with the intent of building relationships with the women who lived there. This same group of women did plant watering, pet sitting, and house sitting for each other when someone was away.

Voluntary simplicity supports the women-centered relational model. It goes even further by calling for the dissolution of boundaries between nature and culture, and demanding that human social life be conceived of and practiced, not just as a set of relations to other human beings, but in relation to nature and all things in the cosmos.

In one way, the voluntary simplicity movement can be understood as a movement that places the often hidden women's work (of building relationships and networks and empowering people through caring, supporting, nurturing, and enabling work)—that is necessary for political action and community organizing for collective action and social movements to be successful—at the center of activity instead of devaluing it.

Stall and Stoecker (1998) point out that social movement literature generally has not considered the importance of community organizing or of gender. The uncritical acceptance of a public and private sphere split that is institutionalized in the dominant culture overlooks the private sphere organizing, network building, relationship building, and nurturing work that is necessary for any organizing, political action, or social movement to exist and take action in the public sphere. The separation between the two spheres serves those who wield power through the reproduction of the illusion of the immutability of separate spheres.

Most of the simple livers I interviewed, both men and women, espoused values in keeping with the women-centered model. But I found that existing institutional structures and other cultural repertoires (the dominant culture; several ethnic cultures including Norwegian, Irish Catholic, and Swedish; cultural variations associated with the eras in which cohorts of simple livers came of age), as well as the emergent culture of voluntary simplicity and biographical histories strongly influenced by gendered identities, play out in voluntary simplicity in much the same way that Stall and Stoecker argue gendered structures and identities play out in community organizing.

Men, it seems largely unwittingly or without reflection, bring characteristics of the Alinsky model into the working of circles. This is an approach named after Saul Alinsky (1971) and is focused on public sphere battles between the haves and have-nots and on connections of local issues to public sphere strategizing that is often linked to national-level change initiatives (Stall and Stoecker 1998, 733). The discussions by men tend to focus on establishing expert status as simple livers, responding against the dominant culture, and criticism of others perceived to be mindless consumers. One man even spoke of his frugality as a form of war against corporate interests. And as chapter 3 discusses, masculine voluntary simplicity moral identities are constructed through a sense of self as independent individuals who stand against the dominant, competitive, and greedy culture much more than on their relations with other simple livers.

Women tend to speak of their voluntary simplicity activity in relational terms of mutuality. For instance, as the last chapter demonstrated, women often describe their voluntary simplicity consumption practices in terms of supporting local business people by buying local products. Men weave into their conversations more concern about frugality, and demonstrating that they can live well at little cost in comparison to those in the dominant culture. The way these women describe their approach to consumption mirrors the ways Stall and Stoecker find women organize at the community level. The women tend to give most of their energy to choices aimed at network building and to talk about generating change out of the private arena, which includes local groups and the neighborhoods they live in. The women focus on relational autonomy (Neitz 1999); that is, they gain a sense of themselves as simple livers less through activities and ideas aimed against the dominant culture and more through supporting relationships with others in the movement that actually create alternative ways of doing things. Some women do volunteer for, contribute to, and advocate state and national level political and organizational agendas but they tend to put most of their energy into more immediate local networks and relationships.

It is important to point out that the men also advocate grassroots community building and contribute to and volunteer for locally based organizations, but they tend to give somewhat more energy in their discussion at circles, in their interviews with me, and in the organizational affiliations they describe in terms of "interests" discourse. Where women talk about empowering themselves and others at the local level, men talk about standing strong against the dominant culture and being experts themselves.

In mixed gender circles, which are most common, men end up coopting circle agendas over time, drawing them back toward a masculine competitive pattern of relating, and establishing themselves as experts and leaders. I theorize that this occurs because of the interaction of the following factors: (1) the power men hold over women through the present configurations of institutionalized structures (Acker 1988, 1990; Dixon 1997; Ferguson 1984; Kleinman 1996; Milkman 1988; Walby 1990) and their desire to both create change and retain power; (2) the poverty of the cultural gender repertoires available to men and women; (3) a lack of adequate models for organizing to generate and use recognition of difference in positive ways and avoid just tolerating or denying differences which can lead to the reproduction of at least some aspects of domination relationships they wish to avoid; (4) the distinct developmental experiences and socialization processes by which men and women in contemporary Western societies are shaped (Chodorow 1978; Dinnerstein 1976; Franklin 1988; Johnson 1988); and (5) a lack of "recognition" of the significance of gender in their lives (Lara 1998).

Since men hold greater power through their connection to the existing institutional structures (they are privileged over women in employment, public policy, the institution of marriage, educational institutions, patriarchal culture, and consumer culture), they tend to orient toward public sphere activities and toward shifting the relative value of simple living in the eyes of those outside the movement. To achieve this goal they jockey for circles to orient toward establishing the members as expert simple livers and encourage a discourse that is critical of affluent people outside the movement. This approach suggests that real power for the men is intuitively still located in the public sphere of the dominant culture. The men orient toward masculine sources of power in the dominant culture found in the public sphere. Women simple livers, too, draw from existing patterns in the dominant culture. They do not fight these shifts or demand that their approaches be heard; instead, they withdraw or acquiesce.

In a circle that had lasted six years at the time of my interviews, the women had joined sewing and knitting retreats that gave them a space without male participation. They said they discussed voluntary simplicity and alternative ways of doing things at these retreats. In another circle that I followed for its whole duration of seven weekly meetings and an eighth meeting to discuss progress a month later, women began dropping out within two weeks as the men began to dominate the agenda and discussions in the meetings. Women's comments on this included the idea that the men were focusing on things they had not anticipated being the focus, such as financial planning for frugality, and the idea the men were setting a standard for simplifying that was beyond the level they felt they were able to achieve or wanted to practice.

Perhaps because they are grateful for the support the circles do provide members, they are hesitant to focus on their differences. In the circles I studied there was a reluctance to compete openly over whose interpretation of social reality is correct or to get into disputes over politics. Schwalbe found similar characteristics in the men's groups he studied (Schwalbe 1996, 100). But competition and efforts to dominate do enter the circles. At times these efforts are overt but more often they are covert.

The circle model dictated by the literature advocates sharing, listening, and support, but it does not provide guidance on how to move beyond tolerance to hashing through differences and establishing common ground on which to stand as a group (Collins 1990). Techniques for generating understanding or recognition (Lara 1998) of difference as important among circle members (beyond differences in ideas about how to reduce consumption, work, and what practices are best for the environment) are missing, as are tools for dealing with covert efforts by some members to dominate the agenda. Drawing from the work of Lara, in which she is concerned with the contribution of feminism to changed definitions of difference and conceptions of the public sphere (Habermas 1987, 1992), I theorize that circles are locations where a struggle takes place over the boundaries between public and private in the culture of voluntary simplicity. This struggle is largely one between women and men embedded in the context of contemporary capitalist patriarchy (Walby 1990).

The idea of tolerance of difference among circle members is accepted. But differences in the cultural and biographical experiences of women and men or the greater power afforded men relative to women through dominant institutions, and how this shapes circle dynamics, are unexplored by them. This undercuts a full recognition of difference and thereby a full understanding of themselves in relation to each other, and others in the world, whom they assume they understand.

Voluntary Simplicity Circles

Ideology, practices, and language are all important mechanisms for establishing a sense of insider status for movement participants. Those who are inside will know what "FI" is. "FI" refers to financial independence, one of the things Dominguez and Robin (1992) set as a goal for simple livers. It consists of saving and investing enough and reducing consumption to the greatest extent possible while still feeling you are able to live comfortably on your investments and no longer have to work for a wage at a job you don't like. Those who are "FIers" are looked to as role models by those aspiring to achieve financial independence. They will often share stories of the "gazingus pins"[2] (nonessential purchases) they have stopped "frittering"[3] (spending what seem to be small amounts on things that are nonessential) their money away on. "Frittering" away money on daily coffee at coffee shops, stopping for a take-out breakfast, and eating lunches out daily are examples of food related purchases that add up quickly and could be reduced by taking a cup or thermos of coffee with you when you leave the house, preparing breakfast at home, and taking a sandwich from home for lunch.

No explanation of what is meant by "mindfulness" will be needed when it comes up among insiders at a circle meeting. The new member who is explaining the stress they feel as they rush from task to task, from their job to the grocery store to their home to cook in a rush will be patiently listened to. There are murmurs of understanding. Someone says, "It's hard to be mindful when you don't have time to think." The initiation has begun.

At simplicity circle meetings people usually greet each other by inquiring about each other's week, picking up on events that they know about in each others lives, and bringing the threads of knowing each other up to date. Sometimes, and more often in some circles than others, someone will share a difficult experience or a particularly good experience that is not directly related to efforts to simplify. Arrivals and greetings are followed by the check-in, a familiar practice in therapeutic groups. Each person is supposed to briefly describe how their week went relative to their simplifying. Then, if there was a reading for the week, it is discussed.

The discussion often digresses from the text at hand. Conversations may shift toward broader societal concerns and critiques of the dominant culture or toward practical concerns that have come up in the lives of circle members. Sometimes conversations takes on a more social tone that appears to be unrelated to voluntary simplicity altogether.

The model of process and participation that Andrews (1997) outlines is drawn from both the model of the Swedish study circle and the Folk Schools of Denmark she studied when getting her Ph.D. in education at Stanford.[4] The model developed by Andrews calls for facilitation of circles to rotate and suggests avoiding having a leader. Ideally, everyone speaks and everyone listens and no one judges or finds fault with anyone else in the circle. Her prescribed model has diffused as the ideal. All of the circles I studied were influenced by the Andrews circle model even if they were using other books. But my findings also suggest that, while the model influences how circles work in some ways, it is rarely the way circles really work over time. That is, leadership does not rotate among all members, topics for discussion are not always mutually arrived at and discussed, and discussion aimed at self-change or mutual support for all members is not always ongoing.

The circles as prescribed are designed to last for a minimum of six or eight weeks depending on the book the circle selects to work with. After that the group can decide to continue or disband. Of the three circles I studied, one has been meeting for over six years, another had been meeting for two years, and one met for seven weeks over the period of a semester.

Most members who stop going to circles or who have been in circles that have ended do not view them as failed. Instead they believe the circles have served their purpose and that they and others who may have left the circles have grown beyond them or in different directions and that it is a normal evolution for them to move to something else. For some this includes finding another circle; for others it involves reaching FI, finding a passion, or getting tired of the way the circle they are in is working. Only two people, both men, mentioned that they left circles because of interpersonal conflicts. Leaving a circle does not mean the person is moving away from voluntary simplicity since it is considered a life encompassing choice that individuals can choose to pursue regardless of affiliation. Voluntary simplicity circles or study groups provide a somewhat safe space for people to work on their alternative individual and collective identities and develop practices without overt negative judgments from others, at least for a period of time.

The highest level of consensus among simple livers regarding practices is relative to the need to reduce consumerism and build an alternative culture starting at the community level. But the specifics of how to reduce consumption, how to handle the need for money, how to build an alternative form of community, and what a desirable community is are very fluid and emergent, and men and women tend to have differing conceptions of how to build the type of alternative community voluntary simplicity implies.

Gendered Visions of Process, Power, and Community

Emily's experience typifies the experiences of women in mixed gender groups. The group process, type of empowerment, and supporting community envisioned by Emily as ideal, and the lack of this ideal in the reality of the way her circle works, eventually caused her to opt to give more energy to other activities. One of the reasons she left was because the men in the circle shaped the agenda away from ongoing work on how to further simplicity for long-term circle participants and instead turned to recruiting new members and asking long-term circle members to serve as expert advisors.

As prescriptions became more narrowly focused on things Emily had already resolved and the circle meetings were taken up with going over stock issues repetitively for new recruits, she lost interest. Emily explains why she is thinking of leaving the circle in the following way:

> This is where it sort of gets dicey because for me I feel like I might be leaving the circle I'm in. Because it is getting kind of more money focused and now I feel like where I'm heading is more of a community-based circle where you can support and help each other around community. Forming community is becoming more important to me in my neighborhood. Basically neighbors are very separate here. And so we don't help each other out and that is the issue—instead of paying somebody to water your plants, having a friend come and water your plants or getting somebody's plant starts instead of buying or capitalizing on each other's expertise, and so that's the part I'm more

interested in. It is sort of a form of collective living without living together. I'm really interested in co-op housing.

The circle was not shifting from problem identification to jointly constructed problem solutions that really met the needs of long-term women members who had moved beyond decluttering, overconsumption, and jobism to the question of how to build alternative community after their rejection of consumer culture and their shift to simple living.

Two of the three women members in Emily's circle whom I interviewed say it no longer meets their needs and they don't go regularly, instead preferring to see one another outside the circle. Emily says:

> Jack's group are all just sharing [stories of how they got involved in voluntary simplicity]. There are so many new people coming in. You tell your story and then next time there are more new people so you tell your story again. You get tired of telling your stupid story. So anyway I think it would be nice if there was sort of an issue, a topic based, you know, how do you do this in the city? Ideas on something like issues—somebody is having trouble with their refrigerator, brainstorming on solutions. Should you get it repaired so that is does not go to the landfill? Yeah, I'm thinking that I'm probably not going to go back to the group for awhile. I tried it out last week again and I was not very happy. Nine o'clock is when we usually end and we had not even gotten through the check-in by nine o'clock.

Emily also recognizes that the needs of the men in her circle are being met by the agenda established in the circle. But she does not consider trying to get the circle to shift the agenda or question whether it should be happening. She accepts it and puts her energy into describing where she is finding support for her interest in community building rather than trying to change the circle:

> I think what happens, probably for all of us, but for men especially, they don't have a lot of relationships in their lives where they support each other so that groups become a way for them to talk and kind of express what they need. And I'm in some needlework groups now and talk to people through those groups; there is some commonality with the simplicity stuff there. Nita and I get together and knit, and I get together with

Joan. So I've formed friendships through the circle where you can get ideas and help each other out.

Nita, a close friend of Emily, expresses a similar feeling about the circle:

> Jack feels like anyone who is interested he can just invite in, which may be OK, but I think that it kind of dissipates the group because you got these people that are starting from ground zero that you don't know. . . . If you are always getting new people it's not just that they are at different places, it's that you . . . I have this theory about meetings, that people go to meetings if they are comfortable with the people who are going. So I don't care if it's about neighborhood planning or what, it's about your need to have built up or be in the process of building up a kind of friendship group, so you're going because you enjoy the people who are there as well as the topic you are discussing. But if there are always new people, the group never kind of stays jelled in a way. And so I feel when I go now I have to say practically nothing or way too much . . . just a couple of simple sentences. There is so much history back there that nobody knows about. Oh, one of the neat sessions we did do is we had agreed that everyone would talk about something they hadn't simplified and maybe wanted to. And that was a really neat discussion and we have talked about things we hadn't simplified and were not going to because we like them the way they were. There are a lot of things you can really discuss that you haven't delved into.

Jack's circle had, according to the long-time women members, become a forum for bringing in new people and telling each person's story of becoming a simple liver over and over. The circle meetings were always held at Jack's home. The circle was used as a place for old timers to influence new recruits and establish status as experts. Particularly revealing was the fact that everyone I interviewed from the circle described it as "Jack's circle," despite the fact the circle approach is ideally supposed to be based on rotating facilitation and agenda setting determined by group process.

A circle I was in from its inception, which ran for seven weeks following the format prescribed by Dominguez and Robin (1992), showed signs of the same sort of dynamic. In this circle the first two facilitators were the two men in the circle. The first was chosen by the organization sponsoring the workshop on circles to serve as the facilitator for the first meeting. The second man volunteered to facilitate the second meeting.

At the third meeting one man suggested the circle discontinue having a weekly facilitator. The other male member immediately agreed this was a good idea but continued to refer to himself as the "leader." Two women present indicated they were content with it. It meant the women who had not yet facilitated did not have to facilitate. It was clear they did not particularly want to. I was the only person who did not immediately agree. But because of my participant/observer role, I did not push strongly against the decision. If I had not already gained knowledge of the tendency of men to come to dominate circles through earlier data gathering, I suspect that I would not have questioned the idea at all. The decision not to have rotating facilitation resulted in all future meetings being covertly dominated by the two men in the circle. The content of the book we were supposedly following was largely discarded or discussed in terms of comparison to nonsimple livers. Discussions by the men shifted toward judgments of the dominant culture and practices of other people. The women were more focused on exploring their own practices. The men established themselves as the experts who were well along on simple living, while the women talked about how their practices fell short of the ideal.

Carol believes her behaviors are like the behaviors described in the readings. She says, "[In] chapter 3 it talks about irrational, addictive, greedy behavior around money and they compare it to that same behavior around food, which I think is real interesting. And it definitely is right on target with me." Carol approaches the discussion with an interest in exploring her practices in comparison to those described as problematic and healthier in the readings the group is preparing to discuss. Roger is the first to speak after Carol:

> Well, like you I thought the analogy between how you spend your money and food was really good. And the thing that really did it for me was, I don't really worry too much about what I eat. I feel like I'm reasonably active and I also kind of feel like I have a pretty healthy diet. So that is not really something that concerns me. But that makes it really easy for me to observe my roommates, or other people I know, who go through these sort of crazy dieting cycles. And I can see how irrational the diet cycle really is, that is really manifest to me. And then to have that compared to how we live our life in

terms of spending money, irrationally acquiring things, just like a binge eater. . . . That just really completed it.

Roger quickly establishes that he is not irrational, greedy, or addictive in his eating behavior. When he discursively distances from these behaviors he uses the word "I." He mentions that he is not really concerned about food. He says he is physically active and eats healthy foods too. He places himself as already being at, or close to, the simple living ideal in terms of food consumption and exercise. He goes on to note that he does observe problematic eating behaviors in others more clearly as a result of doing the readings. He notes their binge and diet cycles and says he sees how irrational they are. While he does not directly say his relationship with money is also already in keeping with simple living values, he subtly shifts from the use of "I" to the use of the more distant "we" when he describes linking problematic eating behaviors to behaviors associated with money. Roger lets the other people in the circle know his practices are those of an expert who is well along in living simply.

Two men and six women participated in this circle but at the time the circle ended only I, two other women, and the two men remained. Three women had dropped out of the circle. I later asked these women open-ended questions about why they left. Two of them commented that the men were interested in different concerns from those they thought the group would be concerned with, that is, gradual, practical, day-to-day ways to simplify. One mentioned she perceived the men as extreme simple livers pushing others to simplify in similar ways. A third woman, who was Hispanic, the only ethnic minority represented among those I encountered in the circles, said she felt the group could not understand her views on the issues of consumption, work, and environmental concerns because her experiences growing up in Latin America were so different from those they were recounting. She said she had no interest in sharing her intimate feelings about these matters with people who had no conception of the different kind of life experience she had had.

The third circle I studied that was made up of women and men also had two unofficial male leaders. Instead of saying the men were the leaders, as was the case in the other two circles, they simply looked to them for guidance and inspiration. This pattern points to a shift back to a separation between leaders and followers and the elevation of achieving goals over maintaining relationships of mutuality that characterize the dominant culture in voluntary simplicity circles. The men initiate this shift employing several strategies that give the illusion of "structurelessness" (Freeman 1974), supplanting the open but somewhat guided formulaic support group processes advocated by Andrews (1997) and Dominguez and Robin (1992) with a more open agenda and format. Some simply advocated for dropping facilitation and planned agendas. Some created alliances with others in the group that enabled them to silence those who might not agree. Some used control over the agenda to achieve the illusion of agreement most of the time. Freeman notes that the concept of structurelessness that was popular during the years in which the women's liberation movement was taking shape served to mask power within the women's movement. She maintains that the strongest advocates of structurelessness were those who were most powerful whether they were conscious of their power or not. She argues that as long as the structure of the group is informal the rules of how decisions are made are known only to a few and shared selectively. Freeman maintains, "for everyone to have the opportunity to be involved in a given group, and to participate in its activities the structure must be explicit, not implicit. The rules of decision making must be open and available to everyone, and this can only happen if they are formalized" (1974, 204). Though men simple livers taking control of circles don't use the word "structurelessness," they use the concept in very much the same way that Freeman found powerful women used it in the women's liberation movement—to assert power. But as men came to dominate circles they did not get other members to take collective actions as a group outside the circle and they did not get members to stay and conform to their desired behaviors and discussions either. And women began to detach.

The way community and power are defined in circles is different for women and men. This comment of Kevin's is a common example of what men think about the discussions in circles: "And you know when you approach voluntary simplicity it is in an independent thinking way of thinking. You can't be influenced by what somebody else thinks when you do this. You have to be influenced by what you think and what you are comfortable with, because you are making your life."

Nita's comments here represent the perspective most often voiced by women:

> I think that you are influenced by other people and what they are doing partly because it gives you a sounding board and some other new ideas. So I think you are influenced by other people and what they are doing partly because it's new ideas and partly because you realize there are things they are doing you may not want to do. And you can pick and choose among your own thoughts as well as what other people are doing.

Women tend to want to extend the relationships built within circles into relationships that bind members into a community of mutual support in daily life with the assurance of support of a high level of personal autonomy. Men tend to want circles to establish expert knowledge that everyone agrees upon or at least does not question openly, to bring in new members, or over time to shift the focus to discussion of the differences between themselves as successful simple livers and the majority of mass consumers in the dominant culture. Men also sometimes describe wanting to have confrontation with the dominant culture or those they view as representatives of it. Women talk more about work aimed at deepening the ties of community among a smaller group of people who know each other over time, including the whole persons of people in the group in the discussions and activities they undertake and supporting others in a variety of activities, some of which they themselves are not necessarily interested in doing. In a few cases, if something a person needs comes into the possession of another person in the circle, they transfer it to the person who needs it without money changing hands. Circles serve in part as a network that extends out and links members to a broader range of possible sources for getting things they need without spending money. For instance, Fred, who did not have a television, got one by mentioning at his circle that he wanted one. Another member, Pam, had an extra television that came from the household of someone who had passed away, and she let Fred have it on indefinite loan.

Sometimes friendships, networks of support, joint involvement in other groups, and, in a few cases, even relationships of quasi-material dependence develop. Women are usually the ones who create and maintain these types of networks. But in other cases the circles are largely the only contact members have with each other. In the circles I studied people don't interact as a collectivity except within the circle context. In those circles people discussed times when some people from a circle may get together for dinner, a concert, to do community and volunteer work, or to knit and sew, or to help each other out by house and pet sitting when someone is out of town.

Nita describes a man who started with their circle but soon left because he wanted to set the agenda of the group and was frustrated that others were not willing to follow. Nita chuckles as she explains, "He was really quite crushed that everyone did not jump on his bandwagon and he did not continue on with the group."

Kevin described his circle's lack of interest in participating in "Buy Nothing Day" with disappointment:

One of the things that has been discussed a couple of times is that whether or not some of the things that were discussed at the meeting should be converted into action and our group has always said no, let everybody go their own way. I don't know whether there are other groups that have taken a different tack. But it has come up. Buy Nothing Day is a good example. Several of us are involved in Buy Nothing Day. But we don't push for somebody else to do it. . . . They never agreed as a group to participate in any action.

Men appear to be more invested than women in influencing the circle to adopt their agendas. This may in part be because men claim circles are important for them as a place where they can relate to others, particularly other men, closely. While women discussed a variety of activities that brought them close to others in the context of group activities, the men tended to discuss the circles as the primary places where they can feel close to other men.

Another striking difference in women's and men's conceptions of power is the different ways women and men assign status in circles. Status for men and among men in the circles I studied was enhanced by having had a high-status occupation and having chosen to give it up because it was not fulfilling. Status in two of the circles also was given to those who were able to live from sources other than paid work. Ultimately having capital, property, or pensions derived from a work-for-pay history are valued and played a role in constructing the moral identity of simple livers, particularly for men. All of these are embedded in the public sphere.

Women are interested in circles so long as they are maintained as nondirective open spaces where individuals can come for support in making choices to simplify. Circles can, and do, become limiting and problematic for women when men shift circle agendas toward a confrontational stance against the dominant culture and discourse shifts toward establishing a closed space with expert knowledge and practices agreed upon by all participants.

The men tend to want to establish a stable body of knowledge rather than engage in an ongoing process of knowledge construction that is deepened and engaged in by equally knowledgeable participants who know each other over time and bring different ideas to the group. The men set about establishing acceptance of a range of practices and values as the basis of the collective identity of the circle as a group. What ideal practices are, and expert knowledge consists of, become objects with which to wield collective power. It is the collectively held object that everyone is supposed to agree is right that will then presumably become the basis for community. In this way the men tend to want to shift the goal to creating the illusion of a collectively held claim of being right that becomes the object for achieving the goal of winning the public sphere struggle for dominance over consumer culture.

Men in voluntary simplicity point out they are pacifists and want to build community and nurture meaningful relationships, just as women do, but seem to be less successful in building intimate networks of relationships that connect them to the kind of community they yearn for (Franklin 1988). Kevin confided he envied his wife because she had such close relationships with several other women from their circle and the women took retreats together to sew and knit. This is a statement made by Kevin that is typical of how men who have adopted voluntary simplicity feel about the typical ways that men in the dominant culture relate:

> I'm kinda jealous [of Nita's women's sewing retreats] you know 'cause I've never been able to figure out a real combination so I can figure out a retreat for the guys I kinda know. We've developed a culture here that cultivates superficial friendships between men so men get together and talk about football games and tell jokes and all this meaningless crap they would be better to leave at home, you know, or at least some place. [Chuckling] For Christ's sake, don't bring it up! Some guys say this is the way men relate to each other but I don't think it is. I think it's a lousy way to relate 'cause it leaves people, us, separated.

Kevin told me that the circle provided him with the closest connections to other men he had. Several other men said the same thing.

Even as men express a desire for community and intimacy (Nardi 1992), and find circles a place where they can have meaningful communication with others, they sometimes also express discomfort with personal things becoming the topic at circle meetings. Fred told me he finally blew up at a woman who just talked about her personal issues in the circle. He ended up leaving the circle because he felt it was taken over by giving therapy to her. His agenda was to critique the dominant cultural practices relative to consumption and he presented himself as a successful simple liver, dedicated to living frugally. When the agenda of the circle became one of supporting a woman on issues outside of the frame he viewed appropriate for the circle, he first tried to shift the agenda back to his interests and when that failed, he withdrew (Sattel 1976). He expressed similar views regarding a woman in the circle he is in presently, complaining that her concern about not being able to afford to go on a trip to Greece with friends to celebrate her birthday as she had in past years, due to her shift toward simplicity, was trivial. She left the circle while I was observing it. Another man also said he left a circle because he could not get the other members to do what he wanted. None of the women mentioned a desire to direct the circle's focus on a particular agenda or limited range of concerns addressed in the circle. But they did leave when the circles didn't meet their needs.

The women tend to accept men's efforts to use circles to form the kinds of male relationships they need. The women don't fight for an agenda that primarily meets their own needs. The men tend to press for their own agenda in the circle but generally don't resort to the extreme tactics of the man discussed above, who left the circle only after his angry demands, aimed at making his agenda the dominant one, failed.

Women are comfortable with supporting people based on the types and levels of their need rather than requiring that everyone demonstrate more or less the same levels of need consistently in the circle meetings (Gilligan 1977; Ruddick 1989). Men prefer to limit the parts of a person's life that are acceptable to bring to circle meetings, and some mention irritation at those who stray outside of the bounds. Women find the different aspects of the lives of others worthwhile and valuable in themselves and for developing strategies for simple living for themselves. They tend to be more involved than men in extending the network of relationships outside of the circles and into their everyday lives. Men tend, in the long run, to center their community-building energies in terms of voluntary simplicity in circles and other organizations rather than in networks or diffuse relationships.

Circles are not important for women in the same way they are for men. Women describe themselves as having multiple networks that support them and view the circles as only one of several. They also elaborate on the connections in terms of personal relationships they have that are of different levels of intimacy. The men tend to speak of relationships in terms of group affiliations rather than in terms of networks and levels of intimacy of relationships with people.

Several women described the importance of their relationships with other women. This is how Emily expressed the importance of other women in her life:

> For me another joy has been the community of women in these needlework retreats and finding a whole different sense of relationship. You just don't have these kinds of depth in work

relationships and very brilliant women who maybe had fabulous careers, maybe didn't, but are still very intelligent and very knowledgeable, getting together over embroidery and talking, supporting each other, and forming community. How do people form community in their lives? You do it through church, country club, that kind stuff, but then it is all based on those values through your work, your church, and then how do you explore those other parts of yourselves and it has just been kinda interesting to start seeing these whole other ways of connection with people. Those [women's groups] are the ones I've been more interested in because, just for me personally in my life, I feel like where my messages need to come from are women; they are more relevant for me.

The focus on mutuality and relating at multiple levels characterizes women's discussions.

Several of the people I interviewed expressed a sense of collective anger at the oppressions they believe they, or others, face. These expressions have fundamentally different foundational assumptions for women in comparison to men. For instance, Nita expresses a sense of participating in a collective response to increasing levels of income inequality in the United States through voluntary simplicity while acknowledging that voluntary simplicity focuses on the individual making change based on values and interests held collectively in this way:

A lot of it has to do with the difference between the lowest and the highest wage. The natives are getting a little restless here. Capitalism, just as communism, in its theoretical form, is very different [in reality]. We don't have a free market economy. We got the rich people getting richer, and the CEO making more money, and the companies doing whatever it takes for the bottom line. And this is not how theoretical capitalism works because you have lost any responsibility to your community and your workers and any notion of the good of all. And when they are telling stock holders that they can't insist on, the business world has trained stock holders to think the only thing they can be concerned with is the bottom line. Well I don't think this is going to last very long, thank you! And then you have things like GATT so we can't enforce environmental and human rights laws. Part of the idea of voluntary simplicity has to do with personal responsibility. People interested in voluntary simplicity are not necessarily concerned about converting someone else. The idea is you live the way you think you should live, and if it is working for you and you are having a good time, other people will notice much more than the Mormons at the door with your Bible. You won't find anyone going door-to-door with the voluntary simplicity stuff. Voluntary simplicity begins and goes on no matter what else happens. Voluntary simplicity is a very individual, person-oriented approach.

Nita has integrated voluntary simplicity into her framing of her own biography in socially and politically meaningful terms. As is typical among women in the movement, she makes clear she is not interested in proselytizing door-to-door but in living her beliefs on a day-to-day basis. She acknowledges structural problems but she emphasizes the importance of personal responsibility and not trying to convert others. This is in keeping with the ideology espoused in voluntary simplicity literature and tends to be adhered to more by women than men in the movement.

Kevin's discussion of his view of free enterprise as greed is typical of the way men talk about their way of thinking about their collective response to issues of concern to them:

If anybody wants to go back to grass roots, let's just chuck these corporations right out the window and make them all responsible for the mess they create and everything else. I have expressed these ideas, I've expressed to you, that free enterprise is greed, in our meetings and although I'm not sure everybody agreed with me, nobody challenged me. Because when you talk in terms of jobs you could talk in terms of, "Why aren't we down to a thirty-hour week at this time?" We would have no unemployment now . . . presumably.

Kevin acknowledges that there may be some in the circle who disagree with his position regarding free enterprise but that no one speaks against his position openly in the circle. He points out that some in the circle may not have agreed with him but they did not challenge him. He is communicating his dominant status within the circle by acknowledging that others in the circle don't challenge him though they may disagree.

Kevin is clearly respected by others in the circle, especially the other men. He and Jack are both mentioned frequently as role models among the younger men. Kevin is in his seventies and Jack is in his eighties. Both say they are pacifists and reject the domination and competition advocated by the dominant culture. The range of attitudes about free enterprise is broad among members of circles. Some hold ideas similar to Kevin's. Others say they have not given much thought to this kind of issue. What is important for understanding the influence of gendered tensions in circles on the collective capacity of circles is that when the Alinsky model becomes dominant, the process of self-empowerment for women and many men who do not agree with the men who establish dominance in the circle gives way to a process that undercuts the ability of the group to achieve greater levels of collective solidarity based on the recognition of difference and comes to rely on the force of the leaders to dominate, narrow the agenda of circles, and discourage oppositional voices.

The inability to sustain a process that allows for recognition (Lara 1998, 120–145) of difference and discussion of alternative understandings of how to achieve voluntary simplicity causes women to reduce their investment in circle activities and undercuts the goals the dominant men say they have of building grassroots community. Critical cultural feminist philosopher Lara writes:

> Transformations entail a "fusion of horizons," a new and novel way of seeing the other that also becomes a new way of understanding oneself. Recognition is a struggle, a struggle that must be fought in relation to others and in the permanent tension of changing prejudice and transforming the symbolic order. This battle plays a major role in how one uses institutionalized channels of communicating with others, and how one redefines the limits on traditional views, enlarging one's own understanding of values and "changing the rules." Dialogue is not only a means of showing what makes one different, but also of showing that those differences are an important part of what should be regarded as worthy.
>
> Solidarity enters here because it is through others that one can define one's own identities, and no solidarity is possible if the discourse does not form a bridge to the other's understanding of what are considered to be worthy features and needs of human beings. Recognition, in this sense, is a performative process of acquiring identity. (Lara 1998, 157)

Lara goes on to caution however, "A model based only on difference might lead one to believe that any difference is as good as any other; if so, one would deny oneself the means to reach a partial consensus on how everyone can live a better life and be respected by others"

(Lara 1998, 157). The men who are dominant are disappointed that they can't establish or find the kind of community they yearn for. Defining themselves and their relationships in terms of differentiation from others and falling back on a zero-sum conception of power is not what these men aim to do, but their behaviors continue at times to follow patterns consistent with such self-definition in the processes they advocate in circles and in the ways they conceive of power.

Tolerance, not recognition of the differences of the other cultures present in the circles, characterizes the circle culture and the voluntary simplicity movement more generally. Because of this, the different values that the women's model and the Alinsky model reflect and the positive and negative aspects that each model may bring to voluntary simplicity activities of participants go uncommunicated, unrecognized, and uncritiqued in the circles.

Tolerance of difference is not enough to produce the kind of solidarity many simple livers say they want to achieve so they can build communities of belonging that value autonomy, participate in grassroots community building in keeping with their environmental values, and influence broad economic, social, and cultural change. Recognition of difference among themselves, beyond just differences in income and consumption that include sensitivity to gender differences, cohort differences, and serious consideration of sexuality and racial and ethnic differences, are essential if the movement is to achieve the kind of change to which many in the movement aspire.

Among women, status comes from being a network builder, from sustaining and supporting ongoing relations with others, and doing creative and practical work. Both men and women value sharing things like tools and expertise and having skills such as gardening, sewing, knitting, cooking, and carpentry. But women give more energy to developing these sharing networks. These activities come out of the private sphere and generate an extended private sphere.

For the women the process of collectively arriving at understandings of ideal practice and constructing knowledge does not necessarily imply arriving at the same understanding or practice as the right one for everyone. Power for them derives from the openness of recognizing differences among people. For them one best way of practice does not exist. It recognizes variation and different needs, and welcomes discussion from an empowered position between people in the movement and with those outside the movement.

Rather than elaborating what the opposition is like, what the right practices are, and how to convince others to change, women tend to want to elaborate ways of building ties with other people in their neighborhoods and circles of friends, acquaintances, and groups to generate lots of different ways of living simply based on the needs of specific, unique people making thoughtful choices. For them it is the networks of relationships that generate both material support and interdependent understandings that produce power and community.

Despite the beliefs espoused by simple living men that all things in the universe including human beings exist in relation to all other things, and their avowed rejection of competition and domination, the men tend to respond to others in circles in terms of wanting to bring them into line with their own ideas and goals rather than to hear, understand, and support others in gaining self-understanding and establishing independent goals. The men act in circles as individuals negotiating their interests while using a language of cooperation and support drawn from the how-to literature. They tend to guide discussion toward critique of a more distant mainstream culture that they locate in the public sphere and to try to build group identity through identifying against mainstream others. This is a subtle but consistent feature of the discourse in circles.

Even though one of the main thrusts of voluntary simplicity is to pull production and reproduction back into the private or local sphere as much as possible, the men in the movement tend to voice an interest in aspects of this shift that are located more closely to the juncture with the public sphere as it is defined by the dominant culture. A good example is Kevin and Jack advocating participation in "Buy Nothing Day," picketing at the local mall where they would confront mainstream shoppers with the simple living alternative.

Women tended to briefly critique the dominant culture and then to discuss their own efforts aimed at local community building and developing networks of relationships across different settings they go into to support them and others in simple living. They talk about how they want to figure out ways to build neighborhood community and the importance of friendship groups and networks to achieving their goals. Women focus on self-change, building close relationships and practical and emotional ties with others, and close community building.

The men are most interested in changing the public sphere. Although they talk about the importance of the private sphere activities of simple livers for outcomes in the public sphere, they intuitively respond to these spheres as separate. Some also feel the need to confront the dominant culture in the public sphere through protest, while others are not involved in organized protest but make meaning of their own individual practices in terms of confrontation with the dominant culture in the public sphere. They view their personal lifestyle as a confrontation. Women rarely describe their voluntary simplicity lifestyle in terms of confrontation in the public sphere or view it as primarily aimed at confronting the dominant culture. Women seem to be trying to reduce the split between the public and private sphere. They create a set of relationships that extend across the boundaries associated with the private/public split.

The men tend to view community as based on joint action against some external element, while women view it as based on relationships among members to achieve common goals together and support each other in daily life (Stall and Stoecker 1998).

Conclusions

People in voluntary simplicity recognize that building relationships with others based on simple living values is desirable. But they don't recognize the importance gender differences are playing in the movement. Nor do they acknowledge how much the possibilities of the movement are limited by their denial that gender-based group interests are relevant in the movement. This prevents them from exploring differences among themselves. Exploring these differences might lead to open conflict, which both women and men want to avoid in order to hold onto the support the circle offers. But it might also lead to a higher degree of recognition of difference and solidarity for the movement.

Part of the problem is linguistic. The same words have different meanings consistently for men and women simple livers as groups. Women may say they view themselves as unique individuals but they go on to describe themselves as relational. When men claim to be unique individuals they go on to describe themselves as strong individuals standing against the mainstream. And perhaps most importantly women tend to view others as relational while men tend to view others as self-interested.

Achieving solidarity across differences based on recognition is better supported by the women-centered model. Resisting the separation of public and private spheres in production and reproduction relative to work and consumption is a clear agenda for all in the movement. If this shift is to succeed then practices that support the continued separation of public and private must also be questioned.

Rather than taking a short-term combative approach, voluntary simplicity implies a long-term commitment, lived daily and embedded in the local context of building local networks of relationships that will endure over time and at times come together in solidarity to fight on given issues, but which is aimed at fundamental change in the way human relationships and the production of life is organized. Not everyone in the circle need participate in all activities but the circle is there as one site for generating and maintaining this kind of network.

To fulfill the potential of the voluntary simplicity movement, participants will need to go beyond saying that feminine relationality is preferable to masculine competition and struggle for domination to recognizing that these ways of relating are embedded in existing institutional structures that they rely on. They will need to gain recognition of ways their very identities are gendered constructions that rely on gendered cultural repertoires. And they will need to gain a recognition of the difference between themselves and others in the movement as important. To shift the basis for community away from the dominant cultural pattern based on the subordination of women and the competition of men also requires a profound shift away from the separation between the public and private spheres in practice broadly not just in terms of reproductive and productive work. It requires change in our acting, not just our thinking. Only by rejecting this split and recognizing how it serves to subordinate women and enables men to dominate can the kind of community men and women in voluntary simplicity say they want become a possibility.

Attempts to put on and take off bad characteristics of stereotypical masculinity and femininity by disclaiming them are clearly only one step in the process. They don't problematize the ability of individuals in the movement to simply reject the bad traits they associate with the dominant culture and adopt the good. Men in circles strive to become dominant despite their claims of rejecting these practices, and try to shift attention to public sphere issues where they will have more authority and power than women. Women tend to either leave the circles as men come to dominate or acquiesce and become less invested in them.

Because gendered power is not discussed as an issue in the everyday lives of simple livers, both women and men draw on available cultural repertoires and don't reflect critically on their behaviors derived from quite different developmental histories and socialization pressures. In the circles simple livers continue to reproduce some of the stereotypical gender behaviors they want to reject. Voluntary simplicity participants overlook the significance of gender differences and unequal gendered power even within the circles they are in, and this undermines the movement's capacity to build solidarity that truly responds to and respects difference.

Many of the men in voluntary simplicity, despite their desire to avoid competition and conflict, tend over time to orient their voluntary simplicity concerns to the public sphere and to articulate them in terms of confrontation, conflict, and compromise that takes place in the public sphere among self-interested groups of individuals. All are features in keeping with the Alinsky model. Stall and Stoecker write, "This makes sense when we consider that the public sphere has been structured to emphasize competition between men—forcing a separation and the ever-present potential for conflict between the competitors" (1998, 737).

Nancy Chodorow's (1978) work, showing that boys raised in contemporary Western nuclear families learn to separate themselves from others and to demonstrate forceful self-interested and autonomous behavior as a result of their early need to differentiate from their mothers to achieve masculine identity, is also helpful in understanding the orientation of these men toward the Alinsky model in circles. This conception of human nature as self-interested individuals and the way the public sphere has been organized as a masculine domain in which these interests are fought over is reflected both in how the men in voluntary simplicity approach building a collective capacity for the movement and the processes they orient toward for generating power to be carried into the public sphere.

In keeping with the women-centered model, women in voluntary simplicity are oriented toward a conception of power that begins in the private sphere of relationships based on human interdependence and "the development of all within the group or the community through collaboration" (Stall and Stoecker 1998, 741). The competitive structures of the public sphere are implicitly brought into question because they do not allow for the sort of process that women want to use. Both men and women simple livers have in a sense politicized the public/private sphere by rejecting its split relative to reproduction and production. But they don't carry this critique into their own extended public sphere found in the circles. Men in voluntary simplicity, like those who use the Alinsky model of organizing, center their energies in the circles as in an enduring organization that can represent the group. This leads to efforts to create a more traditional decision-making structure that mirrors the male-dominated public sphere structures they view themselves as confronting. The men continue to use the language of the literature of the movement that advocates group processes with rotating facilitation, support of differences in opinion and practice, self-understanding as superior to given knowledge, and ongoing group work aimed at self-change as well as community building. But in practice the men end up establishing dominance and setting the agenda of the circle.

The women in voluntary simplicity want to create a safe and nurturing space to discuss issues of concern both personally and politically and to build trust, respect, and tolerance for difference. They focus less immediately on public sphere action and more on building relationships that foster local activities of subgroups in their networks in the community along many different lines. This includes working at elections, volunteering at homeless shelters, helping teach young people how to grow vegetables at community gardens; building relationships with women in local housing projects; collecting egg cartons, plastic tape centers, and other throw-away things for art projects at local schools or day-care; knitting things for people staying at local shelters; and helping people build straw bale homes. The voluntary simplicity empowerment work is being done largely outside of circles by more of the women than men.

The issues that concern women and men in voluntary simplicity are closely linked and they are engaged as a collective in cultural struggle with the dominant culture to define what kind of community is desirable and what values should inform it. But women and men within the movement are also engaged in a struggle over defining what processes and structures create power for the group in relation to the dominant culture.

Because the business and government sectors are structurally organized to be competitive and take the separation of spheres as given, the desire to confront the dominant structures can be important. At the same time the dominant cultural orientation to preserve the private sphere as a haven in a heartless world and to exclude concerns from that domain in the public discourse is at the heart of voluntary simplicity (Walby 1990). People in voluntary simplicity believe that personal daily life practices are the starting point for broad social change. In addition, the women-centered model offers the ability to build relationships that can be sustained over time and can link people doing a diversity of types of change-oriented work together depending upon the context and concerns that prevail at any given time.

The efforts of people in the movement to expand its agenda and bridge into more traditional social movement practices seem to be gaining strength.[5] What this implies for the future direction of the voluntary simplicity movement and the model of organizing that will emerge remains a question. Vicki Robin is concerned with building bridges from the voluntary simplicity cultural movement to other groups across the differences they may have. A more self-conscious examination of the tensions within the movement that tend to fall along gendered lines might help simple livers build bridges across the differences within the movement and to act from power generated by a more complete recognition (Lara 1998) of the significance of those differences rather than tolerance or denial of them. Andrews (1997) offers a study circle model for simplicity circles that could produce a more egalitarian form of support group. But in practice gendered patterns of dominance and subordination enter circles and weaken their transformative capacity.

This analysis supports Stall and Stoecker's (1998) theorization of different styles of community organizing. But Stall and Stoecker don't give much systematic evidence for their claims that the Alinsky model appeals more to men and the women-centered model appeals more to women. This analysis extends beyond their findings at the organizational level and shows that the same differences in style are observed at the individual and interpersonal level in simplicity circles and voluntary simplicity networks. These two ideal-type kinds of approaches of community organizing are actually participated in by both women and men so it is useful that my analysis demonstrates from qualitative data that, in the case of voluntary simplicity participants, men do tend to adopt characteristics of the Alinsky approach more often and women practice the women-centered model more. In this way I provide support for their argument and deepen the evidence that the orientation is not just lodged at the organizational level but is generated from biographical, cultural, and structural locations of men and women.

The ideal-type polarities that I have identified as being gender based among simple livers have been noted in both movements defined as identity (empowerment) movements and formal (political action) social movements. A significant body of literature exists showing that to have a successful social movement, empowerment of individuals and ongoing nurturing of relationships among them must take place. Generally this work has been done by women and has been both invisible and devalued (Barnett 1993; Brandwein 1981; Feree and Miller 1985; Kaplan 1982; Naples 1991; Payne 1989; Robnett 1996).

A key question for simple livers who want to use voluntary simplicity to build alternative culture and community is how to move beyond accepting difference and advocating that each person be able to act based on their difference to transcending difference. The participants in voluntary simplicity are challenged with establishing an alternative form of community that allows for difference and also generates adequate solidarity for collective action.

In chapter 5 the ways simple livers make meaning of gender, racial, ethnic, and class inequalities in society will be described in detail. In order to gain understanding of how inequalities are resisted or reproduced in the voluntary simplicity movement, I examine the class, race, and gender politics in the ideology and practices of movement participants. Chapter 5 explores how power is distributed and patterned in the ideas and practices of voluntary simplicity and what the consequences are, not just the stated intentions of people in the movement but what is made salient and what is left unquestioned.

CHAPTER FIVE

Looking into the Shadows:
The Politics of Class, Gender, and
Race/Ethnicity in the
Voluntary Simplicity Movement

This chapter explores the class, racial/ethnic, and gender politics in the voluntary simplicity movement to gain understanding of how inequalities are resisted or reproduced through the movement and to assess the transformative capacity of the movement. The inequalities politics of the voluntary simplicity movement that I analyze are not the overt politics of party and other political organizational affiliations they claim, but instead rest upon and become evident in people's beliefs about affluence and poverty, gendered power, and racial and ethnic relations, and in the ways they define the primary problems and prescribed solutions for social and cultural problems.[1]

Michael Schwalbe writes, "Every belief or practice will, through some chain of effects, either challenge or help reproduce an unjust status quo. Every belief or practice thus warrants scrutiny. This can be thought of as the sociological equivalent of facing one's shadow" (1996, 144). This chapter faces the shadows of the voluntary simplicity movement. Voluntary simplicity is a movement I am sympathetic to, made up of people I feel connection with, so in part this is also a way for me to face my own shadow side.

People in the voluntary simplicity movement target quite specific pressures of jobism and status-driven consumption from the dominant culture and economy as key problems and tend to gloss over the significance of control over resources and how they are used, such as capital investment, accumulated wealth, and sex and racially and ethnically segregated employment that systematically subordinate women and racial and ethnic minorities. The movement does not claim to try to change racial and ethnic or gender inequality directly, but focuses primarily on voluntary self-change in work and consumer behavior, aimed at attaining a fulfilling lifestyle, that will eventually lead to changes in global patterns of inequality between the poor and consumerist classes through adopting voluntary simplicity. But the ideology and practices of voluntary simplicity raise issues, more often implicitly than explicitly, about power that can't be adequately analyzed sociologically if separated from consideration of class, race, and gender inequality and how people actually relate to each other and other groups.

Simple livers' own accounts of their lives reveal that categories through which power moves and is structured such as the hetero-gender system (Ingraham 1996, 169) and race/ethnicity are intertwined and coconstructed with occupational and consumer status hierarchies that they want to escape and see erased. These categories shape the identities and goals of individuals at the level of their biographies, in many ways forming the options for changes that they can envision and structuring the avenues available through which to achieve them. They leave their traces in the shadows of the simple livers' identities. It is through revealing what remains in the shadows and problematizing it that I believe simple livers will move closer to achieving the highest meaning of the movement and their own goals of being part of a meaningful and just community.

In this analysis I draw upon Sylvia Walby's theoretical perspective that there are six structures of patriarchy which she outlined in *Theorizing Patriarchy* (1990), Ruth Frankenberg's analysis of race in the lives of white women in *White Women, Race Matters: The Social Construction of Whiteness* (1993), David Halle's analysis in *America's Working Man: Work, Home, and Politics Among Blue-Collar Property Owners* (1984) of the whole lives of blue-collar workers, and Rick Fantasia's *Cultures of Solidarity: Consciousness, Action, and Contemporary American Workers* (1988).

I refer to Walby to analyze gender as a constituting element in the relations that characterize the voluntary simplicity movement. Walby defines patriarchy as "a system of social structures and practices in which men dominate, oppress, and exploit women" (20). She rejects the notion that every individual man is in a dominant position and every woman in a subordinate one. She maintains that "patriarchy needs to be conceptualized at different levels of abstraction. At the most abstract level it exists as a system of social relations" (20). But "at a less abstract level patriarchy is composed of six structures: the patriarchal mode of production, patriarchal relations in paid work, patriarchal relations in the state, male violence, patriarchal relations in sexuality, and patriarchal relations in cultural institutions" (20). And it needs to be remembered that in the contemporary United States, it is present in articulation with capitalism and racism.

Frankenberg analyzes how daily experience shapes white women's perceptions of the significance of race in the social structure as a whole and examines the discursive repertoires that "reinforce, contradict, conceal, explain or 'explain away' the materiality or the history of a given situation" (2). I am trying, as she did, to locate those I'm studying in their historic situation and in relation to both the material structures of racism at this time in the United States and to locate them in terms of discourses on race. Race and ethnicity as socially constructed are linked to relations of power and processes of struggle, and their meanings change over time (Omi and Winant 1986). Because of this it is significant that simple livers downplay the importance of racial/ethnic inequality in their own lives.

Instead of whiteness being a neutral or empty category it is a category that is a location of structural advantage or race privilege and is itself a "standpoint" (Frankenberg 1993, 1). Whiteness refers to "a set of cultural practices that are usually unmarked and unnamed" (Frankenberg 1993, 1). By focusing on race as a constituting element in the lives of simple livers, the analysis in this chapter contributes to examining how whiteness is constructed (Frankenberg 1993). I show that the material lives of simple livers and the meaning they make of their situation is influenced by their whiteness, as well as class and gender in interconnected ways. I find that race is an important constituting element in the voluntary simplicity movement, though it is not recognized as such by movement participants.

I use David Halle's and Rick Fantasia's theorizations of class to guide my consideration of class as a constituting element of the voluntary simplicity movement. I do not conceive of class as a fixed set of relations determined solely by the division of labor and organization of production, though these are very important. Halle points to the failure of class analysis to provide an adequate understanding of the lives of the male blue-collar workers he studies and paints a more complex picture of how they are situated within the social world they inhabit. He reveals that class consciousness is connected to production, income level, neighborhood, and consumption. Both Halle and Fantasia point out that class is dialectically constructed from both the economic relations people are situated in and the broader culture they experience. Class consciousness is viewed as situated rather than fixed and found to vary across contexts and over time. Fantasia points out that even when individuals do not express themselves in terms of class interests or consciousness they often have a keen sense of their relative oppression or interests within a given context that is based in a struggle for power derived in part from class relations in that context. This makes it important to ask how simple livers as a group are located in terms of the dominant social hierarchy, how generally secure or insecure their locations are, and how much their move to simple living changes their location.

Nita, a vivacious sixty-five-year-old white woman dedicated to grassroots community building, expresses ideas about the significance of class, gender inequality and sexuality, and race/ethnicity that are typical among participants in the voluntary simplicity movement when she says:

> In [this city] it's hard to know what class [people are]. But I think almost everybody is middle class. Income level does not play a big role. [And people in the movement are] working part time or working fulltime and living on nothing so they can stop working and quit. I have a friend who works at [a software company] and she is living on next to nothing so she can quit before long. . . . This may also be different in other areas, [but here], people, male, female, pretty much do what they want to do here and have for some time. And I don't think there is an awful lot of gender roles. In [this city] male, female, straight, gay, it doesn't matter. I've worked with a lot of groups, including the simplicity circle, that struggle with the racial diversity issue. Crone is not a racially diverse group. The Greens—and I was with the Greens a long time ago—are not a racially diverse group. And it is really a problem because a lot of these groups try. I have difficulty because I don't sort them [by race/ethnicity]. You know, someone asked me if the children in my class were all black and I said, 'You know, I'll have to look tomorrow,' because I really couldn't remember what colors they were. [She laughs] But I think that most of our friends are your basic standard light people.

Nita says that for most simple livers in her community class differences are not that important. She suggests that most people are middle class regardless of how much income they make. This downplays the significance of class differences among movement participants and people in the community in general. Nita says people in her city are not constrained by dominant culture gender roles. Women and men pretty much do what they like. Her focus is on the ability of people to choose not to comply with gender roles rather than on structural aspects of gender inequality. In discussing racial diversity in the movement Nita employs what Frankenberg (1993) refers to as a "power evasive" form of discourse. Nita claims color blindness. She does not see the color of people. In this way she discursively rejects claiming the advantage of white privilege that being in the dominant white group provides. The implication is that white privilege can be neutralized by claiming racial blindness. This is a discursive attempt to downplay the presence of white privilege by denying the significance of racial difference. It overlooks the institutionalized inequalities that shape the life chances of people in the contemporary United States based on race and ethnicity and leaves white privilege unexamined and in place.

Class, gender, and race/ethnicity, as categories through which power is structured presently, shape the movement in significant ways. But how simple livers are situated at the intersections of race and class privilege (they are largely white, middle class, and heterosexual) makes them more likely to overlook public aspects of patriarchy as well as their class and race privilege.

The ideology and practices of voluntary simplicity do tend to shift and alter the dominant cultural patterns for establishing status through work in status occupations and through conspicuous consumption and to establish alternative ways of attaining worth and status. They also shift the dominant cultural patterns of gender relations somewhat by resisting market intrusion into household production and rejecting traditional gendered patterns of household work and the male breadwinner role. Yet access to resources from the market plays a significant role in their negotiation of power relations. In couples in voluntary simplicity access to resources and control over resource distribution is key to their experience of their sense of their relationships in their own households being equal.

The shift the movement implies for racial and ethnic relations involves an inconsistent and very incomplete pattern of recognition of the importance of participants' whiteness in determining their relative positions of power. There are moments of "race cognizance" (Frankenberg

1993, 15) among the informants in the analysis. This term acknowledges differences articulated by people of color. According to Frankenberg, "Difference signals autonomy of culture, values, aesthetic standards and so on" (1993, 14), and inequality in this case does not refer to ascribed characteristics, but to the social structure. Most also demonstrate "power evasive" (Frankenberg 1993, 14) responses to questions about the significance of race/ethnicity in voluntary simplicity or in their lives more generally. The term "power evasive" refers to a "discourse of essential 'sameness' popularly referred to as 'color-blindness' " (Frankenberg 1993, 14). Frankenberg describes this discourse as one that maintains that "we are all the same under the skin; that, culturally, we are converging; that materially, we have the same chances in U.S. society; and that, the sting in the tail, any failure to achieve is therefore the fault of people of color themselves" (14). While simple livers do not express the idea that the failure to achieve is the fault of people of color, some do, at times, use power evasive discourse. The use of power evasive discourse shows that simple livers often do not see the full importance of race/ethnicity and continue to take the category of white as the given category, even as they deny that race is important to them.

The movement does shift dominant cultural and economic definitions of desired levels of affluence versus poverty and changes their meanings. People in voluntary simplicity maintain that Western affluence is actually destructive to human happiness and fulfillment in addition to being responsible for destroying the environment. They assert that living like the "global middle income class" (Durning 1992) at levels most affluent Western people would consider poverty is the best model for ecological sustainability and human happiness.

Simple livers claim that those who are still committed to mass consumption and pursuit of status occupations are deluded and have not reached the higher level of awareness that those in voluntary simplicity have. And they claim that the global poor are so caught up in survival activities they don't have time to think of alternatives. In this way voluntary simplicity reproduces the existing dominant cultural hierarchy that elevates Western (white) middle-class people over Western racial and ethnic minorities, the populations of non-Western countries, and the poor, and reasserts their right to guide the future of the world by claiming that simple livers are ideally situated to understand what choices everyone in the world should make. Drawing on the Puritan heritage and elaborating a voluntary simplicity culture to enrich the empty category of whiteness can in one way be seen as a shift toward remaking what a worthwhile Western (white) person is and does. Simple livers tend to talk about the movement as one made up largely of affluent Westerners rather than highlighting the whiteness of the movement unless asked about it. But the discourse of voluntary simplicity draws on aspects of the Puritan heritage, along with many other traditions, in such a way that it reaffirms the (silent white) Western heritage indirectly and reasserts the superiority of affluent (turned simple liver) Western (silent white) people who adopt voluntary simplicity as the most ideally situated group to understand and lead a global cultural change.

Class: Affluence and Poverty

Class, gender, and race/ethnicity function as parallel and interlocking systems that shape the relationships of domination and subordination in the lives of simple livers by shaping their identities, the structural locations and institutionalized privileges that influence their choices and their understandings of the world, and the ideology of voluntary simplicity that they develop. Certain forms of inequality are apparent to them, and others are hidden in the shadows cast by their privilege. Simple livers identify themselves with the given categories of middle class, white, and heterosexual and they also self-identify as well educated.

Many have worked, or do work, in the caring professions or social services. As social workers, teachers in inner city schools, and staff at shelters for the homeless, a high percentage of simple livers have come into contact with people who were disadvantaged relative to themselves. A number were strongly influenced by religious doctrines aimed at service to less fortunate people in their formative years, and several say they had important formative experiences as activists during the late 1960s and early 1970s. Some also say international travel to Third World countries has influenced them. The younger cohort, between the ages of twenty and thirty, tend to have educational backgrounds in disciplines concerned with environmental and social issues.

As discussed in earlier chapters, most of the people I interviewed view themselves as potentially oppressed by the forces of rationalization that would, or do, enslave them in meaningless work or overconsumption. Many who adopt voluntary simplicity view work as the major source of disappointment and dissatisfaction in their lives. They experience their need to earn money to survive, along with cultural pressures to practice status and identity construction consumption in keeping with the dictates of the dominant culture, as the greatest oppressions they are conscious of suffering under.

For some people in voluntary simplicity, suffering comes from feeling they have to work, not that they can't get or keep a job. But it is more complex than that. Some people in voluntary simplicity have lost jobs as the result of downsizing or because of health problems, and some have worked in jobs they felt were insecure. A number have a pattern of a lot of job turnover in their work history with about equal numbers saying it was or was not by choice. Volunteer work is generally judged more meaningful than paid work. This provides ideological support for being unemployed whether it is by choice or not.

The ideology of voluntary simplicity emphasizes the inequality between the affluent, who are using up the earth's resources, and the poor, who are being socialized to want to do the same thing, shifting the focus away from relative poverty within the United States to differences between Western affluence and extreme Third World poverty. In cases where poverty within the United States is described, the significance of gender and race/ethnicity are often downplayed or overlooked and the differences between classes are redefined in ways that do not emphasize class conflict or structural barriers.

Simple livers do differentiate themselves from the poor in the United States in several ways. Most do so by comparing the attitudes and experiences of poor people with their own. There is also recognition that income earning capacity, regardless of whether they are actually earning that income, makes a difference. Simple livers don't view being a middle-class simple liver as based on income or occupation but upon having control over how one spends one's time and how one obtains resources to survive.

Simple livers also sometimes minimize the significance of their differences with both the rich and the poor, suggesting that everyone in the United States is more or less in the same boat when it comes to simplicity. This is how Kevin says it: "So many people ask, 'How do you get by without spending?' And I say, the other thing is you start from zero and poor people are starting from zero just like a wealthy person starting from zero." Kevin establishes the idea that rich, poor, and middle-class people are really all equal in terms of being able to simplify since all of them can choose to start from zero. Kevin has lived at times with very little and distinguishes between his circumstances when he had little money and the poor who have little money mostly as an attitudinal difference. This is how he explains his beliefs about this:

When I was in Florida the guy that ran the temporary employment agency [and I] were sitting [having] coffee one day in the afternoon and he was apologizing that he had not gotten me out. And he says, "Are you going to be all right?" And I said, "Of course." And he says, "How much money do you have?" and I says, "Fifty cents." And he says, "Have you got any food?" And I says, "Yes, I have some in my room." And he says, "How long have you got your room paid for?" And I says, "Until tomorrow." And he says, "What will you do?" I says, "I have enough food for a couple of days but I'll probably end up on the street." "Don't you feel insecure?" And I says, "No, the security is not in my wallet, it's in my head." I know that I will be all right no matter what I do.

Nita also believes that the poor experience their lack of resources as oppression while simple livers do not. In the passage below she describes the different ways she and other graduate students interpreted similar monetary limits in comparison to people on welfare. She then goes on to describe giving a talk to women getting out of prison about not accepting the dominant culture's materialistic values. Nita believes that these values are at the root of much crime and that the needs are not real but created by advertising. She maintains that one of the roles of voluntary simplicity is to inform people that they don't need "stuff" because a lot of people who don't have much are really doing fine:

I was on a working group—I can't even remember what it was about—and the group had a lot of graduate students and a lot of welfare people on it. And the thing that I noticed, although we were living on the same amount of money, our attitudes were very different because the welfare people felt that they were not in charge and they were trapped by the system, and for graduate students, it's a big game, you know—I have two dollars to get through two weeks. Well this should be interesting. [I] gave a talk at a place that is a living place for women who are getting out of prison. I gave a talk about VS [voluntary simplicity]. And I told them that it may seem to them that not having stuff is a down-trodden condition, but one of the things they need to look at is that a lot of things that get people into legal trouble as into jail have to do with working one way or the other to acquire things, that they need to think about what they really wanted and needed before they just get sucked back up into this materialistic thing. A lot of people who have a lot of stuff are miserable and a lot of people who didn't have much really were doing fine. It is not like the world owed them a lot of stuff and if the world did not give them a bunch of stuff they should get it one way or another. It was that they were being sold a bill of goods by the people who make that stuff that they couldn't really be happy without it. . . . People who worked there thought it was really great too because they could see these people starting to fall back into acquiring one way or another. But to me one of the differences is that the American dream largely created by advertising has convinced people if they just had this they would be happy and that part of the job of voluntary simplicity is to change that concept because we have all these miserable poor people who really think that of course they are not happy because they don't have the stuff. And we have a whole bunch of people in the Third World countries who are being sold a bill of goods so they'll buy Coke and cigarettes and pesticides. And the world cannot support people doing that and we can't live with the discontent of people who don't have the stuff, so it is for voluntary simplicity to get the word out.

Not having enough time to think about issues because you are struggling to work and provide for your family is also a factor simple livers mention as important in preventing people from making conscious choices and being able to live well on little money. Poor people, they say, are too caught up in providing the basics for themselves. This is what Jack says about the poor: "I think too when people are really struggling to make, quote, a 'living' they don't have time to look at this stuff. That is the scary thing about the whole damn economy. Poor people are too busy trying to put bread on the table to be concerned about politics." Jack equates voluntary simplicity with being involved in politics and considers himself an activist because of his involvement in a simplicity circle, a wellness study group, and Buy Nothing Day activities. Simple livers say the affluent are caught up in status consumption and escapism largely because they are drained and numbed by overwork and use consumption and escapist leisure time activities as an addict would use alcohol or drugs.

Linked to the idea that real needs don't require much money or stuff is the idea that the dominant culture fosters greed. Emily discusses greed as a major factor in determining what people want as consumers and believes Western people need to decrease consumption and accept a lower standard of living to rectify imbalances globally:

The whole greed thing, the collecting and the accumulating, it's like the beany babies. You can buy those things for under six dollars but who got paid to make it and what did they get paid and under what conditions do the workers live? If we asked that about everything we bought, there would be a whole different responsibility, but instead it is how many can I get for me and how can I keep you from having it? . . . I think our whole thinking has got to change on that. I personally think the globalization of jobs will bring that about faster because already Detroit is concerned about . . . jobs going to Mexico. So now people are concerned about what people in Mexico are earning. . . . The conditions and pay are of concern. [People are asking], Are people living in poverty? I think [globalization] might be a greater leveler, this whole miserable period in between. But we are becoming a global world and the only way is to do it all, all of us, and do the disarmament globally. If our fates are linked then I have to be concerned about you in a different way of brotherhood and that I show I see hope. I think it is going to downsize the U.S. and we are already seeing this as jobs have left. Only it is mostly seen among working class but will have effect gradually over all. This is where the great boon for voluntary simplicity people is. They are ahead by already doing it.

Emily believes the global future will be one in which the labor market is globalized and the ability of people in the United States to command higher incomes for similar work will be undermined. Like most simple livers, she thinks of accumulation of wealth in terms of earning it, not in terms of inheriting it, because most of them come from working-class backgrounds.

There was only one man whose family were middle class who mentioned that he would probably inherit money from his parents. He said that knowing they might inherit money gave him and his wife an added sense of security against inflation as they prepared to quit work at an early age and live on rental income from investment properties. Another man, whose background was working class, critiqued inheritance laws that enable the rich to pass capital from generation to generation without the need for work. But most simple livers did not critique this aspect of capitalism at all.

As mentioned in chapter 3, eight of the fourteen people I interviewed came from working-class backgrounds and had achieved middle-class income or had moved into middle-class occupations at some point in their lives, though they had not tended to stay there for a variety of reasons, including choosing to make a change, choosing not to begin the consumer lifestyle after completing college, retiring, losing their jobs, having accidents, and having health problems.

For most people their own ability to make choices, change jobs, and, at least in some cases, have the resources to live without working for a wage, makes them experientially distant from those who do not have such economic and cultural power. But the need for money is a basic constraint for everyone interviewed. The patterned ways in which people get money reflect clearly the imprint of the possibilities available. And money is not just a resource for buying needed goods, but continues to be a source of establishing status in circles. Those who have resources that enable them to get by without working for a wage, those who have gained financial independence (Dominguez and Robin 1992), and those who have given up high paying and high status occupations gain status in circles.

In addition, some simple livers invest in interest-bearing stocks, bonds, and treasury bills and use the interest to live on. Dominguez and Robin (1992) recommend investing in treasury bills. Some other well-known figures advocate socially conscious investing. And though a few everyday people in the movement say they invest in socially conscious ways most say they don't for a variety of reasons that range from not wanting to take the time to seek out and evaluate such investments to the belief that there is no way to invest in socially conscious ways because the money will always move in the market in ways that end up supporting things they don't support.

Giving money away and investing money are two areas that simple livers have to deal with, and do make decisions about, but the ideology of the movement does not place as much emphasis on connecting investing capital to the profit-driven economy as it does consumption. Making this connection would highlight the dependence of people who use investment income as a way to stop working in the profit-driven economy and the continued exploitation of other workers who generate profits for investors.

In contrast to consumption practices where spending time researching sustainable goods and devoting time to shopping for them and discussing these issues in circles were common, similar types of discussions of investment practices were not as common. Investments were discussed, but linking those investments to the set of values applied to consumption was missing. The ideology surrounding investments was one of using investment income to free one to do volunteer work. And occasionally someone mentioned the fact that Dominguez and Robin (1992) recommended investing in treasury bills or bonds.

More simple livers make contributions of time and money to the causes they support than invest in socially conscious ways. This may be because they can experience themselves as actors exerting control over time and space more powerfully when they consume causes than when they consume investment services.

Simple livers tend to shift or aspire to shifting ways they obtain money from situations where they feel less freedom (such as the competitive and rationalized wage labor market) into arenas where they have the sense of being less constrained and able to act based on their deeply held values. They rent portions of their homes; cut costs by sharing housing; invest in stocks, bonds, and treasury bills; and do part-time entrepreneurial work like sewing, writing articles, or keeping books for organizations they are in, and they reduce spending on consumer goods.

Some simple livers do very concrete things to help less fortunate people in their communities. Others do not. Volunteer work is suggested as one way to find fulfillment, and some simple livers do end up working in areas that deal with solving problems of social inequality. Six of the simple livers I interviewed do give generously to local efforts to help the poor and do volunteer work that is aimed at helping others in their communities. Most of the people I interviewed do not contribute large sums and shift from using money to giving time as they move into the voluntary simplicity lifestyle.

This ideology advantages those with control over resources because it does not consistently call for altering the legally sanctioned ways resources are distributed but for voluntary change in the way resources are used by those with control over them. The ideology maintains that the structures through which resources are distributed will shift to environmentally sensitive production, distribution, and recycling practices through consumer pressure. And they claim that, at the same time, those who do not have resources will gain access to them in the form of jobs as those who have more, such as themselves, downshift. Though they believe consumer culture driven by the economic drive for profit is the root of the problem, most are not critical of capitalism. Those who are critical are critical of corporate monopoly capitalism in its present form, not of private property, which five of the fourteen people I interviewed rely upon for much of their present income.

Most simple livers maintain that capitalism can be managed to serve the interests of people rather than profit and can be made to work for humanity. A few even say they have never thought about problems with capitalism. These are examples of the ideas simple livers have about the capitalist economy.

> Fred: I've never seen capitalism except on paper. We have such corporate socialism by the corporations among themselves they just take care of themselves. Just hateful, hateful!

> Emily: Capitalism, yeah, I think it breeds the independent thing. Everybody go buy your own lawnmower. You've got to have your own thing. *Market Place* [a program on National Public Radio] yesterday was saying capitalism needs people to buy new, more every year and as long as that is the interpretation of capitalism it [voluntary simplicity] is sort of the antithesis. Voluntary simplicity can be seen as a threat to capitalism.

> Nita: We don't have a free market economy. We've got the rich people getting richer and the CEO making more money and the companies doing whatever it takes for the bottom line. And this is not how theoretical capitalism works, because you have lost any responsibility to your community and your workers and any notion of the good of all. [Exasperated] Well I don't think this is going to last very long, thank you!

> Kevin: The problem is that our government agencies are putting fewer and fewer restrictions on what corporations can actually do without any concern for the fact that when this country was organized, corporations were illegal. Illegal, blatantly, purely illegal! And if anybody wants to go back to grass roots let's just chuck these corporations right out the window and make them all responsible for the mess they create and everything else.

Fred, Emily, Nita, and Kevin offer examples of the types of critiques simple livers make of capitalism. Some simple livers like Pam and Carol perceive problems with the system, but are less certain of the causes of the problems or of how to solve them:

> Pam: I don't know that I have ever given [capitalism] any thought before. I think because we are such a wealthy country with so many wealthy people and yet we have so many people without, I would not know how to fix that either. But I can see those

with the wealth have a way of gathering up whatever they want without much regard to those who don't have anything or any way of getting anything. I don't know if it causes it, but it keeps, it encourages, it keeps poverty thriving because those at the lower end of the scale do not have the resources to gather up the things they need to make things better, to get them out of the poverty that they are in. And the people up here with all the money and all the wealth and the good stuff don't want to let any of it go. They just want to get more and more and more. And the more [the affluent] get the less these people down here have. And I think you can see that every day; you can see it on a global scale and downtown.

Carol: I'm not comfortable with the disparity but I don't know what the solution is. I am in favor of some socialism but not a lot.

Both Pam and Carol are working full time in midlevel professional jobs. Pam does accounting and Carol does social work. Both have done other things during their work lives. Carol was on welfare herself for a period of time and has bad memories of those years. Tears come to her eyes when she discusses them. Pam too has had periods of financial difficulty. Pam, like other simple livers, alternates between identifying with the affluent and with the poor. At one point she says, seemingly placing herself with the affluent, ". . . the people up here with all the money and all the wealth and the good stuff don't want to let any of it go." But only moments later she says, "The more [the affluent] get the less these people down here have." In Carol the same ambivalence is evident. She has suffered from poverty, and believes change to help the poor is needed. But now she has a job and an adequate income so she is reluctant to advocate drastic change that might endanger the position of relative economic security she has worked to get.

Another important feature of the ideology is the belief that no one is to blame for the current situation (not the middle class, or the rich and powerful either) because the process that led here was an evolutionary process that led to the industrial era and that can evolve into the ecological era if human beings globally will adopt simple living. This view is contested and produces tensions even within the thinking of individuals, but it is still espoused, at one point or another, by most of the people I interviewed. These are examples of how people in voluntary simplicity discuss blame and responsibility:

Emily: There are judgments about CEOs' salaries in that group but you know I just don't feel, maybe because I've been there, people want a big salary if they determine that five million is their number that they need to live on that makes them feel secure. . . . I don't have a problem if they want to do what is required to get that amount of money . . . but I think there are judgments in the group about it and certain people have very definite ideas about what people should be living off of. [I know] there are strong judgments because I live in this house by myself.

Peter: I say forgive them for they know not what they do. At the same time I also say, oh my gosh, look how empty they are because of all the stuff they are needing to be filled up. And another part of me that is on the balcony, that is watching me do this labeling and this bullshit judging, says, who the hell am I to say that? Because they may be making the most appropriate choice that their present lifestyle and their present feeling of fear versus in love with life and appreciation gives them this, so what can I do but honor them? Six billion people on this planet, they all have to be right. There is nothing wrong with the people. There is the challenge of the design of the space in which they live.

Peter's description of how he feels about these issues is the most overt expression of the tension, ambivalence, and contradictions that exist in the thinking of most simple livers regarding blame, accountability, and responsibility of the powerful for their inequitable use of resources. The ideology of the movement maintains that simple livers should remain nonjudgmental. But at times simple livers speak with anger about the rich while at other times they maintain that individuals should not be blamed.

Simple livers identify themselves as being among the affluent and they don't want to be blamed for environmental degradation or judged as greedy. Additionally, if they attack the wealthy and powerful they end up attacking those they believe they look similar to, the affluent and white. If the rich are held accountable and are to blame then so are all of the affluent people in the West. I also suspect that some of the people in the movement who went through the 1960s as white liberals are sensitive to such attacks. And if they focus on those who are monetarily wealthy, their own relative lack of control, choice, and power will be made salient instead of the sense of control, choice, and power they desire to feel.

When thinking through the lens of voluntary simplicity provided by core texts and some of their own experiences as frugal livers, they tend to think people in the Western countries are more equal than not. At the same time they recognize the relative differences they witness in their own daily lives and account for them in different ways. Some are sensitive to people who feel their relative poverty as oppression. But simple livers tend to make meaning of these inequalities as the result of cultural oppression that prevents people from knowing they actually have enough rather than the consequence of economic disparities in opportunity and income. Some are angry about the inequalities they see and blame corporate and governmental policies, greed, and media. Some try to change the inequalities they see through volunteer work and local politics as well as personal simple living practices. Others express discomfort with the close inequality they observe but say they don't know what causes it or how to solve the problem. Most focus their energies on self-change aimed at reducing inequalities of consumption through their own voluntary choice of consuming less of the world's resources.

One reason simple livers don't make class inequality in the United States salient in their world view is that they don't use class to think about their own life experiences, which they draw on to construct ideology. They tend to move into and out of middle-class occupations and therefore to have different income levels at different times in their lives. And many say their changes in jobs from higher paying to lower paying jobs were by choice, not from necessity, because they exerted choices regarding free time, time doing nonwaged work, and time for self-actualization.

Simple livers' class location is defined by their being Western, white, well-educated people who often have working-class roots and who are fed up with the pressures of midlevel professional or paraprofessional work and keeping up with the Joneses. As a group their rejection of the nature of work in those jobs points to cultural change that devalues occupational status and consumerist values. Simple livers opt away from centering identity in waged work. Their status as a group is defined by their rejection of consumerist and careerist values held in the dominant culture and by their ability to shift their daily practices away from involvement in waged work and consumerist activities. The high educational levels and histories of income and occupational mobility of many simple livers make them less sensitive to structural barriers.

The Heterogender System

Some simple livers acknowledge that gender inequality is an issue for some people, but most of the people I interviewed maintained that gender inequality was a nonissue for them personally. In the view of simple livers the women's movement, mentioned by some of the core texts (Andrews 1997; Elgin 1993a), is largely seen as having achieved much of what it needed to do to place male and female simple livers on equal footing.

All of the people I interviewed identified themselves as heterosexual. They maintained that the issues of sexuality, sexual orientation, and gender inequality are nonissues in voluntary simplicity. Despite the fact there were no self-identified nonheterosexuals in their circles at the moment (some said there had been in the past), they believed their circles were open to nonheterosexuals. Some said that sexual orientation might be a feature of identity that would never surface in the circles because it was not relevant.

Barbara, a white, twenty-seven-year-old married woman whose energy is presently aimed primarily at becoming "FI", expresses her belief that voluntary simplicity is not about changing gender relations in this way:

> When I look at other couples in our age grouping the guys cook nearly as much as the females or the guy cooks and the woman does not. So I don't think it has altered the way we were before reading *Your Money or Your Life*. I don't think we follow the strictest gender roles. I'll take out the trash. I do think more about organizing the cooking.

Her husband, Lewis, also believes that gender inequality is not the issue in voluntary simplicity. For him, the issue is how to escape the rationalization process of the market economy. Lewis, a white, twenty-seven-year-old who like his wife Barbara is focused on gaining financial independence, says:

> Voluntary simplicity could lead toward more women working in the home. But I think it places a value on that work in terms of a dollar saved is worth more than a dollar earned. Whoever could stay home and save money and do some things on the side once you realize you don't want to spend all of your time. I don't think Barbara would be happy just staying home. And I would not be happy just working.

The idea that women should work for wages along with them, if they are having to work, is an idea held by all of the men informants. In the above discussion, Lewis makes meaning of his preference that Barbara also work by claiming she would not be happy just staying home. This contradicts both her assertion that her goal is to save enough to be able to quit work and his stated belief that work for a wage never allows the worker to be authentic and is fundamentally unhealthy.

Only two of the fourteen people I interviewed, both men in partnerships with women, believe the movement has the capacity to reduce gender inequality. And they, like all the other respondents, maintained that in their own personal life gender inequality was not an issue. These men believe that they came to the movement as men already capable of equal relationships with women. Brad, a twenty-one-year-old white college student who lives with his partner, says:

> I just got through a section on feminism in political philosophy. It is really interesting to me because of the way simple roles are created in society and the most powerful people out there are CEOs or things like that. The simplicity movement would change that and make working at home or taking more time, taking more care about things, which is a more, feminists would call it a more feminist approach to the world. That's kind of what simplicity is all about. So rather than competition which our system rewards sets up right now, simplicity promotes cooperation and encouragement and, yeah, I think it could effect gender relations. I don't have a lot of masculine qualities and I'd not categorize myself as competitive and I don't really want to chase money, chase power. I think [voluntary simplicity] brings you onto more common ground. I guess that, although that is already there in my relationship, it really, really bothers me when it is not [there in the relationships of other people]. My background is very sexist. I just thought it was wrong.

Brad, like most men embracing voluntary simplicity, considers himself different from most men because he is not competitive in terms of wanting money or power. Men in the movement tend to distance themselves from what they view as the negative aspects of masculinity, claiming they don't want money, power, or to dominate women and that they prefer more equal relationships.

There are several features of the ideology of the voluntary simplicity movement that offer insight into gender politics in the movement. First, the ideology puts emphasis on the shared oppression of all middle-class Western people by jobism and overconsumption, not on sexism and racism as relevant for their primary goal of shifting the dominant culture toward more sustainable environmental practices. Second, most of the people I interviewed link gender issues to practices and ideas that have dominated in the industrial era and the masculine and feminine gender roles it fostered. They talk as though they believe individuals can largely do away with gender inequality by rejecting dominant culture gender roles.

The core texts of the movement also support these notions. For example, Elgin (1993a), the person who gave the movement its name in his book, *Voluntary Simplicity: Toward a Way of Life That Is Outwardly Simple, Inwardly Rich*, mentions the "contributions of the feminine perspective" (94). Elgin writes that the feminist movement has contributed to the growth of simpler living by encouraging both women and men to "move beyond traditional roles and expectations" and by "liberating men from the need to perpetuate their half of the polarity of sex based roles;" it thereby offers "both men and women the freedom to be more authentically themselves" (96–97).

Aspects of the women's movement aimed at fighting the inequality and oppression of women under capitalist patriarchy are downplayed in Elgin's discussion. He writes, "If the masculine orientation, with its competitive, aggressive, dissecting, and materialistic approach to living, continues to dominate our perception and actions as a culture, we will scarcely be able to live in relative peace with the rest of the life on this planet. If we are to become whole persons in a cohesive culture, we must consciously integrate more feminine qualities into our lives" (98). Elgin assumes that the contribution of feminism has already been made, not that feminist concerns need to be integrated into the movement to problematize the ideas and practices within the movement further. Balance can be achieved, according to Elgin, if men embrace the positive feminine values of relationality and cooperation.

Barbara Ehrenreich (1983) describes the men's liberation movement of the 1970s as the era when "sex-role" stereotypes became the focus of critique and a tool used by men to disclaim their own interests in maintaining power and their actual behavior aimed at increasing, not decreasing their power relative to women. She writes, "[I]f dominance is really a role that men were forced into, and not a choice, then dominance itself was actually a form of submission—another evidence of men's common oppression. . . . The notion of a male role, distinct from men themselves and imposed on them to their disadvantage, spread quickly in all directions—moving upward to become an item of professional wisdom and downward to become an almost inescapable pop-psychological cliche" (125). Elgin, like those in the Human Potential Movement described by Ehrenreich, assume that "analysis that distanced men from masculinity implied that men could transform themselves suddenly, voluntarily, and seemingly without reference to external circumstances. . . . The male role is a disposable exoskeleton from which the true self, the 'human being inside the man,' is invited to emerge" (Ehrenreich 1983, 126–127).

Elgin focuses on the important contribution the feminist movement has made for men. It has liberated men from having to feel like they have to gain their masculine identity from work in an occupation or from consumption and by pointing out the value of feminine characteristics. The women's movement has demonstrated to men that they need to nurture the feminine characteristics within themselves or nurture their development along with their masculine characteristics. In this way men can claim the good feminine traits along with the masculine traits, equalizing the relationship between men and women. Women as living beings who are systematically disadvantaged and subordinated in the present labor market, family, and dominant culture, and impoverished in large numbers as single mothers, are largely outside of the parameters of this version of gender inequality. Elgin maintains that if voluntary simplicity is adopted and feminine values adopted by men it will result in sweeping change, which he describes in the following passage: "With greater balance between masculine and feminine qualities, our cultures would tend to become less aggressive, contain less disguised competition, be more receptive and open, have more supportive friendships, have a greater mixing of roles among men and women in accordance with innate interests and capacities, be able to nurture and care for others to a greater degree, place greater value on feeling and emotion, express greater concern for unborn generations, and have a stronger sense of the intimate interrelatedness of life. This integration and balance is crucial" (97–98). In Elgin's account, balance is not described as requiring changes in existing institutional arrangements that privilege men but in terms of redistributing the qualities of masculinity and femininity in the selves of people and in the culture.

Barbara Ehrenreich describes how the men's liberation movement emerged in the 1970s from the historical context of the 1950s and 1960s as a response to feminism. But she points out it was also in keeping with an earlier pattern in male responses to their roles in the family and relative to women in "a new disguise, enriched by the insights of the Human Potential Movement and blessed, offhandedly, by the approval of feminism. The male rebels of the seventies, whether or not they felt themselves to be members of a men's liberation 'movement,' could articulate all the old grievances and resentments, but in a way that no longer sounded spiteful or misogynist. Male self-interest could now be presented as healthy and uplifting; the break from the bread-winner role could be seen as a program of liberal middle-class reform" (1983, 118–119). The emotional damage and physical toll on men caused by men's traditional responsibilities were at the heart of the critique of men's "burden of oppression" (Ehrenreich 1983, 119). Elgin draws on the Human Potential Movement's perspectives in developing his ideology of voluntary simplicity, linking the need to practice voluntary simplicity to both removing the burden of oppression from men and saving the environment. Ehrenreich argues, "[W]hat men stood to gain was obvious: what they had to give up was the constellation of attitudes, habits and gestures that had for so long defined adult masculinity. In the ideology of men's liberation, this was not a trade-off, but a double gain. The prospect of shedding masculine traits no longer had the fearful surgical implications it might have had even a decade earlier, when 'castration' still stood as a general metaphor for men's oppression. If masculinity was burdensome, it was also detachable: the authentic self could set aside the 'image' " (1983, 123).

Andrews draws on Carolyn Merchant's (1992) book *Radical Ecology* to describe the importance of feminine ways of relating in the voluntary simplicity movement. Andrews downplays conflict between the interests and values of women and men and makes no mention of applied ecofeminist theory, which often brings women into confrontation and struggle with the drive to use up nature by powerful men in their immediate communities. Instead, Andrews interprets the theory in such a way that she arrives at ideas similar to those of Elgin and others in the movement, that all life exists in relation to all other life and that the feminine principle of relationality needs to be brought back into our thinking about our relations to nature. The conflict between women and men over control and use of resources or the idea that men control most of the wealth in the world is not an explicit part of her argument.

While none of the women I interviewed claimed to be feminists, Cecile Andrews is influenced by liberal feminist thinking. Andrews emphasizes the aspects of the women's movement aimed at gaining acceptance of an authentic self. She writes:

> The civil rights movement, the women's movement, the gay and lesbian movement, the movement of people with disabilities, all these were and are about human rights. But they are also about becoming an authentic self, about being able to say 'This is who I am,' about not having to lie or pretend or hide. The

plight of gays and lesbians shows, I think, the powerful need that people have to be known for who they are. Here is a group of people who risk being outcasts, and maybe even risk their lives, to be able to live an authentic life, to be able to quit hiding and pretending.

Even more powerful is the example of Alcoholics Anonymous, one of the twentieth century's major movements of human growth. It has at its core the affirmation of authenticity, 'I'm Bob, I'm an alcoholic.' Addiction is increasingly being seen as a descriptor of our lives, addiction to work, to shopping, to sex, to food, so maybe our real healing lies in being authentic. We all need to be able to stand and say, 'this is who I am.' (1997, 73)

Here Andrews acknowledges and then glosses over the human rights activism and social conflict that was also a central element in these movements, aimed in large part at demanding structural changes and equality and rights, and interprets the civil right's movement along with the women's movement, the gay and lesbian movement, and the movement of people with disabilities as movements seeking to affirm authentic selves rather than as confrontational political movements. Andrews considers Alcoholics Anonymous, a human growth movement, as being "even more powerful." Her feminist concerns center on resisting gender roles mandated by the dominant culture, but she interprets the resistance in terms of freeing the authentic self, not in terms of attacking the structures that play key roles in enforcing and generating the mandates.

All the people I interviewed feel they are largely free of the dominant culture's prescribed gender roles because they define them narrowly as pressures to practice gendered consumption and work roles.

Many simple livers describe having had multiple significant relationships with members of the opposite sex, but most continue to accept a single long-term relationship as the norm. None had children living at home. Only four of the fourteen people interviewed had children. One person who did not have children said she hoped to have children in the future. Nine of the people I interviewed did not plan to have children but one of the nine plans to adopt a child in the future. Some viewed this choice as primarily personal. They wanted to be free to do other things or they did not believe they were intended to have children. One man cited personal reasons for choosing not to have children and then later in the interview added he also didn't plan to have them because of his concern about the impact of overpopulation on the environment and said he was a member of Zero Population Growth, an organization that advocates population control. Often those who planned to have no children combined the two sets of reasoning, citing both personal and environmental concerns as reasons for their choice.

Even though most simple livers don't experience enduring marriages or have or plan to have children, and many claim they don't establish fulfilling relationships with members of the opposite sex, they don't problematize the heterosexual norm, the idea of enduring marriage or that normal people have children. Instead they see themselves as personally different in this respect.

Most of the people in the voluntary simplicity movement are single. As was described in detail in chapter 3, the descriptions they give of how they feel about partnerships and marriage (intimate heterosexual relationships) differ between women and men. Single women are ambivalent about partnerships and marriage with men because they have lost autonomy in such relationships in the past. The men, on the other hand, view future relationships as desirable but specify that the terms of relationship they want includes shared financial responsibility. Pam's ideas about relationships with men are typical of the single women in the movement:

> I'm not [dating]. And I have not for about three years. I don't make good choices in that direction. I have learned that over the years. And so I am really cautious. [Laughs] I go for these guys that are just kind of really interesting but some other things they don't have besides these really interesting parts, like jobs! So he did have a job and he did have a car but he was so high maintenance. Always having to prop him up and tell him how good he was and how wonderful. So I just got tired of that. Life's too short.

Single women show a pattern of avoiding and being ambivalent about relationships with men. Men who are single show a pattern of wanting relationships with women but wanting them on their own terms of equal financial obligation and low levels of conflict or accommodation. Peter described in detail how finding a partner would improve his financial situation and also his vision of an emotionally nurturing relationship. Two of the single men and three of the men in partnerships said openly that they sought partners who could improve their own financial standing.

Walby (1990) suggests that the dominant location of patriarchy is shifted from private to public in the twentieth century. In terms of the structure of patriarchal production relations in the household, Walby focuses on the way women's household labor is expropriated by their husbands and partners. She examines reproductive technologies, the domestic division of labor, and changing household composition. Simple livers focus their ideological attention on the domestic division of labor. Since most simple livers are single, they tend to do their own household work. But in practice they also are responding to patriarchal reproductive technologies and household composition.

Some of the singles have roommates and share the reproductive work with them in mutually agreed upon ways. But they do use voluntary simplicity as a tool to help them bring some types of production work back into their household and more under their control and to generally resist the rationalization process as the market increasingly provides services for households. In this way they are resisting market intrusion into their production work.

Heterosexual couples discussed their equality with each other in terms of shared household work and equal input into or independent financial decision making. The couples say they have organized housework, gardening, cooking, washing clothes, and other reproductive work in ways that make them equals. Both couples I interviewed did projects together including carpentry and gardening. One couple grew much of their own food and canned, froze, and made preserves together. The couples also practiced some division of labor but it was not strictly organized along traditional gendered lines. In one couple the man did the grocery shopping and cooking and made beer and wine. The woman did the laundry, vacuuming, and mending. They shared gardening, canning, freezing, drying, and making preserves.

Money is important in renegotiating gendered power relations in couples and offers an insight regarding how important existing market relations are to how power is established within households of movement participants. For instance, one woman pointed out that her husband got to do some of the more grungy work around the house because he brought less financially to their household. Barbara said she had given up the idea of writing her dissertation for her Ph.D. when she saw how much fun it was for Lewis to be making money. Even though the ideology of voluntary simplicity rejects money as a measure of human worth, the women in couples and single men discuss monetary income as important to them while the men in couples and the single women downplayed the importance of money. Men in couples said who earned income versus who saved money by doing reproductive work was not important—both should be valued equally.

For these couples patriarchal relations in waged work appeared less intrusive because both women and men were highly educated and the women in couples had higher levels of education or came from higher socioeconomic backgrounds than their husbands. This makes it more likely that they can command salaries or have access to resources equal to those of their partners (Spain and Bianchi 1996; Vogler and Pahl 1993). What actually happens in these couples is that whoever has access to or control over more resources to bring to the relationship appears to exert just slightly more power in the relationship.

Drawing on Pahl (1984), Walby points out, "Today the social class of the husband's job makes no significant difference to the unevenness of the domestic division of labour: middle-class husbands contribute no more than working-class men. However, a woman's class does make a difference. If the husband's class is held constant, then we find that, the higher the class of the woman's job, the less uneven is the domestic division of labour" (1990, 83). Walby goes on to say, "[T]his would suggest that a better job can improve a woman's bargaining position over the domestic division of labour" (83). This research suggests that access to resources, earned or otherwise, influences the bargaining power in partnerships between men and women simple livers.

Men consistently made comments about not wanting relationships with women who were dependent on them economically. In order to have partnerships in which the women are not economically dependent, they end up in partnerships with women who are unwilling to do much more of the reproductive work than the men. Single men rarely say they want relationships with women where reproductive work is shared. But some single men describe their satisfaction in being able to do household tasks well. One even said he liked not being dependent on a woman to do his mending. As was noted in chapter 3, voluntary simplicity supports men in identity work that uses private sphere skills such as gardening, grocery shopping, and cooking to establish masculine voluntary simplicity identities.

Patriarchal relations in paid work are less obvious to simple livers in part because of their higher educational levels which locate them in jobs where they don't personally experience the inequality of sexsegregated work as relevant. The men as well as the women rarely have held or presently hold extremely powerful positions in their work settings and missed the significance of their similarities to those who do. This is particularly important in the case of the men who are privileged by gender, race, and class, but also hides from the women their relative privilege based on race and class.

Women in the movement are avoiding several points of patriarchal control. Most informants not only are not married or in partnerships but they also are not and do not plan to become mothers. In terms of marriage this is in keeping with broader patterns in the United States in which women are less likely to be married and also reflects increasing levels of childlessness. There are sound economic reasons for the decline in the birth rate. Children who once were an economic asset now tend to be an economic drain on households.

These findings are in keeping with Walby's (1990) argument that the increase in paid employment of women gives them other alternatives to marriage, in which they get a raw deal. Women with alternative forms of economic support are less likely to enter a relationship dependent on a man. They are also more likely to leave husbands when they have access to alternative forms of support. The less men have to offer women economically, the less likely women are to marry them. Unlike women, it is men of the lowest social classes who are least likely to marry. The less a husband earns, the more it is in a woman's economic interest to leave him.

The men, for the most part, are not participating in marriage, long-term partnerships, and fatherhood. This can be seen as part of a larger pattern in Western countries in which some men are avoiding fatherhood and the costs associated with it. Patterns in voluntary simplicity also link to the shift away from waged work and the breadwinner role as central for men in defining themselves as men.

Men who are simple livers don't believe they oppress women. After all, they treat the women they know well as equals if in partnerships they share household work and financial decision making. Since they don't hold powerful positions in the workplace if working, they don't recognize their structural advantage. Women simple livers don't believe they are oppressed by men. If they are in couples they say they share financial decision making and household work. Single women believe they control the types of interactions they have with men and experience their lives as free from gender inequality because they have opted to be single. Single men in the movement say they want equal partnerships.

As white, educated, middle-class heterosexuals movement participants don't often experience the oppressive aspects of institutional power in the same way less privileged groups do by being excluded, ignored, harassed, and discriminated against. They construct a version of reality that equalizes the suffering of subordinate and dominant groups. This leads to the idea that men and women suffer from sexism equally, just in different ways. They ultimately have an individualistic view of social life. This fosters a tendency for them to reduce institutionalized power relationships and interpersonal power struggles over resources to struggles for self-actualization.

The identity work being done, discussed at length in chapter 3, is aimed at remaking all simple livers, men and women, so they have similar moral identities that distance them from the negative characteristics they associate with the dominant culture. This includes aspects of masculinity and femininity they interpret as constraining, or destructive gender roles that they link to careerism, consumerism, and environmental destruction, so being a successful simple liver requires balancing masculine and feminine characteristics and subtly encourages this sort of interpretation of gender inequality.

Culturally constructed symbols of femininity associated with buying mass consumer goods, fashionable clothing, makeup, and the most recent household gadget are questioned and critiqued. Masculinity associated with gaining self-worth from work, competition, and status consumption for men is questioned. But the deep structures of patriarchy and key aspects of its intersection with capitalism—of heterosexuality, marriage, and, surprisingly in light of the central concerns of the movement, even gender inequality in the sex-segregated labor market that subordinates women and racial and ethnic minorities disproportionately—remain largely omitted from consideration as relevant for simple livers. There is concern with who makes a product (for example, child labor) and under what conditions but they don't mention concerns about women and racial and ethnic minorities being in the worst jobs. They rarely explore ideas that would lead them to recognize how their own control over resources often rests on institutionalized patterns of gender inequality which are intertwined with the economy they depend upon for investment dividends, for instance.

Neither women nor men are questioning heterosexuality or marriage as the norm. They are trying to pull into the private sphere and gain a higher level of control over household work, pulling productive and reproductive work back into the household somewhat, and rejecting the notion of gendered work in the household. But they fail to note women's dependence upon monetary income or access to income derived from market relations in order to negotiate for more equal relations in household production when they are in partnerships with men. They also fail to see women choosing to remain single as a method of avoiding patriarchal exploitation.

Simple living women and men, whether single or in partnerships, continue to accept the family-household form that characterizes the social structuring of capitalist patriarchy as the given norm within which people make their choices. Walby points out that popular cultural forms represent a very restricted range of possibilities and most women experience tensions around marriage and household in terms of issues of popular culture. This seems to play a significant part in the thinking of simple livers where gender relations are concerned. They focus on resisting gender roles, and many are not married or in partnerships, but they do not experience their behavior as a conscious resistance to the deep structures of patriarchy embodied in contemporary Western society. In the case of couples, those who are married do recognize they are negotiating new ways of relating within marriage in comparison to the traditional marriage associated with the dominant culture of stay-at-home wife and breadwinner husband. And couples in partnerships other than marriage also say they do not follow the traditional gendered division of labor in reproductive work.

By not recognizing the importance of gender inequality in their personal lives they fail to recognize that gendered power struggles are an important part of their daily lives. Women's power is not just determined by their relation to the household but also is mediated by class, race, ethnicity, age, marital status, and position in the labor market.

Overall simple livers feel they are largely free of the dominant culture's prescribed gender roles because they define them narrowly as pressures to practice gendered consumption and work. Most viewed the patterns in their intimate relationships as reflections of personal rather than cultural or social factors and did not link them to voluntary simplicity. Men and women often note that voluntary simplicity helps free them from pressures to find their life's meaning from work. Men feel voluntary simplicity reduces pressures on them to gain their sense of self-worth from occupational status and to be primary bread winners.

Most people in voluntary simplicity conceive of women's issues of inequality in terms of access to jobs and public politics, and freedom from gendered consumption and the need to construct gender identity through traditional female occupations. Most assume that power struggles between themselves and members of the opposite sex are from equal positions and none connected their personal problems in relating to members of the opposite sex with institutionalized patterns of power from the dominant culture.

Most believe they have rejected the construction of masculinity and femininity defined by the dominant consumer culture. It appears that more flexibility in gender roles is supported in voluntary simplicity. Women are valued as skilled carpenters, men as cooks and cleaners. Reproductive work is shared in cases where people live with others. But gender-based power continues to shape the lives of simple livers and goes largely unrecognized or denied.

Simple livers believe that, by rejecting the gender roles prescribed by the dominant culture, they have freed themselves from the last vestiges of gender oppression and largely overlook public patriarchy and gender power struggles in their own households. In this way patriarchy moves into the shadows and is hidden from the direct view of simple livers but continues to shape their lives.

Race/Ethnicity

Simple livers for the most part do not consider racial and ethnic inequality as an issue for them personally. Being predominantly white and not having experience themselves of being marginalized based on race/ethnicity leads many simple livers to underestimate the importance of race/ethnicity as a factor of exclusion for others. Additionally, a number of people involved in voluntary simplicity who are white ethnics have been upwardly mobile in their generation. This contributes to their belief that racial and ethnic minorities can make similar gains with similar effort.

Simple livers acknowledge that the voluntary simplicity movement is largely made up of white people, but they believe the people in their circles are open to racial and ethnic minority participation and assert that they are open to close relationships with nonwhites. Seven of the simple livers I interviewed mentioned their own white ethnicity or immigrant heritage as important for them in some way.

Nita and Kevin met at a Sons of Norway initiation ceremony. Their Norwegian heritage was the basis for part of their social life and artistic interests. Nita sewed authentic Norwegian costumes and went to Norway annually to do volunteer work at a costume museum there. They live in a neighborhood that has a high population of people of Norwegian descent. Jack, also of Norwegian descent, remembered feeling that Norwegians were looked down upon in the community where he grew up in Minnesota. Two other male respondents mentioned that their parents were immigrants, and two men mentioned that they were from Irish Catholic families.

The respondents who had a sense of their own white ethnicity as important tended to interpret racial/ethnic difference in terms of cultural difference. Most drew on their cultural difference as a source of rich culture, not as a cause for their relative subordination or oppression. As white ethnics their experiences were those of assimilation in their generation. They have the capacity to choose when and where they emphasize their cultural difference.

Most simple livers don't talk about themselves in racial terms unless asked questions that relate to race, but their accounts reveal that their lives are indeed shaped by being white in the United States today.

Andrews romanticizes the "rich culture"of impoverished black people in the southern United States which she encountered in civil rights work during the 1960s. She writes:

> I began to see the arrogance and lack of vitality in my own culture. I would go to a black church and hear people singing and see people dancing, and feel the joy and strength of the people. And then I would go to a white church, and I would think, these people must be sick. Their skin is pale, their voices are weak. And of course, these people who were upholding segregation were sick in a way, for their lives were blighted by racism and prejudice.
>
> Prejudice is a part of a wider culture that judges people on the basis of their status, their education, their wealth, their race, their gender, their age, their sexual preference, their disabilities. Prejudice is a symptom of the sickness of the culture of success, a culture that does not value people. I began to understand that the more successful you seemed to become, the more vitality you lost. I saw that the successful middle-class white culture is often repressed and artificial. Somehow all of our life is drained out of us. We become bland and lifeless.
>
> After my experience in the South, I began to understand something else. I felt isolated and alone. I envied the people living in this black ghetto. The civil rights movement had given them something. They had fought together for something they believed in. They had comforted each other in their losses. They had celebrated their victories together. They had something that I didn't have, and I wasn't sure what it was. They laughed together more than I did with my friends. Their conversation was about more than movies and restaurants. (1997, 107)

Andrews says she wanted a community like she felt the community in the black ghetto was during the 1960s. She views being white as being part of an empty culture. Her feelings are in keeping with accounts Frankenberg (1993) describes of "race cognizant" white women who yearn for a culture other than white culture, which they perceive as empty and which they contrast to rich cultures they associate with people of color. This perspective constructs whiteness as something empty. For many in the voluntary simplicity movement, this appears to be one way of thinking about whiteness. But the people in the voluntary simplicity movement do not stop there. Ideological work on whiteness is being done through the movement.

Accounts of informants, in keeping with Andrews's work, reflect two things that voluntary simplicity is doing with whiteness. First, it is taking the empty category, which at times is also constructed as bad, and trying to fill it with something good. Even the upwardly mobile white ethnics in the movement define themselves as affluent white Westerners much of the time. There is a sense that they are particularly sensitive to the shallowness of middle-class consumerist culture because of working class roots or white ethnic identities. They talk as though they lost some true human worth by shifting into the dominant middle-class culture. Second, voluntary simplicity is constructing whiteness and "other" as both suffering (equally, though they don't say this directly) from racism, prejudice, poverty, and global degradation even though the suffering may look different. Ultimately, they reason, all of us stand to suffer the consequences of environmental collapse together. Andrews, for example, points out how white racists' lives are blighted by their prejudice rather than emphasizing how white racist prejudice has blighted the lives of blacks and other ethnic minorities. The history and continued extraction of higher levels of surplus value from blacks, Hispanics, and other ethnic minorities and women in the United States under capitalist patriarchy are not a detailed part of this account (Bielby and Baron 1986; Bonacich 1972; Lieberson 1980; Portes and Manning 1986; Spain and Bianchi 1996).

Most of the simple livers I interviewed live in integrated neighborhoods but do not have close friends who are racially or ethnically different from themselves. There are three notable exceptions. Nita and Emily's community-building efforts bring them into regular social contact with poor and racial and ethnic minorities in their neighborhood. And Pam is friends with two neighbors, Gloria and Ruth, who are black lesbians with whom she shares an interest in frugality and nutrition.

Gloria and Ruth are not participating in a circle but Pam says she shares a lot in common with them. Emily has neighbors who are ethnically diverse too. She says she has "good neighbors" and describes a range of relationships with them. She describes their family compositions and race and ethnicity in detail. There are Asian Americans, blacks, Eastern Europeans, a white yuppie couple, and a white lesbian couple living in her immediate vicinity. She describes friendly though not close relationships with all but one family. She says she had some unpleasant encounters with some members of a black family that lives next door. They called her names and threatened her physically on several occasions. She seemed embarrassed to tell me about this and uncertain about why it had happened. She tried to account for it by their being on welfare and said their children "go to jail instead of to college." Still, Emily likes the working-class neighborhood in which she lives and says she has resisted her family pressures for her to move.

At another point in the discussion Emily mentioned the same family in positive terms. She observed that they always spent a lot of time together as a family and she compared this to her own family, which had grown apart as the children became more affluent. Though none of the people I interviewed said they lived in all-white neighborhoods, all lived in neighborhoods where whites are in the majority.

So how do simple livers account for the whiteness of voluntary simplicity circles? Most explain the absence of nonwhites as the result of the interests and choices made by racial and ethnic minority individuals, which they see as natural and understandable. Some also mention basic demographic differences such as neighborhood and distances of commuting to meetings. Disparities in income between racial and ethnic minorities and whites overall is also mentioned by some. Several expressed the belief that minorities who are affluent may have been affluent only a short time and may be naturally reluctant to simplify, having only recently made it based on the values of the dominant culture. Yet a number of the people I interviewed had become affluent themselves only in adulthood, and only for a time, making this reasoning unconvincing as a complete explanation for the lack of participation of people of color in the movement.

Discussions about racial and ethnic diversity in circles and their personal relations with people of different races and ethnic backgrounds than their own often reveal that simple livers shift between identities as white and ethnic themselves to explain the absence of people of color in the simplicity circles and in their friendship circles.

Jack had married a Pacific Islander and it was in the context of describing himself and his family that he revealed his sense of himself as both white Aryan and Norwegian:

> I met her in Fiji in [World War II] sort of like South Pacific. They had a ball celebrating the surrender of Italy, so I went to the ball and I met her there across a crowded floor. Her father is from Australia, her mother is from Fiji. Her mother is a quarter Fijian so she is one-eighth Fijian, which makes my children one-sixteenth Fijian but none of them have the characteristics. In fact my wife didn't either. She has red hair and freckles. My daughter is the only one of four kids who had red hair. She has wavy red hair, beautiful hair. Cuts it off at times. I don't like that. . . . In terms of ethnicity, I'm of Aryan blood, full blooded Norwegian, I guess you would say. And yet I got the feeling that we were looked down on in that region [Minnesota, where he grew up].

Jack experienced himself as both dominant white and as a subordinated ethnic relative to the dominant culture.

Kevin and Nita drew on their experiences as Norwegian ethnics to explain the absence of racial and ethnic minorities in circles:

> Kevin: I think it's not all about me pointing the finger at myself and saying, why aren't you associating with others? I do think that the other people do go out of their way to associate with their own and that's normal.

> Nita: I mean we are more apt to associate with other Norwegians.

> Kevin: Right, right. And if that means we are a segregated minority, [laughs] so be it. . . .

> Nita: Yeah, yeah. And there are typical ways of doing things among Norwegians, not that we do all of them. People here are very direct. Minnesotans are very circuitous sometimes, Kevin for instance.

> Kevin: They aren't necessarily sneaky; they are nonconfrontational.

> Nita: I do think people do tend to seek out people that they share heritage with. If you think about the difficulties there

would be if you marry someone from a totally different culture where—I mean we all think that there are very basic things that are the same for the whole world but my first husband, who was Norwegian and English, we had been married about three weeks and he swept the table off with a broom and I thought my god, what else don't I know. [Both laugh] I just would not have thought someone who looked reasonably civilized ever would have done that, but he did. I'm sure he did not learn it from his mother but it was a shattering experience.

This account shifts discussion to Norwegian culture, the white ethnic group they identify with when they are thinking about minority status, and away from why nonwhite minorities are not in the circle. It demonstrates a power evasive response to my questions, making use of the white ethnic identities they can shift to. Kevin and Nita, as well as most informants, expressed views that included some "color blind" or "power evasive" and some "race cognizant" aspects (Frankenberg 1993, 14–15).

People who lived in diverse neighborhoods and who worked or had worked in settings that brought them into contact with diversity tended to recognize difference based on both cultural differences and social structural characteristics. Most believed 1) neighborhood demographics; 2) structural outcomes that meant more racial and ethnic minorities were poor; 3) the fact that affluent racial and ethnic minorities had often only recently established affluence and were therefore less likely to be eager to simplify; and 4) a natural tendency to seek others that one is comfortable with all play a role in low numbers of racial and ethnic minorities in the movement. Race-cognizant accounts end up establishing simple livers (who happen to be mostly white but are engaged in trying to alter the meaning of whiteness) as more able and interested in adopting voluntary simplicity than the poor, among whom nonwhite minorities are overrepresented. One reason for this that simple livers mention is their view that the poor are so busy trying to survive they do not have time to think about bigger social issues such as environmental degradation. Another reason often mentioned is that the poor have not had enough as they have, and they suffer from the false belief that they will be happy and fulfilled if they can get more material things and be more affluent.

While at times their own ethnicity is discussed as central, when pressed regarding nonwhite minority involvement in the movement, simple livers shift into discourse that gives their whiteness dominance over their ethnic identities. And many simple livers who do not have dual identities as white ethnics and whites begin with this account.

These are examples of the comments simple livers make about the lack of people of color in circles:

> Peter: [There are] not too many black people [in the movement] and I get nervous about the waspiness, but the high economic thing does not bother me. [There are some] black American Negro, no Asian, yes, one lady and in Jack's, people come and go but have been Asian and Mexican. I'm pretty sure there is an American Indian there now. . . . When you don't have so much it is kind of postsimplicity. . . . It is systematically structured that the median income of blacks is lower than the median income of whites.

> Barbara: I would say economically there are ranges of people, so there is some diversity there. I know up here, I don't [see] this area as being ethnically diverse in the first place. . . . I may overgeneralize here, but traditionally minority groups have not had the most success financially so when people do, you have a split, you know, like you read about where this group disassociates themselves from the group that does not have much money. So they go on to lead these kind of successful lives, so the last thing they want to do is go ahead and simplify. I mean they have made it. They are the American dream and any group who are still in poverty and the white people who are poor are not seeking voluntary simplicity.

> Lewis: I think for the most part white people have had materialism for quite a while now. It's kind of lost its novelty now that other ethnic groups are able to have kind of an access to this world. Well the cost of goods has gone cheaper and the materialism culture now, marketers and advertisers, are finally marketing to them. Yeah this is kind of a world move now. We want to include everyone and while that is such a wonderful thought—you know, it's great to see more diversity in commercials and in television programs—but what does that really mean? Does it mean come join this world? We'll accept you if you'll just give us your life, your dollars. I think a lot of it appeals to people who have seen that materialism is not ultimately fulfilling, but if you haven't been around a lot of people who have been materially successful, it is easier to perpetuate that myth that you are going to be fulfilled by that.

Daniel: I think voluntary simplicity is a bit of a luxury. I don't know that a person or a family that is worrying about where they are going to get their next meal or where they are going to sleep tonight has that luxury of looking at voluntary simplicity. . . . They don't have those choices. So I think that is going to be a bit of a filter for the participants in a study circle and the whole nature of voluntary simplicity is, the first word is "voluntary." . . . I think voluntary simplicity, as directly as its own title, is its own filter and Phinney neighborhood isn't going to get people from, you know, Mount Baker area . . . or Seward Park or Rainier Beach that far across town to that sort of a meeting.

Brad, who grew up in a rural area in the Midwest and lives in a midwestern college town, explained the racial and ethnic composition of his neighborhood near campus in the following way: "You know, probably as diverse as society. Predominantly white." Roger, who also was attending college in the Midwest but spent many of his developing years in the southern United States, expressed his ideas about diversity in circles in the following way:

I'm not sure I would say it is important to have a diverse ethnic and racial group and in some ways if you are talking about what problems you are having and what changes you'd like to make in your lifestyle, it makes it easier if you are communicating with people who are having the same problems and who have the same kind of lifestyle. So for example if we had some welfare people from the inner city in our group, I'm not sure if we would have been that useful to those people. You know, in my life there will never be an issue of how to put food on the table. I think if that was an issue, I might see the whole voluntary simplicity movement differently.

Roger assumes it is the white "we" in the circle who would need to be "useful" to the ghetto blacks if they joined. He does not consider what "we" (with a silent white assumed) might learn from poor black people; rather he justifies the whiteness of the circles by focusing on how little the experience of relatively affluent circle members is to helping poor ghetto blacks, the group he conveniently uses as the example of people of color, allowing him to maintain there is little commonality in the problems of the two groups.

The idea that the civil rights movement had largely achieved its goals and that now time is needed to fully realize those goals also came up as expressed by Fred:

> A neighborhood aspect is part of it. It is only thirty years since the legalities of discrimination and segregation have been shaped and changed. It is just the choices on the parts of all people from the various groups. I guess slowly things are changing. It is going to change not with the wishing or the forcing, and that is not to say I'm against forced busing, but that is not to say people are going to want to hang out together until they come to realize it is them against the boss, that it's them against the other companies.

Simple livers do not identify themselves as prejudiced and don't see themselves as responsible for oppression of racial and ethnic minorities or as benefitting from it. Far from it. They believe they generally act in ways that do not contribute to inequality and that their simple living will benefit less privileged people, including racial and ethnic minorities. Durning (1992) points to Africa as the continent that suffers the most poverty. The simple livers, who are focused on reducing this global disparity through their daily practices, can feel they are addressing racial inequality in their daily practices even though they may not interact directly with racial ethnic minorities or other marginalized groups very much in their daily lives.

But some, like Kevin and Nita, reach out in very personal ways to help. They invited Rita, a black woman living on the street in their neighborhood, to live with them while she got on her feet. She lived with them for four months and then was able to get a job. Nita organizes a weekly sewing circle and tea for women in the neighborhood which is held at the housing project down the street from where she lives. In this way she brings women from the circle and other networks, most of whom are educated and have resources above the poverty level, together with poor women on a regular basis. But Nita and Kevin are exceptional examples within the movement.

Unlike Frankenberg's (1993) respondents, who largely viewed whiteness as an empty category, most white simple livers are doing ideological work on whiteness to address the kind of emptiness in the dominant white culture that Andrews (1997) bemoans. They are trying to reconstruct the definition of being middle-class whites by constituting a rich, worthwhile culture of voluntary simplicity. The ideology of the voluntary simplicity movement shifts the colonial discourse in one way. It points to affluent Western (white) middle-class people as a category. It names them as a group "the consuming class" (Durning 1992, 26) of the Western countries, and it holds them and those who emulate them globally as central in the problem of environmental degradation. It acknowledges the empty category as being filled with something bad by the evolutionary process of industrialism. It then prescribes changes this group needs to make in itself in order to live a right livelihood. The consuming class needs to realize that the values and practices of the industrial era are leading to global environmental collapse and social chaos and they need to change. Simple livers as members of this group choose to change their own practices and "live simply so that others may simply live," as Fred expressed it. The empty category of white, Western, competitive (male), middle-class consumer is first filled with the content of being greedy, mindless, empty, and soulless and then offered the choice of becoming good, mindful, whole, and soulful by adopting voluntary simplicity.

The simple livers shift the definition of the given categories with which they are identified toward change but they don't give up being the dominant group that is seen as being in charge of social change. The dominance of this group is no longer seen as constructed based on racial or ethnic superiority or the ability to exploit resources for its own, constantly increasing personal consumption, but upon its ability to see clearly what is best for all of humanity, its willingness to live cooperatively rather than competitively and to bring about change, not by force, but by example. Simple livers choose to reduce the level of their privileged position relative to being able to consume an unfair proportion of the earth's resources without giving up their position of unequal access to these resources and right to a higher level of control over the use of resources.

The discourse of the movement gives salience to the affluent, Western, middle-class part of the definition, but the way language about this category is used demonstrates that whiteness is the silent companion of middle-class identity and practice. Simple livers tend to unselfconsciously blend whiteness and being middle class at times. At other times they recognize their whiteness as significant. They make the emptiness of whiteness a problem to solve by building community and changing practices so white culture becomes a positive force rather than a negative one. But in terms of themselves personally, they don't generally feel their whiteness as a privilege. Those with ethnic identities shift back and forth between ethnic white and dominant white discourse about themselves. They feel they have rejected white privilege by adopting voluntary simplicity.

This is how Nita articulated her beliefs about the responsibility of simple livers to share their knowledge with others: "I think . . . that voluntary simplicity and the middle class and Americans have the responsibility to let other cultures, other income groups, and other countries know this American dream thing is a bunch of nonsense." That whiteness continues at times to be assumed as given, though it is not mentioned directly, is revealed in the way Nita juxtaposes "other cultures and the poor" to "middle class" and "American" people. The Western (white) self is shifted from a bad form of dominance based on domination and control of resources to a position of dominance based on understanding of the situation and responsibility to make the proper choices to insure the future of humanity and the planet. The dominance assumed here is not acknowledged because it is cloaked in the idea that self-change is what is most important for the consuming class and not judging others is prescribed. In this way simple livers can assert that they are part of a group of cultural change agents who are not telling others what to do but changing their own practices. Voluntary simplicity can, in one way, be seen as a response to the material circumstances generated in large part as part of the unfolding of the industrial revolution and colonialism, but it can also be seen as a method of reasserting the Western (silent white) self as good and in control.

Conclusion

The class, gender, and racial/ethnic politics of voluntary simplicity activity is in many ways an advocacy of the interests of liberal, white, educated heterosexuals who want change that prevents environmental collapse and enables them to be released from economic and cultural pressures to work long hours and practice status and identity construction consumption.

The way of establishing power that they view as central in the dominant culture, through work and status occupation and through conspicuous consumption, is rejected by those in voluntary simplicity. This leads the men to believe they have rejected the primary basis for inequality and that they are cooperative, not competitive. The women believe they have rejected the dominant culture's pressure to practice gendered consumption and to present themselves as feminine in ways defined by the dominant culture.

Men who are simple livers don't believe they oppress women. And women simple livers don't believe they are oppressed by men. They tolerate difference but maintain reasoning that affirms heterosexuality as the norm. True recognition of heterosexuality as a construct in relation and opposition to nonheterosexuality is lacking. Where they are at least questioning some aspects of the dichotomous definitions and the cultural practices linked to them in terms of masculine and feminine gender categories and white/nonwhite racial and ethnic categories, they do not explore heterosexuality as an issue at all beyond simply mentioning the gay and lesbian liberation movements in their lists of movements aimed at self-actualization. They don't see sexual orientation as an issue, claiming that it does not matter to them.

Men and women in the movement agree that women should be treated equally when it comes to paid work and housework. They also tend to believe men should not be judged based on occupational status or income or doing macho things. Many believe they have already dealt with issues of gendered power inequality in personal relationships and they gloss over these issues and distance themselves from exploring ideas that would lead them to recognize how their own control over resources often rests on institutionalized patterns of gender inequality which are intertwined with the economy they depend upon for investment dividends, for instance.

They also tend not to analyze the women's movement or feminist ideas deeply. They touch on them in the texts and will discuss them when asked about them in interviews, but they do so as a way of acknowledging that they know about and are sensitive to these issues. Most accounts also indirectly try to demonstrate that they are not central or have been taken care of and then they turn to their focus on jobism and consumerism, which are the issues they as educated white heterosexuals, with control over resources adequate to meet their perceived needs, feel are the most important forms of oppression they experience.

The way simple livers are located in terms of the intersections of gender, race, and class make the rising collective forms of appropriation through the sex-segregated labor market and welfare, for instance, less obvious to them. In addition, their own shift away from personal patterns that reflect the private forms of appropriation, in which a patriarch exploits the labor of a woman in the household, make them tend to think the culture in general has made this shift or will. And even as the couples continue to negotiate power in their relationships, they do so unaware of the role gender inequality is playing in that negotiation, in their intimate relationships.

In the case of racial and ethnic differences also, simple livers believe they and other movement participants are open to everyone and reject racism and prejudice. They vacillate between mostly "power evasive" and "race cognizant" (Frankenberg 1993, 14–15) thinking regarding race and ethnicity but view themselves as willing to be inclusive and receptive to diversity. One man said that minorities just needed to show up to be accepted and participate. The "other" category of female or racial or ethnic "other" as connected to cultural and economic subordination in the form of poverty vanishes into the shadows too. In two PBS productions that several simple livers played a role in producing, *Affluenza* and *Escape from Affluenza*, which represent one of the ways those in voluntary simplicity have attempted to diffuse the movement, diversity is featured. Blacks, Asian Americans, and Hispanics are included among those adopting simple living, giving the impression the movement is far more diverse in terms of race and ethnicity than my findings suggest.

This way of thinking about the relative status, power, and well-being of women and men, blacks and whites, nonheterosexuals and heterosexuals is political whether people in voluntary simplicity believe it is or not. Many think of gender and race/ethnic inequality as solved by politics aimed at self-definition and demands for recognition as worthy selves since they believe the women's movement and the civil rights movement addressed more basic inequalities successfully.

An important feature of the movement ideology of some simple livers is that they construct a version of reality that equalizes the suffering of subordinate and dominant groups within the movement and relative to themselves. That is, men and women suffer from sexism equally, just in different ways. Whites and blacks suffer from racism equally, just in different ways. The poor and wealthy suffer equally from inequality, just in different ways. By taking an individualistic view of social life, at one extreme in the movement is the tendency to reduce institutionalized power relationships and interpersonal power struggles over resources to struggles for self-actualization.

Simple livers are stuck in some ways between their desire to achieve an environmentally sustainable and more egalitarian world and the desire to feel good about themselves instead of guilty about the world's injustices and negotiate comfortable lives for themselves. They want to retain control over the use of and access to cultural, social, and economic resources that they have, and to feel in control and secure rather than insecure and helpless. Many also want to avoid conflict and contention in their daily lives and to feel comfortable in the relationships they have with others. This makes them reluctant to critique, deconstruct, or advocate the dismantling of structures that provide them relative benefits even as they want to change the outcomes of the processes of these structures.

The implicit message in the ideology of voluntary simplicity regarding inequality is that everyone is in the same boat even if they don't know it. The poor think they want the lifestyle of the consumers and that it will make them happy. The consumer class is caught up on a treadmill of constantly wanting more but people are miserable living greedy, mindless lives devoted to status consumption and occupations. The rich are not separated out as a distinct class but assumed also to be mindless and miserable in their pursuit of more. It is the simple livers and middle-income people in the world who offer a viable model for human fulfillment and evolutionary survival of humanity. And since the middle class is also associated with being white, it is they who continue to be in a dominant position though simple livers, of course, do not couch this dominance in terms of racial superiority, but of a more complete vantage point from which to understand and address the problem.

Through the ideology of voluntary simplicity, simple livers become the ones who know what everyone, globally, needs to do. Affluence beyond what they define for themselves as enough is the cause of the major problems in the world. They say they have learned affluence does not make you happy. Simple livers don't say they are superior, but they talk about their practices as more developed in evolutionary terms than either those of the poor or those who continue to be mindless consumers.[2] They claim they are not judging others. But what results from their ideology is the idea that the poor don't have time to think about the big problems of society because they are so busy trying to survive. Plus they suffer from false consciousness, thinking that if they have more material things they will be happy. Since people of color are over–represented among the poor of the first-world countries and are the majority in third-world countries, the way simple livers make meaning of the situation results, once again, in Western white people developing an ideology that constructs themselves as having superior knowledge and legitimates the absence of people of color from the group. Simple livers, of course, don't associate the form of superiority their ideology constructs for them consciously or overtly with being white. They associate their superior knowledge with their experience and rejection of affluence. They believe they are more clear thinking than those who are still part of the mindless herd, that as simple livers they are the vanguard of the ecological era.

For the most part people in voluntary simplicity don't fully acknowledge their own embeddedness in institutionalized patterns of power, seeing themselves as suffering from jobism, overconsumption, the impacts of environmental degradation, and the prospect of environmental crisis, and believing they need to resist cultural pressures to conform in order to free their authentic selves. The stress, clutter, health problems, lack of fulfillment, and sense of meaning and community belonging felt by simple livers prior to adopting voluntary simplicity are attributed to the lifestyle associated with the dominant culture. Part of the rhetoric includes the idea of freeing the authentic self through voluntary simplicity, just as the women's movement did for women and the civil right's movement did for African Americans. They don't realize that the fact that they can pass as mainstream, something they openly discuss wanting to be able to do, means they have privilege over many in the society who can't. The relative disparities in power of women and men within the movement are overlooked almost entirely. They don't realize that the same techniques that work for them won't necessarily work for others who are excluded or who have less capacity to avoid being dominated and controlled by others.

Elgin writes hopefully of a sustainable future, based on the clear vision of simple livers: "To build a sustainable future, citizens of the earth must see themselves as part of a tightly interdependent system rather than as isolated individuals and nations. With a witnessing consciousness or observer's perspective, citizens cultivate the detachment that enables us to stand back, look at the big picture, and make the hard choices and trade-offs that our circumstances demand. With a reflective consciousness we look at our situation objectively and see how imperative it is to begin the process of healing and reconciliation" (1993a, 187). The language of Western empiricism is used by Elgin in describing this interpretation of a desirable future. The problem of reconciliation expressed this way assumes that people the world over will find common ground in keeping with Elgin's vision of what the future should be for action that moves to a sustainable ecology and that class, gender, racial/ethnic, and nation-based interests will be recognized as less relevant than the interests that unite all humanity through voluntary simplicity.[3] The politics of the voluntary simplicity movement largely omit the living voices and participation of those with whom this reconciliation is to take place. How can such reconciliation take place if recognition (Lara 1998) is lacking? Lara argues that cultures may coexist because they are granted respect-as-tolerance, but if solidarity is to be achieved then other kinds of respect are required. She writes, "Cultures may survive or not, depending on the capacity for transformation which springs from their critical vision and the permanent revision of their legacy, as well as from their utopian projections. However, this challenge, as Habermas points out, cannot come only from the demarcation of an identity of one's own with respect to other identities and cultures. Rather, it must prove itself, as an identity, by undertaking a dialogue of recognition in its interaction with other cultures" (1998, 159). How can a collective, consciously interdependent form of relating as described by Elgin occur when recognition of significant forms of difference are denied, glossed over, and overlooked?

Chapter 6 summarizes the transformative capacity of the movement, examines the highest meanings of the shifts simple livers strive for, and highlights theoretical contributions of the analysis. It also discusses the present limitations of voluntary simplicity and suggests ways those in the movement can extend the emancipatory capacity of the movement in keeping with the central concerns that unify them, the desire for a sustainable human future on the earth and an equitable use and distribution of resources.

CHAPTER SIX

---·•·---

New Tools and Old: Transformation and Reproduction in the Voluntary Simplicity Movement

This chapter summarizes the findings in earlier chapters and extends the analysis to explore the "highest meanings" (Touraine 1981, 1983) of the voluntary simplicity cultural movement in terms of its possibilities and transformative capacity. I draw on the sociological analysis of the movement to point to avenues through which its emancipatory capacity may be extended.

Many in the voluntary simplicity movement believe that it can transform the culture and society of the United States. Andrews expressed her belief in the transformative capacity of the movement at a voluntary simplicity conference in the following way: "The nice thing about voluntary simplicity is we look so benign, we look so harmless. You know, somebody said we're the Trojan horse of change. We'll just sneak right in and they won't notice it! So they think, all those sweet people gathering to talk about simplifying their life, and then suddenly, we'll burst out and transform everything!" (*Escape From Affluenza,* 1998). Are simple livers correct? Will they infiltrate the mainstream and produce dramatic change? What kind of transformation is made possible through the voluntary simplicity movement?

Participation in voluntary simplicity does involve a shift away from consumerist values toward lower levels of consumption and more environmentally conscious ways of consuming. The alternative culture of voluntary simplicity elevates creative work, drawing production back into the household and community, doing volunteer work, and spending time relating to people. Simple livers say they buy time for themselves through reducing consumerist spending. If you buy less, you can work less for a wage. This allows a higher level of control over how time is spent. But the most significant change is in the meanings these activities hold for simple livers. Simple livers believe their practices are also buying time for the planet. Each cut in consumption an affluent Westerner makes is viewed as helping a little.

Even in the early stages of research, I was ambivalent about some of the ideas presented in the literature on the voluntary simplicity movement. I was and am sympathetic with many of the goals espoused, but I was uncomfortable with the seemingly apolitical perspectives found in some of it. I found some of the prescriptions trivial, for instance the focus on organizing "stuff" in your home and getting rid of clutter. It was only after I participated in the movement and ended up getting rid of "stuff," organizing the things I kept, and consciously limiting the things I acquired that I came to understand the value of such practices for simple livers and for myself.[1]

Becoming conscious of consumption is personally empowering for those of us who have resources that allow us at some level to participate in consumerist culture without reflecting on it. In the United States this includes many working-class people and most middle-income people as well as the wealthy. Beyond that any amount of consumption reduction is at least that much less registered market demand. I'm not fooling myself by thinking that the shifts in my consumption[2] over the process of doing this research will prevent the environmental problems that I believe are present due to a complex set of interrelated human practices and the beliefs that support them. Factors central to environmental pressures include overpopulation which, if it is mentioned in voluntary simplicity texts, is glossed over (gender, sexuality, and production, reproduction, and consumption are all linked into this global problem), and contemporary market capitalism aimed at growth and profit for capital itself.

Simple livers face a huge dilemma, one anyone in the United States seeking to resist the ways production and consumption are organized in the dominant economy and culture faces if they want to live their daily lives in opposition to the negative aspects of dominant patterns. The problem is how to get by economically and socially and at the same time participate as little as possible in reproducing the dominant economic relations and culture.

Voluntary simplicity represents a potentially important transformation in the worldviews and identities of well-educated, Western, white people in the face of their emergent understanding of global environmental limits, inequalities of access to resources, and limitations of the satisfactions hyperconsumerism can deliver. Focusing on their own roles in creating the problems and on changing their own personal practices to solve the problems empowers simple livers to feel they can enact change without first having to change massive structures such as the global economy, national policies, and the labor process, all areas that their cultural attack aims to change in the long run. People who may have felt frozen, overwhelmed by the immensity and complexity of perceived problems, and unable to create change become empowered through voluntary simplicity.

When I decided to start using earth friendly products in our home it was an easy change to make. Inspired by a discussion in the women's simplicity circle I belong to, I shifted from environmentally toxic household cleaning products to less harmful ones. I know this act alone is not going to save the planet but I do feel better about cleaning my house knowing that we are not using toxic substances that may harm the environment and people and pets in our home.

I like the smell of the concentrated citrus cleaner that I use in cleaning the kitchen and bath. Its smell brings back memories of outings to my great uncle's orange grove on visits to my paternal grandparents in Florida. The smell gives me tangible proof of a positive choice I have made that links my personal practices with my social values. I gained a much clearer insight into the empowerment simple livers feel through their adoption of voluntary simplicity practices such as these by doing it myself. When I walk in the back door after a day spent in teaching, meeting with students, in committee meetings, and doing research, the smell of a freshly peeled orange welcomes me home, affirming my own power to choose positive personal actions, a sensory and pleasurable affirmation of the self I want to be.

Oranges also always make me think of a field trip my sixth grade class took to Tiahuanaco, an Inca ruin on the Bolivian Altiplano. My family lived in La Paz at that time. My father was working for the State Department doing community development work. I had a packed lunch with me—a cheese sandwich and an orange. A little boy approached me. When he smiled I saw his gums were bleeding. A terrible sense of helplessness, guilt, and confusion came over me, all familiar feelings by that time in my life, having grown up a privileged, white Westerner in third-world countries. He was hawking a four-inch replica of one of the huge statues at the site. I bought the replica made of mud. I got my lunch box and gave him the orange out of it—a typical childhood strategy of mine. I have the statue in my bedroom now. I see it every day. The irony of my cleaning my house with citrus cleaner to reduce environmental degradation while children on the Altiplano have bleeding gums for lack of vitamin C in their diet is not lost on me. And so for me the hopeful hints (scent) of changes that are possible, not just in my home but in the world, are tempered by my strong sense of the constraints which shape our possibilities. The smell of citrus cleaner becomes a reminder that I need to keep reflecting on the processes used to achieve change, to keep the questions open, to deal with the discomfort and ambiguity in knowing the limitations of ideas and practices of the moment, to continue to interrogate my own inner oppressors, to recognize how we are constrained by and can use institutions in the process of change, and to keep acting even with the knowledge of how imperfect those actions may be.

Do most simple livers limit their voluntary simplicity activities to the private sphere of their homes and personal practices? Not really. Though this does appear to be the area where most of the change described by simple livers occurs initially, voluntary simplicity for some crosses over into what they view as community building or social action. This activity is not primarily located in traditional national or state political activities and organizations. Overall, people I interviewed said they had been more active politically in the past but were less so presently. Instead they were now choosing to focus on voluntary simplicity and their own life and immediate communities. A few are involved in party politics. But simple livers don't view their involvement in voluntary simplicity in terms of a strict division of private and public activities. Some are involved in volunteering. One volunteered at a local shelter for street people, another at a community garden, another for Peaceworks (a local organization working for peace, justice, and a sustainable future). Most who were not presently involved in grassroots community activities said they want to be once they get established as simple livers.

Overall people in voluntary simplicity don't emphasize conflict with other people or groups. Instead, they describe being engaged in struggle against the dominant culture and a set of cultural views they oppose. Yet simple livers are struggling with other groups who hold different views. Despite their stated reluctance to try to sway others to their perspective, increasingly their publications, workshops, and television programs such as *Affluenza* and *Escape from Affluenza* clearly aim at diffusion of voluntary simplicity ideas and efforts to teach new ways of action and to develop new "strategies of action" (Swidler 1986).

Voluntary simplicity organizations and the networks established among them and with other types of organizations point to a process of institutionalization underway. And as was discussed in chapter 2, Vicki Robin, Cecile Andrews, and Duane Elgin have each started organizations to promote aspects of voluntary simplicity. There are some indications that connections between key movement participants and elites at the institutional level do exist. For instance, Elgin presented a paper to the State of the World Forum, a gathering of world leaders convened by the Gorbachev Foundation in 1997. Vicki Robin spoke at the Earth Summit in Kyoto, Japan, in December of 1997 when the world's nations met to discuss global warming.

At the highest level of meaning (Touraine 1985), voluntary simplicity is a critique of the social and cultural consequences of contemporary corporate capitalism and a call for social democracy. It is a direct critique of the highly rationalized labor process that characterizes many workplaces and an attack on consumerist culture and McDonaldization (Ritzer 2000, 2001). This critique is launched from a personal desire for a higher quality of life than these structures offer and from concern for the environment. People practicing voluntary simplicity recognize that they must survive presently within the for-profit economy, but they do not accept the existing aims of the economy. Most advocate a major change from a profit-driven economy to an environmentally and socially conscious and sustainable economy. Ideas about how to achieve this shift at the institutional level are not well developed in the ideology of the movement and are varied and sometimes even absent from the thinking of informants. But all advocate a major change in the values that form the basis for organizing the economy.

Simple livers are at least equally concerned with materialist concerns as they are postmaterialist ones. During the era in which the contemporary voluntary simplicity movement emerged, the standard of living overall for Americans was stagnant or falling, and simple livers are well aware of this. Americans were increasingly losing their jobs, working longer, not shorter, hours, and facing reduced benefits and perks. But instead of being concerned with getting more, they are concerned with redefining what is enough at a lower level than the dominant culture and then being fulfilled in nonmaterialist ways. Voluntary simplicity material and postmaterial strands can't be separated out and to try to do so does not increase the ability to understand this movement, but would actually reduce understanding of it. Voluntary simplicity enlists people in trying to act in alignment with their values in everyday personal practices but also invites participants to link all of their actions to their deeply held values.

Simple livers have a consciousness of global inequality in access to resources and a sense of their relative privilege over the global poor. Many say they are uncomfortable living in a world where inequalities are so great. They also argue that if the greed of the affluent goes unchecked it will soon result in environmental collapse. They sometimes also point out that if the global poor seek similar levels of affluence achieved by the global affluent, the environmental crisis will speed up and the quality of life for everyone globally will be endangered.

The interests of simple livers cause them to downplay certain sources of power and certain forms of inequality. The analysis in chapter 5 demonstrates how they underestimate the importance of class, gender, and race and ethnicity in reproducing inequitable control over the use of resources and how they downplay their own economic dependence on institutionalized forms of exploitation and their reliance on dominant cultural repertoires in constructing the voluntary simplicity alternative. At the same time it is important to acknowledge the importance of this group's ideological rejection of even typical middle-class U.S. affluence, and to varying degrees the personal practice of people in the movement.

Simple livers advocate changing the fundamental values that underlie current economic practices and consumerist culture to values of community sustainability and quality of life. They generally accept the idea of a market economy and are supportive of small entrepreneurial businesses, but they want the capitalist economy to be organized to provide basic needs for all rather than aimed at profit. Some mention the importance of using quality of life (QOL), Schor (1998) measures rather than GDP (Gross Domestic Product) or GNP (Gross National Product) in evaluating economic practices.

People in voluntary simplicity do want to get out of the wage labor rat race, even professional jobs in it, because they often find the work unpleasant and want to minimize their sense of the control the need to work has over them. But some also want to reduce participation in waged work because they believe it represents participation and dependence on an economy that destroys the environment and produces social injustice.

Demands of labor for safe and healthy work environments, more paid leave, and more control over the labor process are consistent with demands of simple livers. One big difference is that labor movements negotiate for improved circumstances within an acceptance of a growth economy and consumerist culture, and people in voluntary simplicity don't. They want more fundamental change. The breadth of their demands is actually much greater than those of United States labor unions since World War II, which did tend to focus on increasing wages. More recently, during the period of deindustrialization, unions have focused on maintaining jobs rather than on broad labor initiatives to gain a higher level of control and input into labor policy and labor process (Milkman 1997).

In contrast to those who maintain that new social movements are characterized by noneconomic interests, voluntary simplicity is at the center very concerned with economic matters. But these concerns are addressed by the movement primarily through seeking to support changed values and norms of individuals in rejecting occupational status seeking and consumerist values. They are not demanding higher wages for themselves. They are demanding a better quality of life for themselves and this involves their desire to see better living conditions for others too. At the highest level of meaning of the position they take, they want the labor process to be structured based on compliance with measures of quality of life, not on rationalized profit seeking (Schor 1991, 1998). Those who work tend to shift the meaning of work so that it represents a necessary evil or a transition from the need to work to a fully voluntary simplicity lifestyle once enough has been saved. A few find work they consider consistent with their simple living values but most don't. Those who have retired and depend on social security don't focus on their dependence on the state. They tend to critique the state as unable to respond to the need for change to environmental sustainability and social justice.

Informants rarely articulate their position in terms of gaining higher levels of control over specific labor processes because many have arrived at the belief that no existing workplaces are going to be structured in humane ways until a major shift in the aim of the economy is achieved. Many feel the best way to bring about change is simply to avoid participation in the wage labor market if possible. But when work is discussed, desire for a shorter work week (Schor 1991, 1998), less highly rationalized production organization, and work based on simple living values are viewed as desirable. Developing a clearly articulated policy agenda for voluntary simplicity and mobilizing to enact it is one possible direction some in the movement may devote their energies to in the future.

Though not fulfilled completely in practice, the goal of knowing the details of how, where, under what conditions, and by whom goods they buy are made, the nature of the raw materials the products are made from, and how and where those materials are obtained can potentially also move toward unmasking the true relations in the cycle of consumption and production of consumer goods. Of course, the understandings gained are only as good as the knowledge constructed about these processes, making the knowledge always partial.

For simple livers commodities become more than the use value of the goods and can also be seen as an attempt to resist the fetishism of commodities (Marx [1867] 1978, 319–321) that obscures the labor and natural resources that give consumer goods their value. But simple livers also give goods new symbolic meanings based on the true nature they attribute to them. For Marx, the method and process through which natural resources are appropriated and made use of shape human consciousness. When the social relations that make the production of goods possible are not understood by the consumer, the social relations represented in an object come to appear as given and beyond human control (Lury 1996, 42). As mentioned previously, the meaning making of people within the voluntary simplicity movement does not generally include a knowledge of Marx's conceptions. Yet in one way their efforts to gain a knowledge of who makes a product, under what conditions, and with what resources can be understood to be an effort to unmask the fetishism of commodities and to gain access to the story of the unity between production and consumption rather than experience it as reified. Financial pressures, the availability of products, and knowledge about them limit the extent to which simple livers can achieve their ideal consumption practices. Often these limits generate elaboration of ideology that accommodates them while at other times it sparks innovative responses.

But simple livers are also using the meanings they attach to consumer goods and services in their simple living moral identity construction processes and they are engaged in elaborating these meanings. As chapter 5 demonstrates, they unmask some aspects of production and leave in the shadows other aspects that might lead to unsettling realizations about their own continued privilege or sense of agency. Informants rarely expressed concern over the disproportional numbers of racial and ethnic minorities and women who are relegated to exploitation in jobs in the global labor market, instead focusing the few comments they did make about exploitation of workers on differences between the haves and have-nots more generally and none mentioned consumer boycotts aimed at improving working conditions.

No mention was made by informants of overproduction of consumer goods and mechanisms through which goods are dumped globally, either literally in dumps or at outlet malls, while corporate profits are maintained. To give attention to this aspect of corporate practice would reduce the power to bring about change simple livers attribute to their shifts in consumption and point to the need to institute legal limits on the practices of corporations. Perhaps the 1999 World Trade

Organization meeting protests and the involvement of some in voluntary simplicity in the protests may encourage others in the movement to think about these aspects of institutionalized inequality more deeply.

One couple and one single man whom I interviewed sheltered people in attendance at the November, 1999, World Trade Organization (WTO) meeting protests in Seattle. Four members of one of the circles I studied marched in the protests. They don't view these activities as separate from their voluntary simplicity activities but as interconnected with them. These simple livers participate in "co-optable social networks" (Freeman 1975) of people who have some shared concerns and agendas and can be mobilized for action. Still three others in the same circle said they did not take part in the WTO protests, and claim they have shifted to a more cynical view of the global ecological crisis since I interviewed them in June of 1998. Barbara said they had shifted from practicing voluntary simplicity so that others might simply live to practicing it so they could live good lives themselves and nothing more. Whether these emerging patterns of difference will result in two streams within the movement or splinter it remains to be seen.

Luhrs, the editor of the *Simple Living Journal*, discusses the meeting of the WTO in Seattle in the following way:

> The meeting of the WTO . . . in Seattle at the end of the year provided a massive wake-up call to many of us to rethink our place in life—in this coming new millennium, we truly are citizens of the world. What we do, what we buy, what we don't buy, how we conduct our lives affects not only ourselves, but the globe as well. The WTO and the protests that accompanied it brought home the notion that none of us lives in isolation any longer. We are all connected as a global community. . . .
>
> With this new year and new time, let's ask ourselves if we want to make money at the expense of our souls and our planet. Let's ask ourselves if the way we are conducting our daily lives is the best we can do. Let's ask ourselves about the choices we make every day. (2000, 2–3)

This interpretation of the protests is in keeping with the focus on change in personal consumption that characterizes much of the movement literature and discourse and does not shift to discussion of institutionalized inequalities.

As chapter 4 demonstrates, even in their own daily lives, gender inequality continues to play a role. Recognition of gender difference not only gives a richer and more complete understanding of others who are different but it encourages a deeper and fuller knowledge of self and the group to which one belongs. This is also true in the case of class and racial/ethnic difference. Recognition of difference is needed as the basis for establishing overlapping and consciously negotiated grounds of common interest among women and men in the movement and the power over sexual relations of the hetero-gender system (Ingraham 1996, 168–193). The same is true of racial and ethnic inequality. Doing change is far more difficult than wanting change and embracing stated values that support it. Processes and methods to enact the values are required.

The processes advocated by Cecile Andrews for circles are good, but gender and racial and ethnic differences and the norm of hetero-sexuality need to be the explicit focus of discussion along with issues of affluence and poverty. The types of households, communities, and institutions envisioned by different groups can potentially contribute to a much broader range of possibilities for the voluntary simplicity movement to consider. Differences of all sorts within the movement need to be recognized and used to build strength across them instead of having the significance of gender and racial/ethnic differences downplayed and ignored as relevant in voluntary simplicity.

Simple livers want to achieve a sustainable and more egalitarian world and at the same time to feel good about themselves instead of guilty and to blame for the world's injustices. They need to retain control over the use of and access to cultural, social, and economic resources that they have so they can buy time out of the rat race for themselves and at the same time believe they are buying time for the environment by reducing their involvement in consumerist culture. Their need to get by financially and socially requires them to continue to participate in dominant economic relations and culture to some extent. But many make meaning of this participation from a worldview that is critical of it. Their practices often do end up reducing their participation in consumerist activities in comparison to their earlier consumer practices and result in their working less for pay and more as volunteers or in creative endeavors.

The broader changes simple livers aim to bring about are a sustainable global environment, sustainable communities, increased equality in access to resources (though no explicit demands for equality of control over them or their distribution are laid out), and economies aimed at human quality of life rather than profit. The emancipatory politics of the movement are that of both an identity movement and an emergent movement that seeks cultural and economic change. The voluntary movement is in its infancy. The primary mechanisms used by the movement in its earliest contemporary phase are struggle over cultural meanings and self-change. Yet there is mounting evidence of institution-alization of the movement.

The New Road Map Foundation cofounded by Vicki Robin and the late Joe Dominguez is an organization of central importance for the diffusion of the movement through institutional channels. It is an all-volunteer, nonprofit organization staffed by Robin and six other women who live together and give their time to the organization. Other volun-teers also work there. The first offering of a simplicity program at Peaceworks, in the Midwestern college town where I live, was funded by the New Road Map Foundation. The proceeds of *Your Money or Your Life* (1992) go into the New Road Map Foundation and provide the financial resources that the foundation gives to organizations to foster frugality and simple living.

A teleconference Vicki Robin organized in 1999 that involved communities all over the United States and the periodic conferences she organizes are also important forums for network building. Informants in the Seattle area often attend Robin's meetings and two regularly volunteer at the New Road Map Foundation, so they participate in the networks generated.

Another organization that has been gaining strength is the Seeds of Simplicity and the Simplicity Circles Project which Cecile Andrews is affiliated with. The Seeds of Simplicity, directed by Carol Holst, is a Los Angeles-based secular program of the Center for Religion, Ethics, and Social Policy at Cornell University. Andrews is the director of the Simplic-ity Circles Project, aimed at fostering simplicity circles as tools for social transformation. The Seeds of Simplicity gives special emphasis to devel-oping materials to help parents and educators introduce children to the ideas of voluntary simplicity about the importance of reducing consump-tion, the environmental and personal benefits of being critical consumers, and resisting consumerist values. The project has developed curriculum packets for preschool/kindergarten, elementary, and secondary students. They also have materials designed to help parents encourage children to value what they have and resist pressures from their children to buy, and materials that offer alternative activities to engage young people. For instance they offer a booklet on outdoor education that has ideas for outdoor activities. Andrews edits *Seeds & Circles*, the newsletter of the organization. Articles by Andrews and Holst, the program director of the Seeds of Simplicity and founder of the Learning Place preschool in 1981 in the Los Angeles area provide much of the content. They produce an annual membership directory and their organization networks with the

New Road Map Foundation, Center for a New American Dream, Adbusters, and others. The December 2002 issue of the *Cornell Alumni Magazine* featured a cover story that highlights the voluntary simplicity movement and the role of Cornell's Center for Religion, Ethics and Social Policy in supporting the movement. The article is indicative of increasing acceptance of voluntary simplicity ideas among some in the mainstream.

The Seeds of Simplicity has organized conferences that attract large numbers of voluntary simplicity practitioners. The first was held at the University of Southern California Davidson Conference Center in Los Angeles on September 19, 1998. Over one thousand people attended. On August 14, 1999, Andrews was the featured speaker at a "gathering of the circles" held at Rosenfeld Auditorium in Beverly Hills, California. A conference titled "Simplicity: Redefining the Good Life" was held at the Santa Clara Convention Center in Santa Clara, California, on February 12, 2000. A conference titled "No Purchase Necessary II: Building the Voluntary Simplicity Movement" took place at Cornell University in Ithaca, New York, on April 29, 2000.

In June of 2001 a noteworthy meeting signaling the progression of a shift toward institutionalization of networks took place. The Fetzer Institute funded a meeting of people from the "non-profit, academic, commercial, political and literary sectors of the simplicity field" that resulted in the organization of the Simplicity Forum (Cahn 2001). The New Road Map Foundation and the Seeds of Simplicity jointly produced a report of the meeting titled "The Power of Simplicity: An Invitational Dialogue Among Leaders of the Field." The report points to several important developments in the movement. It does not use the term "movement" in the title, though it appears in the text of the report. The report recognizes an emerging leadership of the movement by using the term "leaders of the field" in the title, giving the suggestion that a somewhat more formal and stronger organizational network may be created. The main goal established at the meeting was to develop a policy agenda for the movement around which people can be mobilized.

Theoretical Contributions

Cultural Work and Cultural Movements: The Significance of Power

This book is primarily aimed at understanding the significance of the voluntary simplicity movement through offering an understanding of what the people in the movement are doing, how they are using the movement, and what they are making with it. "Grounded theory" (Glaser and Strauss 1967) that builds theoretical understandings inductively from the data gathered guided the qualitative research that this book is based on. In analysis of the data I have employed theory elaboration that involves applying, synthesizing, integrating, and sometimes reconstructing the sociological work of others in order to enhance understanding of aspects of the social relations and situations that emerged as patterns in the data.

Theoretically one contribution made by this analysis is bringing together reflexive empirical analysis that explores the coconstruction of race, class, and gender and analysis of cultural movements. This approach fosters balanced consideration of the influence of the dominant culture and institutionalized power (Benson 1978; Bourdieu 1984; Collins 1990), the importance of the dynamic identity work of transformative cultural movements (Neitz 1994; Schwalbe 1996; Swidler 1995; Taylor 1996), and shows how the cultural work of the voluntary simplicity movement is shaped by class, race, and gender relations (Collins 1990; Walby 1990). The consideration of multiple and intersecting forms of power as constituting elements has largely been missing in much of the research on new social and cultural movements. In those cases where inequality has been considered, usually one form of inequality has been given salience rather than the intersecting coconstruction of the categories of class, race, and gender through which power moves and is structured (Fantasia 1988; Schwalbe 1996; Taylor 1996).

This research on the voluntary simplicity movement shows how the practical concerns of this group and the problems they are trying to solve have a major impact in motivating people to become engaged not only in a movement but also specifically in the work of culture making and developing alternative practices of seeking change. These concerns and problems, along with the position of relative privilege and biographies of participants, influence choices among the various possibilities offered by cultural traditions.

Through the lens of this type of analysis of voluntary simplicity, culture does not appear as a tightly woven piece of fabric but as a patchwork of many pieces and threads that is always to one degree or another in the process of being unraveled and rewoven. Some pieces of the patchwork may fit tightly with another, while others may hang by a thread.

I have tried throughout analysis to be sensitive to how social-structural factors and power relationships influence symbolic forms (Collins 1990, 1998; Scott 1988). I have also tried to note how cultural forms affect practical activities. One way the study of the voluntary simplicity movement is important is that the analysis of the movement offers access to seeing culture-making processes taking place with new "strategies of action" (Swidler 1986) being crafted in a particular practical context (Swidler 1995) by a particular group of people. The grounded analysis shows that voluntary simplicity is an extension of ordinary cultural life. It is not just a personal choice made by individuals, though individual biographies play a role in bringing people to voluntary simplicity and in the shape the ideology and practices take. Voluntary simplicity also is not a sudden break with past and existing cultural discourse. But it pushes some of the possibilities of existing cultural forms in new directions.

Movement culture, in the case of voluntary simplicity, draws on external, preexisting culture and traditions that are structured in very significant and limiting ways and the movement is constrained by their influence. At the same time, movement participants make use of the diverse and rich possibilities in the culture at hand as a source of agency to construct an alternative (Hays 1994).

People in the voluntary simplicity movement draw on the Puritan heritage of frugality and simplicity. They also draw on the broad heritage of a unified cosmology of meaning found in a variety of religious traditions and in the enlightenment ideology of human self-determination and progress in constructing the alternative ecological ethic that is the ideological foundation upon which voluntary simplicity ideology and practice are elaborated. They rely on the ideals of individual self-sufficiency, personal autonomy, and democratic principles of community even as they reject competitive individualism and greed. They accept a heterosexual norm and an essential understanding of masculine and feminine based on biological sex even as they question the dominant culture's construction of masculinity through competition, domination, and emotional control and claim voluntary simplicity culture offers an alternative in which men can adopt more feminine qualities by choice.

Along with Lefebvre (1971), new social movements theorists in Europe, such as Alberto Melucci (1985, 1989, 1995) and Alain Touraine (1981, 1983, 1985, 1992, 1995), have pointed to the rising prevalence of movements aimed at identity construction and self-actualization that are embedded in and linked to larger social cultural changes taking place in Western twentieth-century societies. Some theorize that this trend is a distinctively postmodern or late modern form of community that serves to replace weakening structures of family, neighborhood, and large-scale institutions in meeting these needs for people in the

United States and Western Europe. The yearning expressed by simple livers for meaningful community and their efforts to create it are in keeping with these findings.

Some new social movements theorists also claim that new social movements displace protest from the economic and political realms. Poletta notes that "analyses of the cultural dimensions of protest have gone some distance in correcting the structuralist and instrumentalist basis of early resource mobilization and political process models" (1997, 431). But she maintains that many studies that incorporate cultural analysis continue to dichotomize conceptions of culture and structure in the emergence of protest. Much work also dichotomizes cultural and instrumental orientations in ongoing collective action. Some work also dichotomizes cultural and political targets of protest. This leads to the neglect of continuities between structured inequalities and the movement challenges made to them. This study gives insight into the coconstructing processes and relationships of these elements and does not rely on dichotomizing them.

Alberto Melucci writes that movements in the last twenty years "have not expressed themselves through political action, but rather have raised cultural challenges to the dominant language, to the codes that organize information and shape social practices" (1995, 41). In the case of voluntary simplicity, at its highest level of meaning (Touraine 1985) this is not fully the case. Protest is aimed at changing the economic and political realms but is consciously launched out of personal self-change and the household and close community instead of in the public political arena. Control over what can be controlled is exerted and then efforts to extend this control in ways that are consistent with voluntary simplicity values are elaborated. It is true the approach is not couched in combative terms or aimed at single political struggles. Instead it is based on change at the local level that provides a shelter for remaking cultural meanings and figuring out ways to meet real local human needs and reduce dependence on the dominant culture and economy to the extent possible.

Countercultural challenge emerges from the "free spaces" (Poletta 1997) of voluntary simplicity circles but they are not spaces where cultural and economic structure is suspended altogether. The importance of free spaces has been noted by many studying cultural movements. For instance, Fantasia (1988) refers to them as "cultures of solidarity," Buechler (1990) as "social movement communities," Melucci (1989) as "oppositional subcultures," Swidler (1995) as "contexts," Fantasia and Hirsch (1995) as "havens," Scott (1990) as "sequestered social sites," Taylor and Whittier (1995) as "spheres of cultural autonomy," and Mueller (1994) as "cultural laboratories." In the case of voluntary simplicity circles we find there are continuities between structured relations and the challenges made to them. The analysis points to the need for movement participants and those who study movements to be alert to the reproduction of asymmetrical social relations even in the free spaces that circles represent.

Voluntary simplicity does not imply a short-term combative approach but a long-term commitment, lived daily and embedded in the local context with solutions being developed from the context. From this perspective voluntary simplicity is potentially a medium through which enduring solidarity to fight on given issues can develop but which is primarily aimed at fundamental change in the way human relationships and the production of life are organized (Collins 1990; Lara 1988; Polletta 1997; Stall and Stoecker 1998). It points to the need for theory that does not dichotomize consideration of political power and cultural challenge (Schwartz and Paul 1992).

Distinctions between New (Cultural) Identity Movements and Old (Social) Materialist Movements: A Cautionary Note

This analysis suggests caution in focusing too much on distinctions between material and postmaterial concerns, economic and political as opposed to cultural and symbolic goals, or expressive versus instrumental forms of action in trying to understand the transformative capacities of emergent cultural movements (Poletta 1997). The voluntary simplicity movement is clearly a cultural movement with strong cultural, symbolic, and expressive components. Indeed these aspects are salient ones. But my analysis also points to strong economic, political, and instrumental elements that could easily be missed if analysis is not sensitive to power as multidimensional in its constitution (Sewell 1992). A reified distinction between cultural and political spheres neglects strategic possibilities that engage in both spheres simultaneously and reject the demarcations that cultural, social, and political structuring reinforces (Poletta 1997; Swidler 1995). Culture inspires, impedes, and shapes collective action (Fantasia 1988; Lefebvre 1971; Swidler 1995).

Power struggles are central in constituting the voluntary simplicity movement and they involve conflict over both ideology and practice. This moves consideration of culture from the individual minds of actors to social practices and locates culture in part in institutionalized practices, in texts, and in discourse (Bourdieu 1977; Collins 1990; Foucault 1977, 1978; Scott 1988; Swidler 1986, 1995). In this tradition there is a range of emphasis on human agency in making use of culture to produce innovative actions versus the powerful effects of structural inequality (Bourdieu 1984), or how systems of categories are reproduced through the actions of people in institutional contexts (Collins 1990; Foucault 1977, 1978; Scott 1988). Culture and power are linked. Class, gender/sexuality, and race/ethnicity are interrelated relationships at the core of which are ongoing processes of exploitation within the present structuring of capitalism and patriarchy (Collins 1990; Walby 1990). Class struggle continues as a feature of contemporary social relations (Fantasia 1988). But class struggle is best understood as both relations between competing centers of accumulation of capital and a complex process in which groups struggle for power to define the basis for legitimate control over and access to resources. Access to and control over resources, which is at the heart of the voluntary simplicity movement struggle, presently is mediated through gender and race/ethnicity and class as constituting elements of culture and economy.

This kind of struggle cannot be explained by conventional economic concepts but instead needs to refer to compelling patterns of social relations which are as much political, cultural, and psychological in their implications as they are economic. Class struggle cannot be understood as narrowly defined and situated in the workplace. But the collective activity of voluntary simplicity, and perhaps other similar groups, needs to be conceived of as activity within a context of conflict and struggle over the ability to define meanings and relationships in terms of substantive justice, not just political representation within existing arrangements (Collins 1990; Eisenstein 1990; Lara 1998; Poletta 1997).

Examining actors' biographies and experience, the processes through which cultural movements emerge and change over time, and the larger forces that shape the motives, ideas, and identities of participants (Swidler 1995)—with a concern with categories through which power moves to transform, challenge, and reproduce existing cultural and economic conditions—reduces the evidence of a sharp dichotomy between postmaterial and material, economic and political, and cultural and symbolic versus instrumental forms of action in the case of the voluntary simplicity movement.

Pushing outward from this grounded study to broader implications suggests the need to reevaluate the way new social movements have been distinguished from earlier social movements and to follow the development of cultural movements over time. There is a problem in viewing such movements as ideologically homogenous entities because they are fluid and emergent, respond to external opportunities as well as constraints, and are actively worked on by participants whose experiences in networks and with each other in collectivities of circles, meetings, volunteering for voluntary simplicity organizations and other activities elaborate the ideology and practices advocated by the movement.

The community-building process and the ways people relate are important in understanding the type of transformative capacity that movements generate and this is not fixed but, just as grievances that are central may change over time and opportunities in the environment may change, so too ways of relating may change. Presently, the most salient concern of the voluntary simplicity movement is the demand for people (at this point acknowledgedly primarily themselves) to have a higher level of control over the aims toward which the work they do is oriented and the way they spend their life's energy, but in the time I have been studying the movement, shifts toward broader concerns among some subgroups in circles have emerged as have evidence of increasing engagement in the same networks.

The idea that new cultural movements such as voluntary simplicity aim primarily at personal freedom rather than power and that they are expressive rather than strategic needs to be questioned because, as analysis of the sources of personal freedom and autonomy of simple livers shows, some degree of power is needed to achieve it. The greater prominence of new social movements points to the alteration of the form of appearance and quality of struggles for power within capitalist patriarchy and a shift in the balance of forces. This analysis suggests the importance of employing a multilevel analysis that examines the individuals who are carriers of the culture; the ideas and practices that make up the culture (Hall and Neitz 1993, 239); the circles, workshops, and other networks people participate in; and the broader cultural and economic forces that constrain, support, and shape the movement (Benson 1977; Collins 1990) simultaneously (as dialectically related) in order to understand new cultural movements. This form of analysis highlights the importance of nonhomogenous features of cultural movements, as well as those that point to similarities among participants, types of grievances, ways of acticulating concerns, and ways of organizing. Using this approach reveals that cultural challenge, which can play a significant role in destabalizing structural arrangements, is itself structured (Poletta 1997; Swidler 1995).

Gender

Voluntary simplicity also offers the beginning of a profound critique of the cultural construction of gender inequality, but fails to link the critique of polarized masculine and feminine gender roles and gendered household reproductive work and consumption to institutionalized patterns of sex discrimination or to the ongoing need for people to problematize gendered power in all contexts of their lives as an ongoing challenge. Simple livers say they don't want to participate in gender-based domination and subordination, and the gender roles they have rejected represent a significant shift. The breadwinner role is rejected among men in voluntary simplicity. Women and men in couples share reproductive work. Women and men are tending away from marriage, a primary location of institutionalized gender inequality. Women and men are not choosing motherhood and fatherhood and often view these as conscious choices. But they continue to view the heterosexual nuclear family and having children as the norm and see themselves as personally different. They tend to arrange their own lives so they don't have to deal with gender power imbalances overtly.

Walby's (1990) theory that the dominant location of patriarchy has shifted from private to public patriarchy in the twentieth century and that this makes the individual form of appropriation less central and a collective form more prevalent is supported by the gender relations found in the movement. This analysis extends the understanding of how this shift is experienced by a particular group, people in voluntary simplicity circles, based on their intersecting statuses of class, race, ethnicity, and sexuality/gender. The lines between friendship and sexuality drawn by the dominant culture, which Walby points out are historically constructed, hold among simple livers. But their daily practices diverge from the boundaries defined by patriarchy as normal relationships. For instance many of the women are strongly woman identified and ambivalent about having heterosexual relationships with men. Bringing a cultural analysis (Neitz 1994) into the analysis of the patriarchal mode of production, patriarchal relations in paid work, and patriarchal relations in cultural institutions and how they shape and are shifted by the voluntary simplicity movement enriches understanding about the process of crafting a cultural alternative. At the same time this approach provides access to the variable ways the structures of patriarchy described by Walby (1990) are felt and responded to in the daily lives of simple livers by linking the analysis of the intersections of gender, race, and class inequalities with analysis of efforts to bring about cultural change.

The analysis of the significance of gender in the voluntary simplicity movement in this book supports Stall and Stoecker's (1998) theory of gendered styles of community organizing. I drew on their analysis because it supported my findings, but in so doing I was able to extend their findings at the organizational level to an analysis of the individual and interpersonal level in simplicity circles and voluntary simplicity networks. Stall and Stoecker don't give much systematic evidence for their claims that the Alinsky model (emphasizing opposition to other groups, confrontation in the public sphere, individualism, and domination in the form of transforming others) appeals more to men and the women-centered model (which emphasizes community building from the private sphere, collectivism, caring, mutual respect, and self-transformation) appeals more to women. These two ideal-type kinds of approaches of community organizing are actually participated in by both women and men, so it is useful that my analysis demonstrates from qualitative data that, in the case of voluntary simplicity participants, men do tend to adopt characteristics of the Alinsky approach more often and women practice the women-centered model more. In this way I provide support for their argument and deepen the evidence that the orientation is not just lodged at the organizational level but is generated from biographical, cultural, and structural locations of men and women.

Race/Ethnicity

In keeping with Frankenberg's findings about white women, I find that simple livers employ "discursive repertoires" (1993, 2) to conceal their racial privileges. I show that these repertoires sometimes conceal or explain away their relative privilege as white people and that they also sometimes offer "race cognizant" explanations of the disadvantages of racial and ethnic minorities. They are sensitive to the disadvantages of being nonwhite but not to the relationship of that disadvantage to the advantage of whites. This analysis provides a close accounting of the way people in the voluntary simplicity movement engage in trying to redefine the meaning of whiteness even as they conceal the race work they are doing by constructing it as a struggle to replace the category of greedy, middle-class Western people, who they believe they look like, with a caring, frugal, Western (white) identity. Frankenberg examines discourses of individual white women about race. This analysis examines individuals participating in a cultural movement and using the discourse of the movement to engage in a collective struggle to redefine the meaning of whiteness and to reconstruct it through voluntary simplicity as a good, moral, and still-hidden category.

Conclusion

Whether voluntary simplicity movement groups will branch out to more systematically organized collective action, take on more traditional political agendas, build coalitions with a diverse range of other groups, or continue to keep the focus primarily on self-change will be influenced by the political context and actions of people in the movement, and remains to be seen. There are indications, as previously discussed, that formation of a still loosely bounded but somewhat more cohesive and identifiable network of people involved in voluntary simplicity is underway.

The line between cultural and political transformation is not clean or definitive among movement participants. This research suggests that dichotomizing cultural and political protest may not be helpful in understanding the transformative capacity of movements such as voluntary simplicity. Though the circles I studied have not organized for political action in the traditional sense, some members of circles do participate in networks that are more oriented toward political action and they don't draw clear lines between their voluntary simplicity practices and politics. Movement leaders are increasingly interested in developing a movement policy agenda and ability to mobilize movement participants to support policy initiatives. How successful their efforts will be remains to be seen.

As I've said earlier, I chose to study voluntary simplicity because it resonated with me as hopeful. It still does. But I don't believe, as many simple livers, at least at times, do, that self-change in keeping with the prescriptions of voluntary simplicity will result in an evolutionary shift to an ecological era without major political and economic shifts that will need to be achieved through policies aimed at structural and cultural change as well. Voluntary simplicity, as it is lived by the simple livers I studied, offers support for taking action daily, encourages people to look for alternative ways of organizing community, and offers critique of some aspects of the capitalist economy, patriarchy, and consumerist culture. The critique is more powerful, though still incomplete in my view, than the ability of the prescribed solutions to deliver the desired results.

Corporations regularly overproduce, dump the overproduction, and still make a profit. Buying less may produce change in production practices over time, but large numbers of people will have to participate in organized consumer boycotts to put greater pressure on corporations to improve their practices. Quitting midlevel professional jobs is unlikely to open up jobs for the poor since they often lack the educational credentials and cultural capital necessary to be hired for such jobs.

Legislation to limit the ownership capacities of transnational corporations and monopolies needs to be brought about if the economy is going to be moved away from pursuit of profit to social democratic aims, and this will require political action, which can take many forms, among them diffusion of voluntary simplicity ideas through media which has already begun. But the ideas of voluntary simplicity need to be developed to link their complaints and demands to clearly articulated and plausible policies that can be carried into existing political structures to bring about institutional change, as unwieldy and frustrating as such work may be, and as much as we may wish those structures were already different. Protestors against the World Trade Organization and corporate accountability advocates offer such links for voluntary simplicity movement participants. Other movements also offer possible alliances and networking opportunities for people in voluntary simplicity. Greater efforts to organize new workers by the AFL-CIO; increasing antisweatshop organizing by students and labor advocates; increased attention to environmental racism and emerging alliances with labor advocates; and the relative rise in welfare rights and antipoverty activism are presently taking place (Reese 2000, 1, 2001).

The challenge for people in the voluntary simplicity movement, who are committed to achieving the broader goals they claim, is to hold onto their commitment to personal change while they shift their concerns outward to the institutional level to engage in organized resistance and in their communities to engage in a higher level of recognition of difference and commonality. Underestimating the importance of difference all too easily results in slipping into reproducing the inequalities associated with the differences. It all too easily results in discounting the need for input from those situated differently from ourselves in devising our solutions. Too easily we are then able to view ourselves as the given norm. Too easily the solutions arrived at fit what is comfortable for us as a group. Reflexivity benefits our understanding of ourselves as social beings whose very sense of self, group belonging, and others is culturally and economically constructed. If simplicity groups grapple with how to bring about the changes they desire at the institutional level and to find common ground with other groups in the same concrete ways they have used to achieve personal-level change, the movement has great promise.

This sociological analysis points to further actions that those who envision the kind of relationships and practices that voluntary simplicity at the highest level of meaning (Touraine 1985) represents can take to contribute to the shifts they say they want to make. In concluding this analysis I offer the following ideas for improving the emancipatory capacity of the movement in the hopes that they may be useful in bringing us closer to goals we share.

Coalition Building

1. Build an institutional infrastructure that links existing voluntary simplicity organizations and can provide the base for creating networks and coalitions with other groups.

2. Share knowledge and build coalitions with the poor and racial and ethnic minorities based on common concerns such as environmental pollution, environmental dumping, exposure to hazardous materials, and adequate social services. Recognize that the poor and ethnic and racial minorities can contribute to the ideas, practices, and agendas of voluntary simplicity in significant ways and actively seek ways to bring them into the discussions within the movement.

3. Recognize and use overlapping concerns of labor and voluntary simplicity, since working-class laborers are often the victims of the toxic effects of industry, and labor would benefit from a shorter work week and higher levels of control over the aims to which industry is put.

4. Link with political parties that have platforms consistent with voluntary simplicity values and goals without giving up a focus on self and grassroots change and community building. The New Party and Green Party are two that have platforms that are compatible with many of the ideas held by people in the movement.[3]

5. Build coalitions with the academic community and invite research and teaching about voluntary simplicity.

6. Build networks and coalitions with nongovernmental organizations with common concerns.

Improving Participation and Recognition across Difference within the Movement

7. Institute methods for increasing the awareness of difference in circles and create ways of building strength across differences rather than just tolerating, denying, or glossing over them. Figure out ways to use recognition of differences to strengthen the movement and to bring marginalized people, including the poor and racial and ethnic minorities, into the movement as full participants.[4]

8. Recognize the importance of race and analyze whiteness as a feature that is significant to the movement and the people attracted to it. Recognize more completely the relative advantage whiteness provides. Instead of discounting it as significant for the movement, keep the question of being privileged open for review.

9. Recognize the importance of gender inequality as a barrier to equitable decision making about access to and distribution of resources. Problematize the institutions of patriarchy, not just the dominant cultural roles and behaviors of men and women. Question the heterosexual norm and other forms of institutionalized gender inequality.

10. Recognize gender power tensions within the movement and the implications they have for the way the movement is organized and the form it may take if it expands. Follow the women-centered model (Stall and Stoecker 1998) of organizing and question the emergence of competitive, hierarchical ways of organizing so that a voluntary simplicity community will be a model of process that continues to strive to be inclusive, respectful of difference and autonomy, cooperative, and noncompetitive. This is, of course, an ideal that is never perfectly achieved but it is worth striving for. In the short run, those who value the women-centered model which is at the heart of voluntary simplicity ideology (Andrews 1997) need to stand up for their desired approach and encourage those who try to dominate circle agendas to be reflexive and to stop.

Extending the Politics of the Movement

11. Open movement ideology up to recognition of the connections between inequality and sex- and race-segregated work. Recognize how racial and ethnic minorities and women are systematically used as the source for generating surplus value for capitalist corporations as one way of producing profit and investment dividends. Develop practices to reduce participation in these modes of exploitation.

12. Demand the right for all to have work that provides a living wage and humane working conditions with reasonable hours of work. Don't focus just on the right of the affluent to reject undesirable long hours of work and ways of helping them figure out how to opt out.

13. Recognize that in the present economy chances are that your survival and having enough comes from resources derived not only from the earth but at least in part from work—if not your own, then someone else's. Gain a more complete understanding of the relations between investment income and the oppression of others through inhumane work conditions and environmentally damaging practices. Recognize and problematize how simple livers continue to be dependent on a profit-and-growth-driven economy. Adopt socially and environmentally conscious investing if you invest. Imperfect though the options may be, it is potentially just as effective a signal to the market as environmentally sustainable consumption practices are.

14. Recognize that while avoiding consumerist practices is important and helpful, it won't necessarily be enough to change the profit-driven economy or cause corporations to adopt environmentally sensitive production methods in a timely way. Policies that legally limit corporate practices are necessary too. Add boycotts of products and specific corporations to the already highly elaborated guidelines for sustainable consumption practices of the movement. Link with other groups engaged in such boycotts.[5]

15. Develop an important role in crafting policy (perhaps even establish a political party that has a policy agenda based on the values of voluntary simplicity) at the grassroots and more broadly, joining with other groups with similar concerns to advocate beneficial policy changes such as legally limiting corporate practices that damage the environment and are unjust.[6]

The participation in community life, volunteer work, and economic transactions of simple livers—who at the same time take an oppositional stance toward a taken-for-granted profit-driven economy, rationalized waged work, and consumerist culture—is a stance that can generate change since it brings simple livers into contact with many nonsimple livers. It is a balancing act for movement participants since they must constantly do ideological work to establish their difference at the same time they depend on many features of the dominant culture for their survival and sense of identity and draw upon it to elaborate the alternative they are advocating.

Audre Lorde (1984) says you can't dismantle the master's house using the master's tools. But any tools we make, even those that are aimed at opposition, are, at least in part, created in the context of our relations to that house. The people in the voluntary simplicity movement deserve credit for their struggle to fashion new tools. I have tried to acknowledge the limitations of these tools, in their present forms, since in their present embodiment within the lives of simple livers they only partially fulfill the goals simple livers have for emancipatory change. Simple livers are resourceful people with good intentions. They take from the culture pieces that they perceive to fit their purposes, combine them in new ways, craft new meanings with them, and create something new that does shift and transform some relationships. But they don't bring with them only their intended and chosen tools. Their own relative power brings with it aspects of the dominant culture and economy that remain hidden from the full view of simple livers. Even when a group creates an oppositional safe space from which to speak, as those in voluntary simplicity are doing, there are forces at the biographical, cultural, and institutional levels that impinge on the oppositional impulses. At the present moment they are engaged in a dialectical process of changing understandings and material relations (Benson 1977) that holds the possibility of taking many different directions.

Those playing major roles in institutionalizing the movement have begun to create organizations aimed at cultural change through voluntary simplicity and to direct the resources they have toward diffusion of the ideas. The resources they have include their creative use of culture in constructing an alternative ideology and innovative alternative practices that resonate well with increasing numbers of participants whose biographical histories and current social and economic circumstances it both reflects and responds to. Other resources are monies from book sales, highly skilled volunteers who work for no wage, and networks that give them broad access for diffusion of ideas about voluntary simplicity. These are powerful resources.

The voluntary simplicity cultural movement is struggling with dominant cultural definitions of what constitutes right livelihood and what values should direct the economy and culture. This suggests that, at least in the case of this cultural movement, efforts to generate change extend beyond identity work into a struggle to define what right livelihood is and what constitutes desirable community, culture, and economy. At the highest level of meaning people in voluntary simplicity are engaged in a cultural struggle over the power to say what constitutes moral action for those they define as affluent people. People in the movement carry their voluntary simplicity values and practices into their communities. They elaborate the ideology, practices, and agendas of the movement and institutionalization of it is underway.

When I show *Escape from Affluenza* in my classes at the midwestern university where I teach, the students often say they believe the ideas are good and right but that they could never adopt such extreme practices. These practices do not seem extreme to me anymore. I have to remind myself that voluntary simplicity represents a major shift that is presently unthinkable for most people in my sociology classes and the larger society. The breadth of the influence of voluntary simplicity in twentieth-century America remains to be seen. Much depends on how efforts at diffusion proceed, whether deeper recognition of difference is addressed, and how simple livers elaborate the ideology and practices. Much also depends on changes in the broader culture and economy, how the process of globalization impacts the United States, and how other groups seeking change make meaning of these changes and respond to them.

The energy that adopting voluntary simplicity generates in informants and the emergent quality of the ideas and practices of the movement suggest we will be hearing more from the voluntary simplicity cultural movement in the months and years to come.

Appendix

Selected Voluntary Simplicity Resources

Organizations

Center for a New American Dream
6930 Carroll Ave., Suite 900
Takoma Park, MD 20912
Phone: (Toll Free) 1-877-68-DREAM or 301-891-3683
Fax: 301-891-3684
E-mail: newdream@newdream.org
Internet: www.newdream.org

New Road Map Foundation
P.O. Box 15981
Seattle, WA 98115-0981
Internet: http://www.newroadmap.org/default.asp

Seeds of Simplicity
P.O. Box 9955
Glendale, CA 91226
Phone: (Toll Free) 1-877-UNSTUFF or Phone & Fax: 818-247-4332
Internet: http://www.seedsofsimplicity.org

Journals, Magazines, and Internet Sites

Enough!: A Quarterly Report on Consumption, Quality of Life and the Environment
Published quarterly by the Center for a New American Dream
6930 Carroll Ave., Suite 900

Takoma Park, MD 20912
Phone: (Toll Free) 1-877-68-DREAM or 301-891-3683
Fax: 301-891-3684
E-mail: newdream@newdream.org
Internet: www.newdream.org

Seeds & Circles: Quarterly Newsletter of Seeds of Simplicity/
The Simplicity Circles Project
Published quarterly by Seeds of Simplicity
P.O. Box 9955
Glendale, CA 91226
Phone: (Toll Free) 1-877-UNSTUFF or Phone & Fax: 818-247-4332
Internet: http://www.seedsofsimplicity.org

Simple Living: The Journal of Voluntary Simplicity
Published quarterly by the Simple Living Press
4509 Interlake Ave. N., PMB 149
Seattle, WA 98103-6773
Phone: 206-464-4800
Internet: http://www.simpleliving.net/default.asp
The Web of Simplicity internet site at http://www.simpleliving.net/
resource–database/introduction.asp makes available an extensive
bibliography of books and other resources on voluntary simplicity
and provides reviews.

Selected Annotated Bibliography of Voluntary Simplicity Literature

Andrews, Cecile. 1997. *The Circle of Simplicity: Return to the Good Life.* New York: Harper Collins. Andrews is a central figure in the voluntary simplicity movement. She started the first simplicity circles in Seattle. This book discusses the ills of contemporary consumerist society and suggests how to simplify one's life, reduce environmental degradation, and build community in seven steps using support groups called simplicity circles. Many simplicity circles use this book to guide the circle discussions. Andrews is director of the Circles of Simplicity project affiliated with the Seeds of Simplicity Program of the Center for Religion, Ethics and Social Policy at Cornell University that she and Carol Benson Holst head.

Blix, Jacqueline, and David Heitmiller. 1997. *Getting a Life: Strategies for Simple Living, Based on the Revolutionary Program for Financial Freedom, Your Money or Your Life*. New York: Viking. Blix and Heitmiller, self described former yuppies, describe how they used Dominguez and Robin's (1992) nine-step program successfully. The introduction is by Dominguez and Robin. Blix and Heitmiller explain how they gained financial independence, quit work, and reduced consumption. They say they now are able to spend more time with family, volunteering, and on personal growth. The book includes the stories of over forty people, including themselves, who have used the *Your Money or Your Life* program to gain financial independence.

Callenbach, Ernest. 1993. *Living Cheaply with Style*. Berkeley, Calif.: Ranin Publishing, Inc. Callenbach offers advice and prescribes ways to live cheaply. The introduction links frugality, health and happiness, and environmental sustainability with the green triangle, a model Callenbach first described in his 1975 futuristic utopian novel, *Ecotopia*, which is cited by Dominguez and Robin (1992) and Andrews (1997).

Dominguez, Joe, and Vicki Robin. 1992. *Your Money or Your Life: Transforming Your Relationship with Money and Achieving Financial Independence*. New York: Penguin. This book outlines a nine-step plan for gaining financial security, escaping the rat race, reducing conspicuous consumption, and living in keeping with your values. The book is based on self-help seminars that the late Joe Dominguez and Vicki Robin, who runs the New Road Map Foundation in Seattle, developed to share the method conceived by Joe Dominguez. The process involves analyzing the use of money in one's daily life, calculating the life energy cost of working for a wage, and reducing consumption based on understanding how much life energy each purchase costs and deciding if it is really worth it. The authors advocate reducing expenditures and increasing savings so that over time you can live off of investment income, which they suggest be put in Treasury bonds. The crossover point where your investment income meets your expenditures brings financial independence. This book is central for most people in the voluntary simplicity movement and is used in many circles. The organization that the authors formed, the New Road Map Foundation, funds organizations and projects that focus on educating people about simple living and frugality or promote such practices with proceeds of book sales.

Elgin, Duane. 1993. *Voluntary Simplicity: Toward a Way of Life That Is Outwardly Simple, Inwardly Rich*. New York: William Morrow. This book was first published in 1981 and reprinted in 1993. It gave the contemporary voluntary simplicity movement its name. Elgin borrowed the term from the work of Richard Gregg, a Quaker and student of Ghandi's whose writings about voluntary simplicity in the 1930s inspired him. Elgin argues that an evolutionary cultural shift toward voluntary simplicity is underway and that simple livers are on the front edge of this shift. He writes that the choices human beings make will determine the direction that evolutionary change takes. Environmental apocalypse can be prevented if human beings orient themselves toward sufficiency, not overconsumption on a global scale. Elgin has since published *Awakening Earth: Exploring the Evolution of Human Culture and Consciousness* (1993) and *Promise Ahead: A Vision of Hope and Action for Humanity's Future* (2001) with an introduction by Vicky Robin. Elgin codirects Our Media Voice *(www.ourmediavoice.org)*, an organization aimed at fostering media accountability.

Fogler, Michael. 1997. *Un-Jobbing: The Adult Liberation Handbook*. Lexington, Ky.: Free Choice Press. Fogler, who works part-time as the director for the Central Kentucky Council for Peace and Justice, guides readers to reject the cultural obsession with jobs and consumption because it is destroying the planet and makes people miserable. He employs Callenbach's (1993) green triangle concept in arguing for the benefit of working less and only earning what you need to live with sufficiency. But he suggests making Callenbach's green triangle into a square that includes the need to create community. This book represents an approach to finding your "right livelihood" that is in the voluntary simplicity genre. Fogler was a speaker at the Seeds of Simplicity Conference in Los Angeles in September 1998, one of the first efforts to bring people involved in voluntary simplicity together to develop a collective agenda.

Heffern, Rich. 1994. *Adventures in Simple Living: A Creation-Centered Spirituality*. New York: Crossroads. Heffern, assistant editor of *Praying*, a bimonthly magazine on prayer and spirituality published in Kansas City, advocates voluntary simplicity as a way to lead a spiritually rich life that is also just and environmentally benign. He asks some questions that are characteristic of the voluntary simplicity literature, such as "What is enough?" He discusses the joys of frugality. But he puts more emphasis overall on the wonder of the natural world and the joys of living in relationship to the earth. He writes about his experience of the power, beauty, bounty, and peace offered by living close to the earth during the time he spent living on a communal farm in the Missouri Ozarks and encourages readers to capture the wonder of their relationship to all creation in their daily lives, no matter where they live, by adopting simple living. Heffern emphasizes the simple living connection with spirituality.

Levering, Frank, and Wanda Urbanska. 1993. *Simple Living: One Couple's Search for a Better Life.* New York: Penguin. Levering and Urbanska are another couple who decided the psychic cost of being in the fast lane was too high. They moved back to the Blue Ridge Mountains of Virginia to run an orchard owned by Levering's family. They describe their experience and offer suggestions for others wanting to simplify their lives. Urbanska, a former journalist, narrated much of *Escape from Affluenza,* the PBS television show about problems with the affluent lifestyle that presents the voluntary simplicity perspective.

Longacre, Doris Janzen. 1980. *Living More with Less.* Scottdale, Pa.: Herald Press. Longacre points to compassion for those in need as a reason to practice voluntary simplicity. She rejects the "me oriented" culture, placing the spiritual aspects of a simple life at the center of her concern. She discusses how to simplify in the areas of food, housing, clothing, and celebrations. Her book includes letters from people describing how they have simplified.

Luhrs, Janet. 1997. *The Simple Living Guide: A Sourcebook for Less Stressful, More Joyful Living.* New York: Broadway Books. Luhrs, a former lawyer, has gathered together materials from the *Simple Living Journal,* of which she is editor and publisher, and organized them under the topics of time, money, inner simplicity, work, simple pleasures and romance, virtues, families, holidays, cooking and nutrition, health and exercise, housing, clutter, gardening, and travel. Because Luhrs is the mother of young children she also takes an interest in issues of how to be a successful simple living parent. Luhrs is well known among simple livers and central in the movement.

McKibben, Bill. 1998. *Hundred Dollar Holiday*. New York: Simon and Schuster. McKibben offers suggestions on how to limit holiday spending to one hundred dollars and reclaim Christmas as a time for family happiness and reflection about how our lifestyles impact on the earth. He developed the idea for his rural United Methodist church conference a decade ago but it has become popular in voluntary simplicity more recently. He describes family traditions of giving that can replace market goods. For instance, he carved walking sticks as gifts and his wife has a tradition of painting him a plate featuring the highlights of their year. McKibben is an environmentalist who has written another book titled *Maybe One* (1998) in which he calls for limiting family size.

Nearing, Helen, and Scott Nearing. 1989. *The Good Life: Helen and Scott Nearing's Sixty Years of Self-Sufficient Living*. New York: Schocken Books. The Nearings were leaders in the back-to-the-land movement in the 1930s and many in the contemporary voluntary simplicity movement mention them as important role models despite the fact that the contemporary movement is primarily urban. This volume brings together in a new one-volume edition *Living the Good Life* (1954) and *Continuing the Good Life* (1979).

New Road Map Foundation. 1990. *How Earth-Friendly Are You? A Lifestyle Self-Assessment Questionnaire*. Seattle: New Road Map Foundation. This thirty-one-page pamphlet invites readers to examine how their lifestyle choices impact on the environment. It provides questions about the following categories: energy, consumption, living space, money/work, diet, health, recreation, education, religion/spirituality, family, and community participation. Each category asks questions from three perspectives: ecological (how your behavior affects others); economic (your financial choices); and personal values (what you value and believe). At the end of each section of the questionnaire readers are asked to rate their level of satisfaction with their practices and to outline changes they will make in the next six months, with an action plan for the coming week. This booklet is often used in study groups.

Pierce, Linda Breen. 2000. *Choosing Simplicity: Real People Finding Peace and Fulfillment in a Complex World*. Carmel, Calif.: Gallagher Press. Breen includes accounts from over two hundred people in forty states and eight countries who have simplified their lives. She offers advice for those who may want to simplify and recounts the experiences of people who have done so. Vicki Robin wrote the forward. This book advocates adopting the simple life and documents how people of different ages, circumstances, and backgrounds have chosen to live simply.

Notes

———•◦•———

Chapter 1. Voluntary Simplicity: A Cultural Movement

1. Joe Dominguez and Vicki Robin's voluntary simplicity book titled *Your Money or Your Life: Transforming Your Relationship with Money and Achieving Financial Independence* (1992) advocates cutting consumption, saving, and investing to reduce dependence on income from waged work and have more time doing fulfilling activities such as volunteer work. By 1999 over 750,000 copies had sold and a new edition was published. The book advocates making conscious choices that align how you use your money and time with your values. The authors call this "financial integrity." The book aims to help the reader achieve financial independence by tracking all expenditures, evaluating them based on financial integrity, and reducing consumption to the point that the individual establishes as enough. Meanwhile the person saves as much as possible and invests it (the authors recommend investment in Treasury bills). They provide a method of putting in place and carrying through a plan that reduces consumption, increases savings, and allows the reader to create a plan for not working for pay or reducing work significantly through living frugally and saving enough to live off of investment income.

2. Here, Etzioni (1998) is referring to Joe Dominguez, one of the authors of *Your Money or Your Life*, a book used by many in simplicity circles as a guide to simplifying their lives. Joe Dominguez was a major player in the voluntary simplicity movement until his death in 1997. Vicki Robin, coauthor of the book, continues to devote her time to giving away the proceeds from book sales through the New Road Map Foundation, which contributes to organizations that promote simple living. I am unclear as to why Etzioni (1998) classifies Dominguez as a "stong simplifier" rather than a part of the "voluntary simplicity movement." Those in voluntary simplicity certainly claim him as part of the movement. This points to the limitations of trying to understand an unbounded cultural movement such as the voluntary simplicity movement by imposing categories onto the movement participants without doing grounded research that offers access to understanding how they establish the boundaries of the voluntary simplicity movement.

Chapter 2. The Ecological Ethic and the Spirit of Voluntary Simplicity

1. I had first read about the movement in a *New York Times* article. Carey Goldberg's September 21, 1995, article was titled "Choosing the Joys of a Simplified Life." The article mentioned a guide for simple living circles by Cecile Andrews, whose book, of course, had not yet been published.

2. A key informant from the movement in Seattle has consulted with me on the analysis of the literature and has confirmed what my research indicates, that these are the three core texts of the movement.

3. They were produced in Seattle by KCTS/Seattle and Oregon Public Broadcasting and made possible by a grant from the Pew Charitable Trusts.

4. Vicki Robin, Cecile Andrews, and Duane Elgin have developed an interest in Brian Swimme and Thomas Berry's book *The Universe Story from the Primordial Flaring Forth to the Ecozoic Era: A Celebration of the Unfolding of the Cosmos* (1992) and Swimme's (1996) *The Hidden Heart of the Cosmos: Humanity and the New Story.* Swimme, characterized as an "empirical mystic" (Scharper 1997, 30) and Berry, termed a "cultural historian" (Blewett 1993, 28), describe a new period in history called the Ecozoic era in which changes in the environment and the major role of humans converge and humanity has taken over control of the earth's life systems to a much greater extent. The Ecozoic period must emphasize the interrelationship of all life in the universe rather than the separateness of things. They view the earth, the universe even, as an organism which cannot survive in fragments. The natural community exists in balance and humans have not practiced reciprocity with the earth; this is the cause of the environmental problems. Swimme and Berry (1992) maintain that humans are destroying the conditions for the renewal of life, and the world humans have created is worse than the natural human condition it sought to replace.

5. In *The Protestant Ethic and the Spirit of Capitalism*, Max Weber ([1904] 1958) maintians that it was Protestant value for salvation through hard work in a calling, frugality, and self-denial that lead to the accumulation of capital that enabled Western capitalism to emerge as dominant. In one way voluntary simplicity can be seen as an attempt to resist the rationalization process associated with the industrial revolution and modernity described by Weber as the "iron cage." Perhaps even more appropriately, the efforts to resist jobism and consumerism on the part of simple livers can be seen as resistance to "McDonaldization" or hyperrationalization that characterizes present day consumerism described by George Ritzer in *The McDonaldization of Society* (2000).

6. The shift from traditional to modern modes of production, of course, was not accepted easily in the first place, as Marx (1978), Polanyi (1944), E. P. Thompson (1963), and Sonya Rose (1992) as well as others have demonstrated. There was considerable resistance to the great transformation (Polanyi 1944). There is sociological evidence that another such transformation from Fordist and modernist economic relations and culture to postindustrial and

postmodern ones is well underway (Aronowitz and DiFazio 1994; Baudrillard 1975, 1988; Bauman 1992; Bell 1973; Clegg 1990; Giddens 1990; Habermas 1987, 1992; Harvey 1989). Bauman suggests consumption is replacing earlier forms of repression in contemporary Western societies as a form of control. In one way the voluntary simplicity movement can be understood as a form of resistence to this repression.

7. In *An Essay on Culture: Symbolic Structure and Social Structure* (1995), Bennett Berger describes his development of the concept of ideological work while doing research on counterculture communes in rural California:

> I developed the concept of 'ideological work'—in part to describe the efforts of communards to cope intellectually with discrepancies, discontinuities, and apparent contradictions between the beliefs that they brought to communal life and the constraints of actually living with those beliefs in a communal environment. But I also used 'ideological work' to defend myself (and, by extension, any ethnographer so situated) against the passion with which my communards were telling me what they believed as persuasively as they could. When people talk passionately about what they believe regarding matters on which several beliefs are possible, plausible, available, and accessible, sociological interpretation is invited by that fact, and it seemed to me that I could not thoroughly understand the meanings of what they were telling me unless I could relate those beliefs to the structure of the specific circumstances in which the believers were more or less stuck (that cognitive tactic, of course, helped me defend myself against their passion). Although "more or less" is an important qualifier, "stuck" is the operative term here because it is seldom easy to change one's basic social situation. It is usually less difficult to alter or modify one's beliefs (probably imperceptibly or gradually but sometimes quite suddenly or abruptly) so that they seem more reasonable, prudent, or realistic (or otherwise persuasive) given the limits and possibilities of one's position. (79)

8. Weber's theory of rationalization is used here to refer to the way formal rationality that emphasizes calculability, efficiency, predictability, bureaucratic control, and use of nonhuman technology is a central constituting element of contemporary capitalist economy and organizations that simple livers experience as oppressive. However simple livers also draw upon formal rationality in seeking to escape the "iron cage." For instance, some keep detailed records of their expenses and savings, work to make the most efficient use of food, clothing, and other consumables, and calculate the time it took them to earn the amount of money before spending on an experience or product so they can evaluate whether it is worth the cost. But they tend to reject bureaucratic ways of organizing and to critique the unquestioning adoption of nonhuman technology.

Chapter 3. Getting a Life: Constructing a Moral Identity in the Voluntary Simplicity Movement

1. The definition of hegemony that I use is drawn from Connell's discussion of it: " 'Hegemony' means (as in Gramsci's analyses of class relations in Italy from which the term is borrowed) a social ascendancy achieved in a play of social forces that extends beyond contests of brute power into the organization of private life and cultural processes. . . .

'[H]egemony' does not mean total cultural dominance, the obliteration of alternatives. It means ascendancy achieved within a balance of forces, that is, a state of play. Other patterns and groups are subordinated rather than eliminated" (1987, 184).

2. My conception of hegemonic masculinity draws from Connell's theorization of "hegemonic masculinity" and "emphasized femininity":

> [T]here is an ordering of versions of femininity and masculinity at the level of the whole society, in some ways analogous to the patterns of face-to-face relationship within institutions. The possibilities of variation of course, are vastly greater. The sheer complexity of relationships involving millions of people guarantees that ethnic differences and generational differences as well as class patterns come into play. But in key respects the organization of gender on a very large scale must be more skeletal and simplified than the human relationships in face-to-face milieux. The forms of femininity and masculinity constituted at this level are stylized and impoverished. Their interrelation is centered on a single structural fact, the global dominance of men over women.
>
> This structural fact provides the main basis for relationships among men that define a hegemonic form of masculinity in the society as a whole. 'Hegemonic masculinity' is always constructed in relation to various subordinated masculinities as well as in relation to women. The interplay between different forms of masculinity is an important part of how a patriarchal social order works.
>
> There is no femininity that is hegemonic in the sense that the dominant form of masculinity is hegemonic among men. (183)

3. But where Connell theorizes that there is not a hegemonic femininity, I draw on Ingraham (1996), who offers a feminist critique of institutionalized heterosexuality. She argues that the "material conditions of capitalist patriarchal societies are more centrally linked to institutionalized heterosexuality than to gender and, moreover, that gender (under the patriarchal arrangements prevailing now) is inextricably bound up with heterosexuality" (169). In her view, gender or " 'heterogenders,' is the asymmetrical stratification of the sexes in relation to the historically varying institutions of patriarchal heterosexuality" (169). She maintains that "reframing gender as heterogender foregrounds the relation between heterosexuality and gender. Heterogender confronts the equation of heterosexuality with the natural and of gender with the cultural, and

suggests that both are socially constructed, open to other configurations (not only opposites and binary), and open to change" (169).

Chapter 4. Gendered Visions of Process, Power, and Community in the Voluntary Simplicity Movement

1. Other sites where voluntary simplicity collective identity is constructed include workshops, the literature, websites on voluntary simplicity, Internet-based simple liver groups, and most recently efforts to bring leaders of the movement and practitioners together in large numbers to lay the groundwork for a more action-based collective identity for the movement. Virtually all of the major players in the voluntary simplicity movement spoke at the September 19, 1998, free conference titled "No Purchase Necessary: Building the Voluntary Simplicity Movement" held at the University of Southern California in Los Angeles. A thousand people attended. The conference was sponsored by the Seeds of Simplicity and the Simplicity Circles Project, which is a program of the Center for Religion, Ethics and Social Policy at Cornell University headed by Carol Benson Holst and Cecile Andrews. A video tape of the conference was made available to members of the Seeds of Simplicity Project for $3.50. Another gathering aimed at creating a movement collectivity was a national live satellite video conference on "Your Money or Your Life" and the simplicity movement organized by the New Road Map Foundation on November 13, 1999.

2. This is a term used by Dominguez and Robin (1992) to refer to purchases of nonessential and nonutilitarian things that please you in some way at the moment of purchase but tend to lose their appeal fairly quickly.

3. A term widely used among simple livers and also by consumer credit counselors to refer to practices of spending what seem to be small amounts on things that are nonessential.

4. Andrews (1997) traces the study circle model she advocates back to the Chautauqua movement, a nineteenth-century American educational movement that included home-based study circles. She describes how Sweden adopted the Chautauqua model of study circles and aimed at peasant self-education and governance. In Denmark folk schools emerged as a response to poverty and social change in the 1860s, according to Andrews. Folk schools continue to be important in Denmark, offering no degrees or credits and having no admission requirements other than a desire to learn. The schools aim at helping people "discover how to be responsible for their own learning, how to live together cooperatively, and how to solve personal and societal problems" (Andrews 1997, 208). Andrews credits study circles and folk schools with playing significant roles in the high standard of living, high literacy rates, and commitment to welfare of citizens found in Sweden and Denmark.

5. Vicki Robin writes:

In building the movement, do we include only people who have been through the "school" of simplicity and frugality? Do we insist that our allies, in some measure "walk the talk"? Or do we recognize that the shift from the "myth of more" to an "ethic of enough" will also require the cadre of sophisticated, highly educated professionals and lobbyists that has moved the environmental movement and civil rights agendas along—people who may care more about changing the world than they do about changing themselves? If a broad coalition is needed, how can it be built with respect on all sides?

I think [voluntary simplicity is] pervasive and way beyond mere downshifting. It has tendrils in many other lifestyle change movements as well as in suburbia and corporations. I believe that becoming visible to one another is the next step in taking ourselves seriously and gaining confidence in our contribution to society. I believe that the integrity of "walking the talk" is part of our strength, and telling our stories of struggle and transformation is a way we show our strength to one another. At the same time, I believe that we need to build a very broad coalition for change, infused with savvy and compassion, courage and critical thinking, community and fun. And I believe that our changes are essential to equity and peace in the global family and that we will need to be helpful to our stuff-starved brothers and sisters as they go through their material maturation. (1999, 7)

Chapter 5. Looking into the Shadows: The Politics of Class, Gender, and Race/Ethnicity in the Voluntary Simplicity Movement

1. In an interview Chinua Achebe, political activist and author, is quoted as saying, "I don't live in a world in which politics is something alien to life or to art. What I call politics is the way people treat each other" (Henderson 1999, E1). His conception of politics captures the essence of the meaning of the way in which I use the term in this chapter.

2. As has been discussed previously, Etzioni's discussion of voluntary simplicity arrives at a similar understanding of the position of those in the movement:

> The rise of voluntary simplicity in advanced (or late) stages of capitalism, and for the privileged members of these societies, can be explained by a psychological theory of Maslow (1968), who suggests that human needs are organized in a hierarchy. At the base of the hierarchy are basic creature comforts, such as the need for food, shelter and clothing. Higher up is the need for love and esteem. The hierarchy is crowned with self-expression. Maslow theorized that people seek to satisfy lower needs before they turn to higher ones, although he does not deal with the question of the extent to which lower needs have to be satiated before people move to deal with higher-level needs....

Maslow's thesis is compatible with the suggestion that voluntary simplicity may appeal to people after their basic needs are satisfied: once they feel secure that their needs will be attended to in the future, they may then objectively feel ready to turn more attention to their higher needs—although their consumeristic addiction may prevent them from noting that they may shift upwards, so to speak. Voluntary simplicity is thus a choice a successful corporate lawyer, not a homeless person, faces; Singapore, not Rwanda. Indeed, to urge the poor or near poor to draw satisfaction from consuming less is to ignore the profound connection between the hierarchy of human needs and consumption. It becomes an obsession that can be overcome only after basic creature-comfort needs are sated. (1988, 632)

3. Dr. Mary Jo Neitz, my advisor on my dissertation research that this book is based upon, pointed out that this ties in with Puritan ideas regarding the "City on a Hill" and the idea of being a moral elite. Voluntary simplicity can in one way be seen as the revival of millenarianism in our day, and Seattle as the new "City on a Hill."

Chapter 6. New Tools and Old: Transformation and Reproduction in the Voluntary Simplicity Movement

1. Kleinman and Copp (1993) say that feelings we experience as we do research and writing can be resources for analyzing data. As mentioned in chapter 1, I have written "reflexive" notes throughout the course of the research and use them as a resource in data analysis.

2. Those shifts include buying locally grown and organic foods as much as possible within my budget; using biodegradable cleaning products; fewer clothes purchases, more attention to durability and source, and more thrift-store shopping; increased recycling, more attention to purchasing goods made locally, and making a conscious effort to use locally owned services; and repairing things rather than buying new when possible. I had shopped at the local farmer's market and a local health food store sometimes in the past but over the last few years have shifted to buying most fresh vegetables at the farmer's market in season and to buying much more organic food. I have observed that local grocery store chains have increased the locally produced and organic products they carry over the last few years. The local health food store has opened a second store in town. Having access to the farmer's market and stores that carry local and organic products makes food consumption in keeping with voluntary simplicity guidelines much easier. Recycling in my community was made easier in 1998 when the city instituted a more extensive recycling program. The Seeds of Simplicity publication authored by Fiona Heath titled *Bringing Simplicity to the Table* and readings and discussions in the circles I've participated in helped to shape the changes I've made in food consumption.

3. Three respondents were Green Party members and two had worked on the campaign of a Green Party candidate in Seattle. Juliet Shor, whose work is read by some in the voluntary simplicity movement and whose ideas about changes needed in the economy and culture are compatible with voluntary simplicity, is a member of the New Party, which works primarily at the local level and was organized as a response to the grassroots political efforts of the Christian right. The New Party platform (http://www.newparty.org/) includes among its many goals the creation of a sustainable economy based on "the responsible and reverent use of earth's resources"; full employment, a shorter work week, and a guaranteed minimum income for all adults; a universal social wage to include basic health care, child care, vacation time, and lifelong access to education and training, and comparable worth. The platform outlines policies to achieve these goals.

4. In the fall 2001 issue of *Seeds & Circles* Carol Holst reported on a new program initiated by Seeds of Simplicity and Dr. Lourdes Arguelles of Claremont Graduate University held early in 2002 setting up discussions between simplicity circles and "marginalized" communities. The goals of these dialogues, according to Holst, were to strengthen the social-justice pillar of the simplicity movement, and to broaden its predominantly middle-class focus by linking the practitioners of voluntary simplicity with those involved in involuntary simplicity. In a telephone conversation on December 12, 2002, Holst said, "Strengthening the social justice component of voluntary simplicity has always been in the Seeds of Simplicity's planning and it is now blossoming thanks to the opportunity brought forward by Claremont University and as a response to critiques." This suggests that key people in the movement such as Carol Holst are looking for opportunities to broaden the base of the movement and are quite open to constructive critiques aimed at enhancing the transformative capacity of the movement. It suggests a vital and responsive approach to bringing new ideas into the movement.

5. The participation of some highly respected circle members in the World Trade Organization protests in Seattle in November 1999 offers an example of an opportunity for collective action that has engaged some in the movement in political activism and shifted the focus of grassroots participants.

6. In 2001 fifty people drawn from the voluntary simplicity movement, the private sector, and research institutions met to begin the process of developing a policy research agenda for the movement. A second meeting to include a broader representation of people was held in 2002, and a third scheduled for 2003.

Bibliography

Acker, Joan. 1988. "Class, Gender, and the Relations of Distribution." *Signs* 13(3):473–97.

———. 1990. "Hierarchies, Jobs, Bodies: A Theory of Gendered Organizations." *Gender & Society* 4(2):139–58.

Affluenza, hosted by Scott Simon, 57 min., KCTS/PBS Seattle's public television station, 1997, VHS videotape.

Alinsky, Saul. 1971. *Rules For Radicals*. New York: Vintage.

Andrews, Cecile. 1997. *The Circle of Simplicity: Return to the Good Life*. New York: Harper Collins.

Appadurai, Arjun. 1986. *The Social Life of Things: Commodities in Cultural Perspective*. New York: Cambridge University Press.

Aronowitz, Stanley, and William DiFazio. 1994. *The Jobless Future: Sci-Tech and the Dogma of Work*. Minneapolis: University of Minnesota Press.

Barnett, Bernice McNair. 1993. "Invisible Southern Black Women Leaders in the Civil Rights Movement: The Triple Constraints of Gender, Race, and Class." *Gender & Society* 7(2):162–82.

———. 1995. "Black Women's Collectivist Movement: Their Struggles During the Doldrums." In *Feminist Organizations: Harvest of the New Women's Movement*, edited by Myra Marx Feree and Patricia Yancey Martin. Philadelphia: Temple University Press.

Baudrillard, Jean. 1975. *The Mirror of Production*. St. Louis: Telos Press.

———. 1988. *Selected Writings*. Stanford: Stanford University Press.

Bauman, Zygmunt. 1992. *Intimations of Postmodernity*. London: Routledge.

Bell, Daniel. 1973. *The Coming of Post Industrial Society*. New York: Basic.

Benson, J. Kenneth. 1977. "Organizations: A Dialectical View." *Administrative Science Quarterly* 22:1–21.

Berger, Bennett. 1981. *The Survival of a Counterculture: Ideological Work and Everyday Life Among Rural Communards*. Berkeley: University of California Press.

———. 1995. *An Essay on Culture: Symbolic Structure and Social Structure*. Berkeley: University of California Press.

Bernard, Jessie. 1981. *The Female World*. New York: Free Press.

Bielby, William T., and James N. Baron. 1986. "Men and Women at Work: Sex Segregation and Statistical Discrimination." *American Journal of Sociology* 91:759–99.

Blanchard, Elisa G. 1994. "Beyond Consumer Culture: A Study of Revaluation and Voluntary Action." M.A. thesis, Department of Urban and Environmental Policy, Tufts University.

Blewett, Jane. 1993. "The Universe Story: From the Primordial Flaring Forth to the Ecozoic Era—A Celebration of the Unfolding of the Cosmos." *National Catholic Reporter* 29(14):28.

Blix, Jacqueline, and David Heitmiller. 1997. *Getting a Life: Strategies for Simple Living, Based on the Revolutionary Program for Financial Freedom, Your Money or Your Life.* New York: Penguin.

Blumstein, Philip, and Pepper Schwartz. 1983. *American Couples: Money, Work, Sex.* New York: William Morrow.

Bonacich, Edna. 1972. "A Theory of Ethnic Antagonism: The Split Labor Market." *American Sociological Review* 37:547–59.

Bookman, Ann, and Sandra Morgen. 1988. *Women and the Politics of Empowerment.* Philadelphia: Temple University Press.

Bourdieu, Pierre. 1977. *Outline of a Theory of Practice.* Cambridge: Cambridge University Press.

———. 1984. *Distinction: A Social Critique of the Judgement of Taste.* Cambridge: Harvard University Press.

Brandwein, Ruth A. 1981. "Toward the Feminization of Community and Organization Practice." In *Community Organization for the 1980s,* edited by A. Lauffer and E. Newman. Special issue of *Social Development Issues* 5(2–3).

Buechler, Steven M. 1990. *Women's Movements in the United States: Woman Suffrage, Equal Rights, and Beyond.* New Brunswick, N.J.: Rutgers University Press.

Burawoy, Michael, Alice Burton, Ann Arnett Ferguson, Kathryn J. Fox, Joshua Gamson, Nadine Gartrell, Leslie Hurst, Charles Kurzman, Leslie Salzinger, Joseph Schiffman, and Shiori Ui. 1991. *Ethnography Unbound: Power and Resistance in the Modern Metropolis.* Berkeley: University of California Press.

Cahn, Christine Gray. 2001. *Report from the Power of Simplicity: An Invitational Dialogue among Leaders in the Field.* Seattle: New Road Map and Glendale, Calif.: Seeds of Simplicity.

Callenbach, Ernest. 1975. *Ecotopia.* Berkeley: Banyan Tree Books.

———. 1993. *Living Cheaply With Style: Live Better and Spend Less.* Berkeley: Ranin Publishing.

Campbell, Colin. 1995. "The Sociology of Consumption." In *Acknowledging Consumption: A Review of New Studies,* edited by Daniel Miller. New York: Routledge.

Chodorow, Nancy. 1976. "Oedipal Asymmetries and Heterosexual Knots." *Social Problems* 23(4):454–68.

———. 1978. *The Reproduction of Mothering: Psychoanalysis and the Sociology of Gender.* Berkeley: University of California Press.

Clegg, Stewart. 1990. *Modern Organizations: Organization Studies in a Postmodern World.* London: Sage.

Collins, Patricia Hill. 1990. *Black Feminist Thought: Knowledge, Consciousness and the Politics of Empowerment.* New York: Routledge.

————. 1993. "Toward a New Vision: Race, Class, and Gender as Categories of Analysis and Connection." *Race, Sex & Class* 1(1):213–23.

Combahee River Collective. 1982. "A Black Feminist Statement." In *All the Women Are White, All the Blacks Are Men, But Some of Us Are Brave: Black Women's Studies*, edited by Gloria T. Hull, Patricia Bell Scott, and Barbara Smith. Old Westbury, N.Y.: Feminist Press.

Connell, Robert. 1987. *Gender and Power*. Stanford: Stanford University Press.

Dacyczyn, Amy. 1999. *The Complete Tightwad Gazette: Promoting Thrift as a Viable Alternative Lifestyle*. New York: Random House.

De Graff, John, David Wann, and Thomas N. Naylor. 2001. *Affluenza: The All-Consuming Epidemic*. San Francisco: Berrett-Koehler Publishers, Inc.

Devall, Bill, and George Sessions. 1985. *Deep Ecology: Living As If Nature Mattered*. Salt Lake City: Peregrine.

DeVault, Marjorie L. 1991. *Feeding the Family: The Social Organization of Caring as Gendered Work*. Chicago: University of Chicago Press.

Dinnerstein, Dorothy. 1976. *The Mermaid and the Minotaur: Sexual Arrangements and Human Malaise*. New York: Harper and Row.

Dixon, Kathleen. 1997. *Making Relationships: Gender in the Forming of Academic Community*. New York: Peter Lang.

Dominguez, Joe, and Vicki Robin. 1992. *Your Money or Your Life: Transforming Your Relationship With Money and Achieving Financial Independence*. New York: Penguin.

Donald, James, and Stuart Hall. 1986. *Politics and Ideology: A Reader*. Philadelphia: Open University Press.

Durning, Alan. 1992. *How Much Is Enough? The Consumer Society and the Future of the Earth*. New York: W. W. Norton.

Ehrenreich, Barbara. 1983. *The Hearts of Men: American Dreams and the Flight From Commitment*. London: Pluto.

Eisenstein, Zillah. 1990. "Specifying U.S. Feminisms in the Nineties: The Problem of Naming." *Socialist Review* 20(2):45–56.

Elgin, Duane. [1981] 1993a. *Voluntary Simplicity: Toward a Way of Life That Is Outwardly Simple, Inwardly Rich*. New York: William Morrow.

————. 1993b. *Awakening Earth: Exploring the Evolution of Human Culture and Consciousness*. New York: William Morrow.

————. 1997. "Collective Consciousness and Cultural Healing" (online). Available from: http://www.awakeningearth.org/ccreport_asciversion.html.

————. 2001. *Promise Ahead: A Vision of Hope and Action for Humanity's Future*. New York: Quill/William Morrow.

Elgin, Duane, and Arnold Mitchell. 1977. "Voluntary Simplicity." *Co-Evolution Quarterly* (summer):4–19.

Escape from Affluenza, hosted by Wanda Urbanska, 57 min., KCTS/PBS Seattle's public television station. 1998, VHS videotape.

Etzioni, Amitai. 1998. "Voluntary Simplicity: Characterization, Select Psychological Implications, and Societal Consequences." *Journal of Economic Psychology* 19:619–43.

Fantasia, Rick. 1988. *Cultures of Solidarity: Consciousness, Action, and Contemporary American Workers*. Berkeley: University of California Press.

Fantasia, Rick, and Eric L. Hirsch. 1995. "Culture in Rebellion: The Appropriation and Transformation of the Veil in the Algerian Revolution." In *Social Movements and Culture,* edited by Hank Johnston and Bert Klandermans. Minneapolis: University of Minnesota Press.

Ferguson, Kathy E. 1984. *The Feminist Case against Bureaucracy.* Philadelphia: Temple University Press.

Ferree, Myra Marx, and Frederick D. Miller. 1985. "Mobilization and Meaning: Toward an Integration of Social Psychological and Resource Perspectives on Social Movements." *Sociological Inquiry* 55:38–61.

Fogler, Michael. 1997. *Un-Jobbing: The Adult Liberation Handbook.* Lexington, Ky.: Free Choice Press.

Foucault, Michel. 1977. *Discipline and Punish: The Birth of the Prison.* New York: Vintage Books.

———. 1978. *The History of Sexuality: An Introduction.* Volume 1. New York: Vintage Books.

Frankenberg, Ruth. 1993. *White Women, Race Matters: The Social Construction of Whiteness.* Minneapolis: University of Minnesota Press.

———. 1997. *Displacing Whiteness: Essays in Social and Cultural Criticism.* Durham, N.C.: Duke University Press.

Franklin, Clyde W. II. 1988. *Men and Society.* Chicago: Nelson-Hall.

Freeman, Jo. 1974. "The Tyranny of Structurelessness." In *Women in Politics,* edited by Jane Jacquette. New York: John Wiley.

———. 1975. *The Politics of Women's Liberation: A Case Study of an Emerging Social Movement and Its Relation to the Policy Process.* New York: David McKay.

Giddens, Anthony. 1990. *The Consequences of Modernity.* Cambridge: Polity.

Gilligan, Carol. 1977. "In a Different Voice: Women's Conceptions of Self and of Morality." *Harvard Educational Review* 47(4):481–517.

Glaser, Barney G., and Anselm L. Strauss. 1967. *The Discovery of Grounded Theory: Strategies for Qualitative Research.* Chicago: Aldine.

Goldberg, Carey. 1995. "Choosing the Joys of a Simplified Life." *New York Times,* Sept. 21.

Goodwin, Neva, Frank Ackerman, and David Kiron, eds. 1997. *The Consumer Society.* Washington, D.C.: Island Press.

Gregg, Richard. 1936. *The Value of Voluntary Simplicity.* Wallingford, Pa.: Pendle Hill.

———. 1977. "Voluntary Simplicity." *Co-Evolution Quarterly* (summer):20–27. Reprinted from *Visva-Bharti Quarterly* August 1936.

Habermas, Jurgen. 1987. *The Theory of Communicative Action.* Vol. 2, *Lifeworld and System: A Critique of Functionalist Reason.* Boston: Beacon Press.

———. 1992. *The Structural Transformation of the Public Sphere: An Inquiry into a Category of Bourgeois Society.* Cambridge: MIT Press.

Hall, John R., ed. 1997. *Reworking Class.* Ithaca, N.Y.: Cornell University Press.

Hall, John R., and Mary Jo Neitz. 1993. *Culture: Sociological Perspectives.* Englewood Cliffs, N.J.: Prentice Hall.

Halle, David. 1984. *America's Working Man: Work, Home and Politics Among Blue-Collar Property Owners.* Chicago: University of Chicago Press.

Harding, Sandra. 1986. *The Science Question in Feminism.* Ithaca, N.Y.: Cornell University Press.

———. 1987. *Feminism and Methodology: Social Science Issues.* Bloomington: Indiana University Press.

Harvey, David. 1989. *The Condition of Postmodernity.* Oxford: Blackwell.

Hays, Sharon. 1994. "Structure and Agency and the Sticky Problem of Culture." *Sociological Theory* 12(1):57–72.

Heath, Fiona. 2001. *Bringing Simplicity to the Table: Sustainable Food Choices.* Glendale, Calif.: Seeds of Simplicity.

Heffern, Rich. 1994. *Adventures in Simple Living: A Creation-Centered Spirituality.* New York: Crossroads.

Henderson, Joan. 1999. "African Literary Giant Comes to St. Louis to Accept Prize." *St. Louis Post-Dispatch* Oct. 27.

Hochschild, Arlie Russell. 1983. *The Managed Heart: Commercialization of Human Feeling.* Berkeley: University of California Press.

———. 1989. *The Second Shift.* New York: Avon.

Ingraham, Crys. 1996. "The Heterosexual Imaginary: Feminist Sociology and Theories of Gender." In *Queer Theory Sociology,* edited by Steven Seidman. Cambridge, Mass.: Blackwell.

Johnson, Miriam M. 1988. *Strong Mothers, Weak Wives: The Search for Gender Equality.* Berkeley: University of California Press.

Johnston, Hank, and Bert Klandermans, eds. 1995. *Social Movements and Culture.* Minneapolis: University of Minnesota Press.

Kaplan, Temma. 1982. "Female Consciousness and Collective Action: The Case of Barcelona, 1910–1918." *Journal of Women in Culture and Society* 7(3):545–66.

Kleinman, Sherryl. 1996. *Opposing Ambitions: Gender and Identity in an Alternative Organization.* Chicago: University of Chicago Press.

Kleinman, Sherryl, and Martha A. Copp. 1993. *Emotions in Fieldwork.* Newbury Park, Calif.: Sage.

Lamont, Michele. 1992. *Money, Morals, and Manners: The Culture of the French and the American Upper-Middle Class.* Chicago: University of Chicago Press.

Lara, Maria Pia. 1998. *Moral Textures: Feminist Narratives in the Public Sphere.* Berkeley: University of California Press.

Laraña, Enrique, Hank Johnston, and Joseph R. Gusfield, eds. 1994. *New Social Movements: From Ideology to Identity.* Philadelphia: Temple University Press.

Lasch, Christopher. 1978. *The Culture of Narcissism: American Life in an Age of Diminishing Expectations.* New York: Norton.

Lefebvre, Henri. 1971. *Everyday Life in the Modern World.* New York: Harper and Row.

Levering, Frank, and Wanda Urbanska. 1993. *Simple Living: One Couple's Search for a Better Life.* New York: Penguin.

Lieberson, Stanley. 1980. *A Piece of the Pie: Blacks and White Immigrants since 1880.* Berkeley: University of California Press.

Longacre, Doris Janzen. 1980. *Living More with Less.* Scottdale, Pa.: Herald Press.

Lorde, Audre. 1984. *Sister Outsider*. Freedom, Calif.: The Crossing Press.

Luhrs, Janet. 1997. *The Simple Living Guide: A Sourcebook for Less Stressful, More Joyful Living*. New York: Broadway Books.

———. 2000. "A Time of Wonder & Reflection." *Simple Living Journal* (winter):2–3.

Lury, Celia. 1996. *Consumer Culture*. New Brunswick, N.J.: Rutgers University Press.

McAdam, Doug. 1988. *Freedom Summer*. New York: Oxford University Press.

———. 1992. "Gender as a Mediator of the Activist Experience: The Case of Freedom Summer." *American Journal of Sociology* 97(5):1211–40.

McCracken, Grant. 1988. *Culture and Consumption: New Approaches to the Symbolic Character of Consumer Goods and Activities*. Bloomington: Indiana University Press.

Madison, Cathy. 1998. "Don't Buy These Myths." *Utne Reader* 90 (November–December):52–57

Marx, Karl, and Friedrich Engels. 1978. *The Marx-Engels Reader*. New York: W. W. Norton.

Maslow, Abraham H. 1968. *Toward a Psychology of Being*. Princeton, N.J.: Van Nostrand.

Melucci, Alberto. 1985. "The Symbolic Challenge of Contemporary Movements." *Social Research* 52:781–816.

———. 1989. *Nomads of the Present: Social Movements and Individual Needs in Contemporary Society*. Philadelphia: Temple University Press.

———. 1995. "The Process of Collective Identity." In *Social Movements and Culture*, edited by Hank Johnston and Bert Klandermans. Minneapolis: University of Minnesota Press.

Merchant, Carolyn. 1992. *Radical Ecology*. New York: Routledge.

Milkman, Ruth. 1988. *Gender at Work: The Dynamics of Job Segregation by Sex During World War II*. Urbana: University of Illinois.

———. 1997. *Farewell to the Factory: Auto Workers in the Late Twentieth Century*. Berkeley: University of California Press.

Miller, Daniel, ed. 1995. *Acknowledging Consumption: A Review of New Studies*. New York: Routledge.

Miller, Stuart. 1983. *Men and Friendship*. Boston: Houghton Mifflin.

Mueller, Carol. 1994. "Conflict Networks and the Origins of Women's Liberation." In *New Social Movements: From Ideology to Identity*, edited by Enrique Laraña, Hank Johnston, and Joseph R. Gusfield. Philadelphia: Temple University Press.

Mukerji, Chandra. 1983. *From Graven Images: Patterns of Modern Materialism*. New York: Columbia University Press.

Naples, Nancy A. 1991. "Contradictions in the Gender Subtext of the War on Poverty: The Community Work and Resistance of Women from Low Income Communities." *Social Problems* 38(3):316–32.

———. 1998. *Community Activism and Feminist Politics: Organizing Across Race, Class, and Gender*. New York: Routledge.

Nardi, Peter M., ed. 1992. *Men's Friendships*. Newbury Park, Calif.: Sage Publications.

Nearing, Helen, and Scott Nearing. 1989. *The Good Life: Helen and Scott Nearing's Sixty Years of Self-Sufficient Living*. New York: Schocken Books.

Neitz, Mary Jo. 1994. "Quasi-Religions and Cultural Movements: Contemporary Witchcraft as a Churchless Religion." *Religion and the Social Order* 4:127–49.

———. 1999. "Contemporary Witchcraft: Gendered Spiritual Paths and Empowerment and Ecstasy." Manuscript prepared for Religion Outside the Institutions Conference, Princeton University, Princeton, New Jersey.

———. 2000. "Queering the Dragonfest: Changing Sexualities in a Post-Patriarchal Religion." *Sociology of Religion* 61(winter):369–92.

———. 2002. " 'Walking Between the Worlds' Permeable Boundaries, Ambiguous Identities." In *Personal Knowledge and Beyond: Reshaping the Enthnography of Religion*, edited by James Spickard, J. Shawn Landres, and Meredith McGuire. New York: New York University Press.

New Road Map Foundation. 1990. *How Earth-Friendly Are You? A Lifestyle Self-Assessment Questionnaire*. Seattle: New Road Map Foundation.

Omi, Michael, and Howard Winant. 1986. *Racial Formation in the United States*. New York: Routledge and Kegan Paul.

Pahl, Jan. 1989. *Money and Marriage*. New York: St. Martin's Press.

Pahl, Ray E. 1984. *Divisions of Labour*. Oxford: Blackwell.

Payne, Charles. 1989. "Ella Baker and Models of Social Change." *Signs: Journal of Women in Culture and Society* 14(4):885–99.

Pierce, Linda Breen. 2000. *Choosing Simplicity: Real People Finding Peace and Fulfillment in a Complex World*. Carmel, Calif.: Gallagher Press.

Polanyi, Karl. 1944. *The Great Transformation: The Political and Economic Origins of Our Time*. Boston: Beacon Press.

Polletta, Francesca. 1997. "Culture and Its Discontents: Recent Theorizing on the Cultural Dimensions of Protest." *Sociological Inquiry* 67(4):431–50.

Portez, Alejandro, and Robert D. Manning. 1986. "The Immigrant Enclave: Theory and Empirical Examples." In *Comparative Ethnic Relations*, edited by Susan Olzak and Joane Nagel. Orlando, Fla.: Academic Press.

Prus, Robert, and Lorne Dawson. 1991. "Shop 'til You Drop: Shopping as Recreational and Laborious Activity." *Canadian Journal of Sociology* 16(2):145–64.

Ray, Paul H. 1997. "The Emerging Culture." *American Demographics* February:29, 31.

Ray, Paul H., and Sherry Ruth Anderson. 2000. *The Cultural Creatives: How 50 Million People Are Changing the World*. New York: Harmony Books.

Raymond, Janice G. 1986. *A Passion for Friends: Toward a Philosophy of Female Affection*. Boston: Beacon Press.

Reese, Ellen. 2000. E-mail to author. Jan. 15.

———. 2002. "Resisting the Workfare State: ACORN's Campaign to Improve General Relief in Los Angeles." *Race, Gender and Class* 9(1):72–95.

Ritzer, George. 2000. *The McDonaldization of Society: An Investigation into the Changing Character of Contemporary Social Life*. Thousand Oaks, Calif.: Pine Forge.

————. 2001. *Explorations in the Sociology of Consumption: Fast Food, Credit Cards and Casinos.* Newbury Park, Calif.: Sage Publications.

Robin, Vicky. 1999. What's Next For Sustainable Living?" *Simple Living Journal* (autumn):7, 9.

Robnett, Belinda. 1996. "African-American Women in the Civil Rights Movement, 1954–1965: Gender, Leadership, and Micromobilization." *American Journal of Sociology* 101(6):1661–93.

Rose, Sonya. 1992. *Limited Livelihoods: Gender and Class in Nineteenth-Century England.* Berkeley: University of California Press.

Rubin, Lillian B. 1983. *Intimate Strangers: Men and Women Together.* New York: Harper & Row.

Ruddick, Sara. 1989. *Maternal Thinking: Toward A Politics of Peace.* Boston: Beacon Press.

St. James, Elaine. 1994. *Simplify Your Life: 100 Ways to Slow Down and Enjoy the Things That Really Matter.* New York: Hyperion.

————. 1996. *Living the Simple Life.* New York: Hyperion.

Sattel, Jack W. 1976. "The Inexpressive Male: Tragedy or Sexual Politics?" *Social Problems* 23(4):469–77.

Saulnier, Beth. 2002. "The Simple Life." *Cornell Alumni Magazine* 105(3): 48–55.

Scharper, Stephen B. 1997. "The Hidden Heart of the Cosmos: Humanity and the New Story." *National Catholic Reporter* 33(38):30–1.

Schor, Juliet. 1991. *The Overworked American: The Unexpected Decline of Leisure.* New York: Basic.

————. 1997. "Summary of New Analytic Bases for an Economic Critique of Consumer Society." Paper delivered at conference on "Consumption, Global Stewardship, and the Good Life" at the University of Maryland, September 29–October 2, 1994. In *The Consumer Society,* Frontier Issues in Economic Thought, edited by Neva R. Goodwin, Frank Ackerman, and David Kiron. Washington, D.C.: Island Press.

————. 1998. *The Overspent American: Upscaling, Downshifting, and the New Consumer.* New York: Basic Books.

Schwalbe, Michael. 1996. *Unlocking the Iron Cage: The Men's Movement, Gender Politics, and American Culture.* New York: Oxford University Press.

Schwartz, Michael, and Shuva Paul. 1992. "Resource Mobilization versus the Mobilization of People: Why Consensus Movements Cannot Be Instruments of Social Change." In *Frontiers in Social Movement Theory,* edited by Aldon D. Morris and Carol McClurg Mueller. New Haven, Conn.: Yale University Press.

Scott, James. 1990. *Domination and Acts of Resistance.* New Haven, Conn.: Yale University Press.

Scott, Joan. 1988. "Deconstructing Equality versus Difference: The Uses of Poststructuralist Theory for Feminism." *Feminist Studies* 14:33–50.

Seager, Joni. 1993. *Earth Follies: Coming to Feminist Terms with the Global Environmental Crisis.* New York: Routledge.

Seeds of Simplicity. 1998. *No Purchase Necessary: Building the Voluntary Simplicity Movement*. Video Highlights of the Seeds of Simplicity National Conference, September 19, at the University of Southern California Davidson. 60 min. VHS videotape.

———. 2002. *National Directory of Member Circles, Seeds and Stories of the Seeds of Simplicity Project*. Glendale, Calif.: Seeds of Simplicity.

Segal, Jerome M. 1996. "The Politics of Simplicity." *Tikkun* 11(4):20–7.

Sewell, William H. 1992. "A Theory of Structure: Duality, Agency, and Transformation." *American Journal of Sociology* 98:1–29.

Shi, David. 1985. *The Simple Life: Plain Living and High Thinking in American Culture*. New York: Oxford University Press.

———. 1986. *In Search of the Simple Life: American Voices Past and Present*. Salt Lake City, Utah: Peregrine Smith Books.

Simmel, Georg. 1950. *The Sociology of Georg Simmel*. New York: Free Press.

Smith, Dorothy E. 1987a. "Women's Perspective as a Radical Critique of Sociology." In *Feminism and Methodology*, edited by Sandra Harding. Bloomington: Indiana University Press.

———. 1987b. *The Everyday World as Problematic: A Feminist Sociology*. Boston: Northeastern University Press.

———. 1990. *Texts, Facts, and Femininity: Exploring the Relations of Ruling*. New York: Routledge.

Spain, Daphne, and Suzanne M. Bianchi. 1994. *Balancing Act: Motherhood, Marriage, and Employment among American Women*. New York: Russell Sage Foundation.

Stall, Susan, and Randy Stoecker. 1998. "Community Organizing or Organizing Community? Gender and the Crafts of Empowerment." *Gender & Society* 12(6):729–56.

Swidler, Ann. 1986. "Culture in Action: Symbols and Strategies." *American Sociological Review* 51:273–86.

———. 1995. "Cultural Power and Social Movements." In *Social Movements and Culture*, edited by Hank Johnston and Bert Klandermans. Minneapolis: University of Minnesota Press.

Swimme, Brian. 1996. *The Hidden Heart of the Cosmos: Humanity and the New Story*. Maryknoll, N.Y.: Orbis Books.

Swimme, Brian, and Thomas Berry. 1992. *The Universe Story from the Primordial Flaring Forth to the Ecozoic Era: A Celebration of the Unfolding of the Cosmos*. San Francisco: Harper.

Taylor, Verta. 1996. *Rock-A-By Baby: Feminism, Self-help, and Postpartum Depression*. New York: Routledge.

———. 1999. "Gender and Social Movements: Gender Processes in Women's Self-Help Movements." *Gender & Society* 13(1):8–33.

Taylor, Verta, and Nancy E. Whittier. 1992. "Collective Identity in Social Movement Communities: Lesbian Feminist Mobilization." In *Frontiers in Social Movement Theory*, edited by Aldon D. Morris and Carol McClurg Mueller. New Haven, Conn.: Yale University Press.

———. 1995. "Analytical Approaches to Social Movement Culture: The Culture of the Women's Movement." In *Social Movements and Culture*, edited by Hank Johnston and Bert Klandermans. Minneapolis: University of Minnesota Press.

Thompson, E. P. 1963. *The Making of the English Working Class*. New York: Vintage Books.

Touraine, Alain. 1981. *The Voice and the Eye: An Analysis of Social Movements*. New York: Cambridge University Press.

———. 1983. *Anti-nuclear Protest: The Opposition to Nuclear Energy in France*. London: Cambridge University Press.

———. 1985. "An Introduction to the Study of Social Movements." *Social Research* 52(4):749–87.

———. 1992. "Beyond Social Movements?" In *Cultural Theory and Cultural Change*, edited by Mike Featherstone. Newbury Park, Calif.: Sage.

———. 1995. *Critique of Modernity*. Cambridge, Mass.: Blackwell.

van Gelder, Sarah. 1996. "Upshifters: Pioneers of an Awakening Culture." *Yes! A Journal of Positive Futures* (online). Available from: http://www.awakeningearth.org.

Vanderbilt, Tom. 1996. "It's a Wonderful (Simplified) Life: Is the 'Voluntary Simplicity' Movement True Liberation, or Diminished Expectations under Another Name?" *The Nation* 262(3):20–3.

Veblen, Thorstein. [1899] 1965. *The Theory of the Leisure Class*. New York: A. M. Kelley.

Vogler, Carolyn, and Jan Pahl. 1993. "Social and Economic Change and the Organization of Money within Marriage." *Work, Employment & Society: A Journal of the British Sociological Association* 7(1):71–95.

Walby, Sylvia. 1990. *Theorizing Patriarchy*. Cambridge, Mass.: Basil Blackwell.

Wachtel, Paul. 1989. *The Poverty of Affluence*. Philadelphia: New Society Publishers.

Weber, Max. [1904] 1958. *The Protestant Ethic and the Spirit of Capitalism*. New York: Charles Scribner's Sons.

Weinbaum, Batya, and Amy Bridges. 1978. "The Other Side of the Paycheck." In *Capitalist Patriarchy and the Case for Socialist Feminism*, edited by Zillah R. Eisenstein. New York: Monthly Review Press.

Weiss, Penny A. 1993. *Gendered Community: Rosseau, Sex and Politics*. New York: New York University Press.

———. 1998. *Conversations with Feminism: Political Theory and Practice*. New York: Rowman and Littlefield Publishers, Inc.

Weiss, Penny A., and Marilyn Friedman, eds. 1995. *Feminism and Community*. Philadelphia: Temple University Press.

West, Guida, and Rhoda Lois Blumberg, eds. 1990. *Women and Social Protest*. New York: Oxford University Press.

Index